Sources Of
American Spirituality

Horace Bushnell

SERMONS

Edited by Conrad Cherry

PAULIST PRESS
New York ◆ Mahwah

101970

Library of Congress
Catalog Card Number: 85-60410

ISBN: 0-8091-0362-1

Published by Paulist Press
997 Macarthur Boulevard
Mahwah, N.J. 07430

Printed and bound in the United States of America

CONTENTS

INTRODUCTION

The life and work of Horace Bushnell (1802–1876) have spawned a profusion of studies in the twentieth century. Bushnell has been examined as a minister to an America seeking to cope with the emergence of modern ideas, institutions, and values; as a theologian bent on reconciling diverse schools of thought in the nineteenth century; as a religious thinker devoted to the recasting of Protestant orthodoxy into an aesthetic mold; as a precursor of Christocentric Liberalism, the Social Gospel, modern theories of religious education, and post-critical biblical scholarship. Bushnell's views of blacks, women, language, and the social order have recently come under careful critical scrutiny.[1]

What, from Bushnell's own perspective, held together the various roles he performed and ideas he entertained was the Christian religion understood as a life in process. As David L. Smith has remarked, Bushnell believed that all of the expressive vehicles of Christianity—its doctrines, symbols, traditions, and rites—should serve one primary function: "to evoke or encourage growth in the life of the spirit."[2] In *Aids to Reflection*, an aphoristic book which exerted an enormous influence on Bushnell, the English poet and philosopher Samuel Taylor Coleridge wrote that "Christianity is not a theory, or a speculation; but a life;—not a philosophy of life, but a life and a living process."[3] That observation, so simple on the face of it but so

---

1. For an overview of interpretations of Bushnell see James O. Duke, *Horace Bushnell: On the Vitality of Biblical Language* (Chico, CA: Scholars Press, 1984), 1–6.

2. David L. Smith, *Symbolism and Growth: The Religious Thought of Horace Bushnell* (Chico, CA: Scholars Press, 1981), x.

3. Samuel Taylor Coleridge, *Aids to Reflection*, 4th ed. of 1840 (New York & London: Kennikat Press, 1971), 201.

packed with implicit criticisms of nineteenth-century Protestantism, was one which Horace Bushnell made very much his own. It was an observation which summarized a meaning of Christian spirituality, framed a theological task, and warned of false views of religion. The Christian religion was for Bushnell, as for Coleridge, a particular kind of life—a life of growth, of struggles of the free human spirit, of the counterforces of darkness and light. Such a dynamic phenomenon could never be captured by dogma nor preserved by a moral code; it could only be symbolized by imaginative metaphor and nurtured by vital persons and institutions.

THE MAN

Bushnell did not grasp the full meaning of Christianity as a living process until his mid-forties. Born in Litchfield County, Connecticut in 1802 to a family that earned its living by farming, weaving, and carding, he was urged by his mother to adopt the vocation of the ministry. But Bushnell was to reach that decision by a more circuitous route. Not until 1821 did he join the church, and his teen years were marked by episodes of religious doubt and skepticism. He entered Yale College in 1823 and was admitted to membership in the church there, but, as one early biographer said, ''the growing spirit of doubt took strong possession of his mind as he advanced in college life.''[4] After graduating from Yale, he taught school for a while in Connecticut and then worked for a New York daily newspaper, but within two years he was back at Yale as a tutor of undergraduates and a student in the law school. In 1831 Yale was swept by a religious revival. At first Bushnell was unaffected by the fervor, but eventually he was won over to a conversion. It is apparent from Bushnell's own testimony that this conversion sprang at least in part from social pressure, from a sense of guilt that the students in his charge were imitating their tutor's skepticism and indecision. Bushnell remarked to a friend at the time, ''I must get out of this woe. Here am I what I am, and these young men hanging to me in their indifference amidst

---

4. Noah Porter, ''Horace Bushnell,'' *New Englander* 36 (1877): 154.

this universal earnestness on every side."[5] Later in life Bushnell was to say that his move from religious indifference to religious trust was tied to a vocational decision: "And now, as I look back on the crisis here passed, it seems very much like the question whether I should finally *be*. No other calling but the ministry of Christ, I am obliged to feel, could have anywise filled my inspirations and allowed me to sufficiently *be*."[6] After completing theological studies at Yale Divinity School, Bushnell became minister of the North (Congregational) Church in Hartford, Connecticut, the only parish he would serve.

As important as the personal experience of 1831 was for Bushnell's vocational choice and religious development, it was not the event which was to open a new world of understanding to him. That was to come in 1848. In February of that year, according to Bushnell's wife, after a long period of hard study and "mental struggles, trials, and practical endeavor," he reached a quiet but decisive turning point in his life. When asked by his wife what had occurred, he replied that he had seen the gospel of the New Testament from a fresh perspective.[7]

It is difficult to say for certain what mental struggles preceded this breakthrough, but Bushnell's wife did mention the death of their young son five years earlier.[8] And, as H. Shelton Smith has remarked, the turmoil which followed the publication in 1847 of Bushnell's *Discourses on Christian Nurture* could certainly be construed as one of the personal trials.[9] That book, which challenged then conventional ideas of sin and regeneration by arguing for the steady development of a Christian within the organic structures of family and church, brought such an outcry from orthodox Protestant ministers that the publisher suspended the sale of the book, and Bushnell responded with a caustic pamphlet. Although Bushnell later rebuked himself for his intemperance, he was deeply affected by the controversy.

---

5. *Life and Letters of Horace Bushnell*, ed. Mary Bushnell Cheney (New York: Harper & Brothers, 1880), 56.

6. *Ibid.*, 33.

7. *Ibid.*, 191–92.

8. *Ibid.*, 191.

9. H. Shelton Smith, *Horace Bushnell* (New York: Oxford University Press, 1965), 24.

Whatever events led to the spiritual turning point of 1848, Bushnell much later—in 1871—was to describe its critical nature:

> I seemed to pass a boundary. I had never been very legal in my Christian life, but now I passed from those partial seeings, glimpses and doubts, into a clearer knowledge of God and into his inspirations, which I have never wholly lost. The change was into faith,—a sense of the freeness of God and the ease of approach to him. [10]

Bushnell was ever scornful of the tendency of nineteenth-century American Protestantism to make the whole of Christian existence hinge on a single conversion experience. Revivalism, in particular, denied the manner in which one could *grow* into faith and thereby ignored the need for the structures of family, church, and society which nurture the person into the religious life. Still, the 1848 experience remained crucial for Bushnell's development, and he believed that if the whole of the Christian religion could not be collapsed into a datable conversion, as a life of growth it *could* certainly be marked by critical events. Bushnell's view of the matter is summarized in the following words from one of his sermons:

> The importance of living to God, in ordinary and small things, is seen in the fact that character, which is the end of religion, is in its very nature a growth. Conversion is a great change; old things are passed away; behold all things are become new. This however is the language of a hope or confidence somewhat prophetic, exulting, at the beginning, in the realization of future victory. [11]

What Bushnell's religious vision entails and what his 1848 change into "a sense of the freeness of God and the ease of approach to him" underscores, is that Christianity is best understood not as something that explodes violently within human experience but, rather, as a life into which one grows, even if by fits and starts. The

---

10. *Life and Letters*, 192.
11. "Living to God in Small Things," *Sermons for the New Life* (New York: Scribner, Armstrong & Co., 1873), 292–93.

image of God in this vision is less of one who demands earth-shaking, urgent decisions than of a person who is gentle, accessible, and patient.

Bushnell's own personal life seems to have embodied this understanding of the Christian religion. Despite his occasional contentiousness in the midst of theological debate, despite his frequent extolling of the virtues of manly industriousness, those closest to him described him as a gentle but engaging person. His children found him warm, playful, and spontaneous; his daughter wrote that "it was always the winning, never compelling side of religious experience, which he presented to us."[12] Those who heard his sermons discovered a solemn, vital, moving, intense preacher whose aim was to persuade his auditors gently into growth in the Christian life.[13] Friends, particularly those who joined him in his coveted walking tours of the New England countryside, described Bushnell as an engaging conversationalist who, even in his later years, revealed "a mind *still in movement* on the central theme of the Christian faith; not doubtful so far as he had discovered, yet not resting in ultimate convictions."[14]

That restlessness of mind—Bushnell would have said its constant *growth*—led him to yearn for, and at times feel he had attained, a mystical union with God in which the only discernible activity is the direct interchange between God and the human spirit. In a letter to his wife in 1852, he reported having reached an immediate confrontation with God, one which transcended all images and constructs of the human mind.[15] Later he was to report a similar experience which broke through even revelation in Christ:

> O my God! what a fact to possess and know that he is! I
> have not seemed to compare him with anything, and set him
> in a higher value; but he has been the *all*, and the altogether,
> everywhere, lovely. There is nothing else to compete; there
> is nothing else, in fact. It has been as if all the revelations,
> through good men, nature, Christ, had been now through,

---

12. *Life and Letters*, 465.

13. Theodore Munger, *Horace Bushnell, Preacher and Theologian* (Boston & New York: Houghton, Mifflin & Co., 1899), 275–92.

14. *Life and Letters*, 533.

15. *Ibid.*, 277.

and their cargo unloaded, the capital meaning produced,
and the God set forth in his own proper day,—the good,
the true, the perfect, the all-holy and benignant.[16]

This mystical strain competed with Bushnell's theological/philo-
sophical position (which he never abandoned) that religious truth is
available only by a "right beholding of the forms or images by which
it is expressed"[17]—that is, only in and through the forms of language,
nature, ritual, doctrines, and persons. The truth of the matter is that
this contradiction within the life and thought of Horace Bushnell was
never resolved.[18] Bushnell continued to hold that infinite truth is accessible only in finite forms, but his restless spirit drove him to feel
that the human spirit can meet God in this life without the mediation
of those forms.

For all of his intense religiosity, Horace Bushnell was a man of
broad and varied interests. An accomplished surveyor, he laid out a
park in Hartford which still bears his name, forecast the route of the
transcontinental railroad, and as president pro tempore of the University of California surveyed and recommended the site for the cam-
pus at Berkeley. During the Civil War he followed the details of the
military campaigns and, as a sort of armchair general, planned the
conduct of the war and the movement of armies. He delighted in music, helping to found the Beethoven Society at Yale during his student
days. At home he joined his wife and children in singing tunes of
many kinds and surrounded himself with musician friends. As a ro-
bust youth he was fond of athletics, earning the nickname of "Bully
Bush" from his classmates. When tuberculosis curtailed his activities
in middle age, he took to fishing, hunting, and walking. He read
widely—in science, history, philosophy, and English literature particularly. Although he disdained systematic theology and the metaphysics of the eighteenth and nineteenth centuries, he did read in the

---

16. *Ibid.*, 516.

17. "Our Gospel a Gift to the Imagination," *Building Eras in Religion* (New
York: Charles Scribner's Sons, 1881), 266.

18. For an elaboration of this contradiction see Conrad Cherry, *Nature and
Religious Imagination: From Edwards to Bushnell* (Philadelphia: Fortress Press,
1980), 178–80; and Robert A. Schneider, "Form, Symbol, and Spirit: Religious
Knowledge in the Thought of Horace Bushnell" (M.A. thesis, Pennsylvania State
University, 1974), chap. 2.

history of doctrine and in modern European, British, and American theological literature.

There is considerable evidence that his reading was wider than it was deep. He was less inclined to research a subject or author than to read selectively for what ideas could be generated in his own mind. And he read not in order to refute an author in detail but to obtain the gist of a position which could then be readily accepted or rejected. One acquaintance recalls Bushnell saying this about his reading habits: "It is very hard for me to read a book through. If it is stupid and good-for-nothing, of course I have to give it up; and if it is really worth reading, it starts my mind off on some track of its own that I am more inclined to follow than I am to find out what the author has to say."[19] Many other nineteenth-century American intellectuals shared with Bushnell this attitude toward reading. They were all caught up in the Romantic conviction that knowledge should be original rather than borrowed (especially borrowed from European thinkers). Ralph Waldo Emerson announced, for example, "Books are the best of things, well used; abused, among the worst. What is the right use? What is the one end which all means go to effect? They are for nothing but to inspire."[20] Bushnell voiced a similar sentiment in an essay on the meaning of language: Words "do not literally convey, or pass over a thought out of one mind into another, as we commonly speak of doing. They are only hints, or images, held up before the mind of another, to put *him* on generating or reproducing the same thought."[21]

Bushnell's impatience with the details of another person's thoughts owed as much to his overriding interest in preaching as to his theory of knowledge. He sought, above all else, to be an effective, imaginative preacher rather than a scholar. Even after ill health forced him to retire from the Hartford church in 1859, he became a "minister at large" and looked for opportunities to preach. He wrote in 1862, "As my old pulpit is now vacant, I am trying to put in a sermon a week there. How long I shall stand so much, I don't know. I could

19. *Life and Letters,* 295.

20. "The American Scholar," *Selections From Ralph Waldo Emerson,* ed. Stephen E. Whicher (Boston: Houghton Mifflin Co., 1957), 67.

21. "Preliminary Dissertation on the Nature of Language," *God in Christ* (Hartford: Brown & Parsons, 1849), 46.

go on to the world's end, or to mine, for there is nothing I so much delight in as preaching.''[22] This chief delight infused the numerous theological works which flowed from his pen. Many of his theological essays and treatises were first cast in the form of sermons. Others were written to ground theoretically ideas which he would express from the pulpit.

This feature of Bushnell's work has led even his friendly critics to point to the limitations of his theological style. His theology possesses flashes of intuitive insight, quick discernment of fundamental issues, provocative figurative language, a personal tone, and hints of genuine originality—all qualities which Bushnell sought to embody in his sermons. As a consequence, however, his theological writings tend to dismiss too easily logical contradictions, fail to define key words and ideas, render judgments before intensive investigation of a subject, and refuse to engage theological opponents with sustained argument.[23] Bushnell would have defended the style of this theology, limitations and all, not simply by claiming that he was principally a preacher rather than a scholar, but also by insisting that the theology of his day stood in dire need of being enlivened by the art of imaginative preaching. Indeed, he firmly believed that scholarly, scientific Protestant theology should be *replaced* by a mode of reflection more akin to poetry than to science.

THE CONTEXT

Horace Bushnell's nineteenth-century America was awash with conflicting religious currents. Revivalists of different Protestant denominations clamored for the commitments of people in all regions of the country. Old-line Protestants who had enjoyed a religious hegemony were confronted, and threatened, by the appearance of such ''outsiders'' as Catholic immigrants, Mormons, religious commu-

---

22. *Life and Letters*, 478.
23. See Frank Hugh Foster, ''Horace Bushnell as a Theologian,'' *Bibliotheca Sacra* 59 (1902):601–7; Munger, *Horace Bushnell,* 275–76; Donald A. Crosby, *Horace Bushnell's Theory of Language* (The Hague & Paris: Mouton, 1975), 142–43; Barbara M. Cross, *Horace Bushnell: Minister to a Changing America* (Chicago: University of Chicago Press, 1958), 87, 157.

nitarians, and foreign-language-speaking Protestants. Theologically the country was virtually at war. Deism and other Enlightenment philosophies challenged orthodox beliefs; Unitarianism departed from the traditions of mainline Congregationalism; Romanticism and Transcendentalism repudiated dogmatic mindsets; colleges and theological schools adopted conflicting theological positions. Whatever hopes for a group of states united around religion may have still been entertained in the nineteenth century were utterly dashed by a Civil War in which religious groups and leaders aligned themselves with sectional interests. Horace Bushnell responded to the forces in his setting. His view of Christian spirituality is especially illuminated by his responses to the theological situation, to the current styles of preaching, and to his own section of the country.

Bushnell expended a great deal of his intellectual energy questioning the rationalism of the New England Protestantism of his day. In setting out the doctrines of the faith, many New England theologians sought to be as scientific in their claims as any modern observer of the natural world. And in defending the faith against the welter of religious options emerging in nineteenth-century America, those same theologians attempted to state with unmitigated authority the truths of the Christian religion. The consequence was, to the mind of Bushnell, the abstraction of theology from the tangible realities of the human spirit. This was the essence of Bushnell's argument with Edwards Amasa Park of Andover Seminary.

Park had intended to mediate between the rationalist and the revivalist factions in New England Protestantism by elucidating the respective roles of the "theology of the intellect" and the "theology of the feelings." He defined the theology of the intellect as the stating of truth "just as it is," the development of theological ideas in propositional form, and the preference for the literal, as opposed to the figurative, use of language. He defined the theology of the feelings as a matter of the heart which expresses itself in metaphors and other "vague, indefinite representations." Although Park (unlike most of the contentious parties of the time) claimed that the two approaches to religious truth could complement each other, he clearly deemed the theology of the intellect to be the superior of the two. He held that "the intellect must be the authoritative power, employing the sensibilities as indices of right doctrine, but surveying and superintending them from its commanding elevation'' and framing into propositional form the one, consistent meaning symbolized by the diverse feelings.[24]

Bushnell found that Park's argument, however irenic its intention, revealed a misunderstanding of religious expression widespread among New England theologians. Above all, Park and his kind failed to recognize how all rational propositions are themselves ''packed full of figures and images''; they refused to admit that human language ''has no exact blocks of meaning to build a science of.'' All language, in other words, is referential and symbolic and does not contain or capture truth. The denial of the fluidity of language with claims about the intellect's ability to state truth ''just as it is'' in propositional form can only serve to produce a theology even more ambiguous than its metaphorical language already makes it.[25] Furthermore, propositional theology, even if it could capture truth, would thereby abstract truth from the vital, experiential Christianity of the New Testament. Bushnell believed that John Bunyan had correctly understood the fundamental question about religious discourse:

> But must I needs want solidness, because
> By metaphors I speak? Were not God's laws,
> His gospel laws, in olden time, set forth,
> By Shadows, Types, and Metaphors?[26]

To replace the rationalistic, propositional theology of so many of his American contemporaries, Bushnell called for a theology that was deliberately an art form, a kind of poetry of the divine and the human spirits. The theologian, instead of attempting to dissolve mystery with propositional language, should make every effort with his words to preserve religious mystery, thereby calling attention to the manner in which the truths of God surpass human comprehension. Such a theologian will employ ''a symbolism, through which the infinite and the unknown are looking out upon us, and by kind signif-

---

24. Edwards Amasa Park, ''The Theology of the Intellect and That of the Feelings,'' *American Philosophic Addresses, 1700–1900*, ed. Joseph L. Blau (New York: Columbia University Press, 1946), 627–58.
25. ''Gospel a Gift to the Imagination,'' *Building Eras*, 269–80.
26. *Ibid.*, 285.

icances, tempting us to struggle into that holy, but dark profound, which they are opening.''[27] The theologian as poet knows the limits of human language: it cannot encapsulate truth. But he also knows its power: it can, if used imaginatively, enliven human existence. ''The poetic forms of utterance are closer to the fires of religion within us, more adequate revelations of consciousness, because they reveal it in flame.''[28]

Bushnell takes into this poetic understanding of theology the central doctrines, persons, and events of Christianity. Christ is ''God's last metaphor,'' the best display in human history of God's mystery and a personal symbol calling for an imaginative, life-transforming appropriation from the ''reader'' of history. The Atonement is the expression of God's character as love and unites the humanly subjective and the divinely objective aspects of religious symbolism. The Trinity is a symbol of the being-of-God-in-action, a symbol *''that God is a being practically related to his creatures.''*[29] Sacrificial rituals in the Bible are metaphoric enactments of the mysterious, redemptive activity of God within the human spirit. The Lord's Supper is a pledge of God's special presence as humanized, a symbolic pledge that reaches behind thought to the sympathies of the imagination.[30] Indeed, the whole of nature and history function for Bushnell as a language of God, a vast storehouse of religious symbols designed to prompt an imaginative response from the human beholder. That response is, when accompanied by thoughtful, metaphoric expression, theology at its best.

Although Bushnell's poetic theology was developed most explicitly as an alternative to the rationalism of Protestant orthodoxy, he offered it as an alternative to other theologies as well. Unitarians, who had departed the orthodox camp of the Congregational Church because certain traditional doctrines could not be reconciled with human reasonableness and a sense of fair play, were, according to Bushnell, just as guilty as the orthodox of an unimaginative interpretation of Christian doctrine. In rejecting the Trinity or ancient creeds, for

---

27. ''Dissertation on Language,'' *God in Christ*, 88.

28. *Christ in Theology* (Hartford: Brown & Parsons, 1849), 87.

29. ''The Christian Trinity a Practical Truth,'' *Building Eras*, 136.

30. ''The Meaning of the Supper,'' *The Spirit in Man. Sermons and Selections* (New York: Charles Scribner's Sons, 1903), 278–79.

example, the Unitarians were unwilling to look for the symbolic meaning of Christian traditions because they assumed that those traditions expressed fixed, literal, antiquated ideas.[31] Proponents of "natural theology," those who argued that a Divine Designer could be inferred directly from the harmonious operations of the natural world, combined literalism with wishful thinking. How, Bushnell asked, could one argue that nature serves the end of demonstrating the harmonious designs of God or the well being of creatures when nature is so obviously filled with gratuitous poisons, destructions, and pain?[32] Better, and more realistic, to let the imagination play upon the full symbolic range of nature's harmony and disharmony, beauty and ugliness, good and evil, darkness and light.

The effort to liberate theology from all forms of literalism led Bushnell to insist that theology is best understood and practiced as an art form. And the effort at such liberation was motivated in turn by Bushnell's view of Christianity as a dynamic life process. Only a theology sensitive to the fluidity of human language, only a theology devoted to the imaginative expression of Christian doctrine, only a theology in which the human mind plays upon the diversity of nature and history could hope to conform to the Christian life conceived as a painful, joyful, free struggle of the human spirit.

Bushnell meant the style of his preaching, quite as much as the style of his theology, to provide an alternative to dominant practices of his time. In particular, he sought a way between two extremes: the dull doctrinal discourses of the Protestant orthodox and the manipulative, urgent pleadings of the Protestant revivalists. Neither extreme, in his judgment, cultivated a life of spiritual growth. And neither lifted before the minds of the auditors the imaginative wonder of the Christian tradition. Preaching should be an art form which stirs the symbolic consciousness and invites one to undertake the pilgrimage of faith. To achieve those ends, the minister should not hesitate to make his own personal presence felt in the pulpit, and he should carefully develop homiletical strategies. Above all, he should strive

---

31. "Dissertation on Language," *God in Christ*, 82.
32. *Nature and the Supernatural* (New York: Charles Scribner's Sons, 1877), 191–92.

to perfect the gifts of direct expression, lively images, and a tone of persuasion.[33]

In recommending such "pulpit talents," Bushnell identified his purposes with those of a host of nineteenth-century liberal ministers and lyceum orators. Bushnell, quite as much as an Emerson or a Channing or a Parker, sought to cultivate the art of eloquent discourse.[34] The art of speaking should attend self-consciously to the rules of the beauty of style, and its aim should be to inspire, edify, and persuade. Yet Bushnell held that authentic preaching was more than eloquence; it was, essentially, a call to faith. When devoid of that essence, preaching was not preaching at all but ethical oratory.[35] The chief shortcoming of ethical oratory is that it breeds subjectivism and a narcissistic preoccupation with self-culture. "Any strictly subjective style of religion is vicious," Bushnell said. "It is moral self-culture, in fact, and not religion. We think of ourselves abundantly in the selfishness of our sins. What we need, above all, is to be taken off the self-center and centered in God."[36] What can take us off our own center, what can direct our attention away from ourselves toward God, is the symbolism of the Christian religion. Symbols, when made lively by the preacher, speak to human needs and provoke struggles of human growth in such a way that the objective reference of the Christian religion is ever held in view. Then ethical oratory and its subjectivistic project of self-culture are transcended.

For all of his successful efforts to take American Protestantism in a series of new directions, Horace Bushnell was very much a man of his time and place. That is nowhere more apparent than in his assessment of New England. Bushnell was incurably and unapologetically a New Englander, at times a quite parochial one, and his New England bias was reflected in a number of his religious views. In his opinion New England had developed virtues, perfected attitudes, and attained achievements worthy of emulation by the nation as a whole.

---

33. Bushnell's views of preaching are summarized in "Pulpit Talent" and in "Training for the Pulpit Manward," *Building Eras*, 182–220, 221–48.

34. See Cross, *Horace Bushnell*, 75–85; and Crosby, *Horace Bushnell's Theory of Language*, 135–42.

35. "Pulpit Talent," *Building Eras*, 212.

36. *The Vicarious Sacrifice* (New York: Charles Scribner & Co., 1866), 542.

He was convinced, above all, that New Englanders had managed to balance civilization and nature. They had understood that the way of maintaining that balance is to adopt the ideal of the cultivated garden. Such an ideal implies that human beings are co-creators with God, finishing off with acts of beauty what God supplies in the rough:

> Thus God creates in the rough—land, sea, rivers, mountains, and wild forests. So far only does he make scenery, but he never creates a proper landscape. The rich fields, and gardens, and green meadows and lawns, the open vistas of ornament, the road-ways, bridges, cottages and cleanly dressed shores of water—all that constitutes the special beauty of the world, is something added, as finish, after the world is made.[37]

By perfecting what God had supplied, New England had established a model for the remainder of a nation struggling to become "civilized." California, by contrast, had not yet tamed nature with the human will, and its natural wildness symbolized the barbarism engulfing the state. For all of his paeans to the beauties of Minnesota's raw nature, Bushnell's most enthusiastic reports during a year in that environment concerned a New England family with well-filled bookcase who maintained the manners and customs of their origins.[38]

The virtues which Bushnell believed accounted for New England's successful cultivation of the garden of God were those of the Protestant work ethic. Industriousness, dutifulness, thriftiness, and the wise use of time were, for Bushnell, the practical expressions of religious faith and the very springs of the modern social order. He found in the simple, earnest, industrious, tough-minded, family-centered lives of his forebears in Litchfield County all of the characteristics suitable to a nation which would dare to become the seat of Western civilization.[39] He was convinced that the nation in its west-

---

37. "Our Advantage in Being Finite," *Sermons on Living Subjects* (New York: Scribner, Armstrong & Co., 1872), 340.

38. For Bushnell's reports on California and Minnesota see *Life and Letters*, 365–405, 423–38.

39. "The Age of Homespun," *Work and Play* (New York: Charles Scribner, 1864), 368–402.

ward expansion could avoid a headlong rush into barbarism only if the education, manners, Protestant religion, and industriousness of New England were transported in the process.[40] And though he warned of the vices of avarice, ostentation, and selfishness attendant upon the accumulation of wealth through work, Bushnell held that "it is the duty of every man to be a prosperous man, if by any reasonable effort he may."[41] The avoidance of prosperity itself, whether by individual or by nation, is simply a repudiation of God's call to hard work and thrift.

It is no wonder, given his celebration of this ethic, that Bushnell differentiated the human from the natural order with the principle of the will. Humans are "beings supernatural" because of their freedom to act from themselves rather than merely being acted *upon* in a deterministic series of cause and effect.[42] Although humans differ from God in the limits placed on their wills and in their choosing evil, they share this trait with the divine being: the freedom to transform nature, the ability to make choices which set the natural scheme of cause and effect into new combinations with new consequences. Bushnell's view of religious character presupposed this understanding of the nature-transforming capacity of the will.

There is another side to the religion of Horace Bushnell, however—one which illuminates the manner in which the meaning of human nature is exhausted by neither will nor work. Central to Bushnell's perspective on the human spirit is the principle of *inspirability*, a principle quite as definitive of human nature as that of the will. Persons are set apart from nature by their ability to receive revelation from God, as well as by their ability to transform nature. Other creatures "can be shaken, melted, exploded, annihilated by [God's] will, but they are not vast enough, or high enough in quality to be inspired by him. Spirit only can be inspired."[43] By the same token, the natural world functions not simply as a dumb piece of clay to be molded by human labor. It also serves as a vehicle of inspiration, as a means of religious communication. "The highest aspect of grandeur in God,"

---

40. "Agriculture at the East" & "The Day of Roads," *ibid.*, 227–61, 403–39.

41. "Prosperity Our Duty," *The Spirit in Man*, 138.

42. *Nature and the Supernatural*, 37, 40.

43. "The Spirit in Man," *Sermons for the New Life*, 33.

Bushnell said, "is beheld not in his knowledge or in his power but in his publicity"—a publicity apparent in a nature that is "laid and inlaid with types of thought" of the Infinite Mind.[44] Indeed, Bushnell discovered in his own New England natural environment stimuli to his religious imagination, a collection of symbols communicative of religious truth.[45] Nature could betoken more than the virtues of the Protestant work ethic. Context could serve as symbol as well as limit.

CHRISTIANITY AS LIFE PROCESS:
THE DYNAMICS OF SPIRITUALITY

Bushnell's personal turning point in 1848 was crucial for the development of his understanding of Christian spirituality. His wife recorded the event, writing of herself in the third person:

> On an early morning of February, his wife awoke, to hear
> that the light they had waited for, more than they that watch
> for the morning, had risen indeed. She asked, "What have
> you seen?" He replied, "The gospel." It came to him at
> last, after all his thought and study, not as something rea-
> soned out, but as an inspiration,—a revelation from the
> mind of God himself.[46]

What this report hints at, and what Bushnell himself later confirmed, is the conviction that human spirit and divine spirit may meet in easy, free accessibility, and that the meeting cannot be worked up by reason or by will. The implications of this understanding were expanded by Bushnell later that same year in a sermon entitled "Christ the Form of the Soul" and in a Phi Beta Kappa address at Harvard, "Work and Play."

In the sermon Bushnell suggests that in the phrase of Galatians 4:19, "Until Christ be formed in you," Paul summarizes the grand object of the New Testament message, namely that Christ is incar-

---

44. "Revelation," (MS in Yale Divinity School Library, 1839), 1–2, 27–28.
45. See, for example, *Life and Letters*, 531; & Cherry, *Nature and Religious Imagination*, 221–27.
46. *Life and Letters*, 192.

nated in the world by dwelling in the soul of every disciple "and giving it a form out of his own."[47] The form of the human personality is "character"; to have Christ indwell the personality, to have him "united to us and habited within us," is to be "charactered to Christ." The sermon stresses Bushnell's own recent religious discovery: God is easily accessible by virtue of the indwelling of Christ, and there is direct communion between the human and the divine spirits. God takes the initiative in forming the union; the human contributes to the accomplishment of God's work by emptying the soul of all hindrances.[48] Yet—and this was to be a constant refrain in Bushnell's version of Christian spirituality—the habiting of Christ within us is *the beginning of a life process:*

> The sublime reality is that the divine has made a junction with our nature, and Christ has begun to be formed within us—only begun. Henceforth the great object and aim of the Christian life is to have what is begun completed. Whether we speak now of growth, of sanctification, of complete renovation, or redemption, everything is included in this, the having Christ formed within us.[49]

Implicit in this sermon is the notion that the Christian life is a life of freedom, a life of spontaneity, an existence that transcends the strict plotting of one's being according to rules, duties, mandates. That idea is developed at length in the address "Work and Play." In so many ways the address may be taken as the key to the spirituality of Horace Bushnell. In it he looks beyond the limits of the work ethic, elevates the principle of inspirability over the principle of will, succinctly expresses the liberation he experienced in February 1848, and sketches the contours of much that he would later explicate respecting the meaning of freedom, spirit, love, and imagination.

The central claim of "Work and Play" is that "the highest and complete state of man, that which his nature endeavors after and in which only it fulfills its sublime instinct, is the state of play."[50] Work

---

47. "Christ the Form of the Soul," *The Spirit in Man*, 40.
48. *Ibid.*, 44–45, 49.
49. *Ibid.*, 41.
50. "Work and Play," *Work and Play*, 15.

is activity *for* an end; play is activity *as* an end. Work springs from a deliberate act of the will; play springs from inspiration or from an overflowing fund of vitality. Work, quite as much as play, is constitutive of human nature, and more often than not work is required to lead one to the point where the spontaneity of play can take over the human spirit. Still, play is a higher human state than work. In sports, philosophy, ethics, or the arts, we are not satisfied until we have moved from labor to enjoyment, until our activities are engaged in as ends in themselves rather than as means to other ends. Play, in other words, is the freedom to which every person aspires. And the Christian religion, which in its essence is liberty, is the consummate expression of play:

> As childhood begins with play, so the last end of man, the pure ideal in which his being is consummated, is a state of play. And if we look for this perfected state, we shall find it nowhere, save in religion. Here at last man is truly and completely man. Here the dry world of work and the scarcely less dry counterfeits of play are left behind. Partial inspirations no longer suffice. The man ascends into a state of free beauty, where well-doing is its own end and joy, where life is the simple flow of love, and thought, no longer colored in the prismatic hues of prejudice and sin, rejoices ever in the clear white light of truth. Exactly this we mean, when we say that Christianity brings an offer of liberty to man; for the Christian liberty is only pure spiritual play. Delivered of self-love, fear, contrivance, legal constraints, termagant passions, in a word, of all ulterior ends not found in goodness itself, the man ascends into power, and reveals, for the first time, the real greatness of his nature.[51]

The mental play involved in Christian liberty, that "rejoices ever in the clear white light of truth," is described by Bushnell in his other writings as the activity of the imagination. Religious imagination is the play of the human mind upon historical and natural symbols in such a way that religious meaning is found *within* those symbols. Rather than attempting to abstract propositional truth from the sym-

---

51. *Ibid.*, 38.

bols (the aim of nineteenth-century Protestant orthodoxy), Bushnell wants through his imaginative response to stay "by the symbols or in them." This means "ceasing to be busied *about* and *upon* truth, as a dead body offered to the scalpels of logic, and the giving ourselves *to* truth as set before us in living expression, under God's own forms."[52] Religious imagination, therefore, is first of all a passive act: it receives meaning from a symbol in much the same way that we receive from the face of a friend a message about his mood.[53] Yet Bushnell also attributes to religious imagination a more active function, one that probes beneath the surface of a symbol in order to stand before a truth transcendent of the form of the symbol.[54] This more active role of the imagination prevents the confusion of God's own truth with the finite form of the symbol. In both its active and its passive modes, religious imagination is spiritual play: it enjoys religious truth discovered within symbols as an end in itself.

Similarly, acts of the will may become activities of Christian play, described in "Work and Play" as "the simple flow of love." The labor of living according to precepts and legal constraints is surpassed when the object of one's love is treated as an end in itself. To call this self-transcending act of love a form of play is not to deny its utter seriousness, for it it essentially suffering love, a love that is "vicarious in its own nature, identifying the subject with others, so as to suffer their adversities and pains, and taking on itself the burden of their evils."[55] Yet it is a free flow of will toward the one loved and is, therefore, a form of play. As a free flow such love is not a passing sentiment dependent upon how the object of love responds; it is, rather, an act of character, a motion of the entire personality. "Love, in short, is not emotion, but motion rather; not some jet of feeling raised by objects and occasions, but the practical drift and current of the man."[56]

Inspiration of the human spirit by the divine spirit, continuous growth into the character of Christ, freedom to enjoy the other without ulterior motive, knowledge of religious truth through the play of the

---

52. *Christ in Theology*, 32, 91.
53. See "The Gospel of the Face," *Sermons on Living Subjects*, 73.
54. "Dissertation on Language," *God in Christ*, 82.
55. *The Vicarious Sacrifice*, 42.
56. "The Eternity of Love," *The Spirit in Man*, 244.

imagination, the free flow of the self beyond its constricting boundaries—these are the dynamic features of Horace Bushnell's view of
Christianity as a life process. Yet Bushnell was keenly aware that the
process is undertaken by imperfect beings set within an imperfect
world. Sin within the self and evil within the world are also parts of
the dynamics of Christian spirituality.

With human liberty comes the freedom to sin: the freedom to
repudiate self-transcendent love, to deform the highest form of human
character, to entrap the free flow of the imagination. Hubris, con-
cupiscence, destruction, and idolatry describe the human lost condition. "God wanted possibly, in the creation of men, free beings like
himself, and capable of common virtues with himself—not stones,
or trees, or animals—and that, being free and therefore not to be con-
trolled by force, they must of necessity be free to evil."[57] Bushnell
saw in the human choice of evil an act of cosmic consequences. Sin
infects the entire social order: as a "medley of common selfishness"
it takes on an organic, self-perpetuating life within the institutions
and customs of society.[58] Nature also is disrupted by the Fall. The
one system of nature (the fixed realm of cause and effect) and su-
pernature (the realm of freedom) is thrown into discord by human
sinfulness: "given the fact of sin, what we call nature can be no mere
embodiment of God's beauty and the eternal order of His mind, but
must be, to some wide extent, a realm of deformity and abortion;
groaning with the discords of sin and keeping company with it in the
guilty pains of its apostasy."[59] Bushnell had no sympathy for the
buoyant Transcendentalists who read the beauties of God and man
directly from nature. Nature was too ambiguous, too "carbuncled and
diseased," too disordered to serve as a direct correlate to the divine
beauty or to the human self made in the image of God. He found
within nature clearer images of the ambiguities and disruptions of
human existence.

It follows from this view of the radical and pervasive quality of
sin that human growth cannot mean a smooth progress or the attainment of fixed ends with mechanical regularity. Growth in the life of

---

57. "Salvation for the Lost Condition," *Christ and His Salvation* (New York:
Charles Scribner, 1864), 75.

58. *Nature and the Supernatural*, 135, 180.

59. *Ibid.*, 190.

the spirit is a constant struggle that carries no guarantees of success. Despite his preference for organic metaphors when describing both sin and redemption, Bushnell recognized the danger of adopting analogies from nature and applying them without qualification to a life governed by freedom:

> The growth of Christian virtue is no vegetable process, no mere onward development. It involves a struggle with evil, a fall and a rescue. The soul becomes established in holy virtue, as a free exercise, only as it is passed round the corner of fall and redemption, ascending thus unto God through a double experience, in which it learns the bitterness of evil and the worth of good, fighting its way out of one, and achieving the other as a victory.[60]

Although Bushnell was confident that with the divine spirit indwelling the human spirit victories against sin could be won, he held that the struggle to grow was a constant battle and that a blissful, unstruggling perfection was an impossibility this side of the grave.[61]

Bushnell did not balk at drawing the imaginative implications from a world torn by sin, suffering, evil, and frustrated growth. The reality of evil forces us to recognize that God can present a dark side of himself, that the goodness of God is no "mollusc softness" but a disturbing presence. "Whatever else may be true, God has created venom, and we must not scruple to say it. If we have any conception of goodness that forbids this kind of possibility in God, then our God plainly enough does not exist, or the God that does exist is not he."[62] In the teeth of those who would prove the beauty of God from the harmonious beauty of the world, Bushnell hurls the dark things of nature and history. Insanity, bad government, disgustful sights, severe winters, storms at sea—such things have their "uses" in the divine scheme. They can build moral character, and they can symbolize the darkness within the human breast. But their darkness certainly should not be passed over by the religious imagination. Evil,

---

60. *Christian Nurture* (New York: Charles Scribner's Sons, 1912), 23.

61. "God's Meaning in Probation," *The Spirit in Man*, 288–300.

62. *Moral Uses of Dark Things* (New York: Charles Scribner & Co., 1868), 281–82.

even the pursuit of evil for evil's sake, should be appropriated by the imagination. "Evil for evil's sake, disinterested evil, is the fearful possibility and fact that must have signs and language provided. In this office all the venomous animals do service, and more especially such as do not use their functions for self-defense, or the conquest of supplies, but distill their poison *gratis* or without reason."[63]

The darkness of Bushnell's vision is held in dialectical tension with its light. Fall and rescue, sin and redemption, darkness and light attain their full meaning when each member of the pair is seen in relation to the other member. Even the idolatry of the unredeemed imagination, that fixing of the mind and heart on an earthly form rather than on the infinite reality expressed within the form, indicates a yearning for God on the part of every person, a yearning that makes more delightful the enjoyment of God when he is found. Yet when union with God is achieved, the yearning is illuminated for what it is: a blind, sinful groping.[64] Bushnell best captures this complementary nature of opposites in his sermon "Dignity of Human Nature Shown from its Ruins." The dignity of the human self is evident in its tragic fall. "All great ruins are but a name for greatness in ruins, and we see the magnitude of the structure in that of the ruin made by it, in its fall. So it is with man. . . . How sublime a creature must that be, call him either man or demon, who is able to confront the Almighty and tear himself away from his throne."[65] Yet the Fall is not fully appreciated as a tragic lapse apart from the restoration of human nature in redemption; a tragic salvation illuminates a tragic fall.[66]

R.W.B. Lewis has correctly placed Bushnell in the tradition of the "Fortunate Fall."[67] The dynamic quality of Bushnell's spirituality is expressed in the words of an ancient hymn: "O happy sin! to deserve so great a redeemer." Sin, seen from the standpoint of redemption, is fortunate since it anticipates that redemption. And, as

---

63. *Ibid.*, 291.

64. "Religious Nature, and Religious Character," *Sermons on Living Subjects,* 134–35, 141–42.

65. "Dignity of Human Nature Shown from its Ruins," *Sermons for the New Life,* 54.

66. *Ibid.*, 66–67.

67. R.W.B. Lewis, *The American Adam: Innocence, Tragedy, and Tradition in the Nineteenth Century* (Chicago: University of Chicago Press, 1955), 61, 71.

Lewis observes, the idea of the Fortunate Fall has potent implications for understanding the development of the human psyche. Maturity is attained through the abandonment of innocence—that is, through the trials and tragedies of experience. This interpretation of Bushnell is important in differentiating him from a host of nineteenth-century American writers who sang praises to the innocence of the American Adam. Yet Bushnell would insist that one be careful not to lose sight of the full dialectical character of the Fortunate Fall. The Fall of Adam, that symbol of growth through experience in the loss of innocence, is not to be celebrated in itself. It is happy only because of the appearance of the New Adam. Darkness makes the light all the more enjoyable, but darkness is doom apart from illumination. To ignore that religious truth is, for Bushnell, to miss the full dynamic nature of Christian spirituality.

NOTE ON SELECTIONS AND SOURCES

The following selections were chosen to represent the chief features of Horace Bushnell's view of Christian spirituality as a life process. They are grouped thematically rather than chronologically under the conviction that the reader of this volume will be more interested in the relation among Bushnell's ideas than in the sequence of their emergence. But they are so grouped, also, in deference to Bushnell's insistence that his thought be approached as an organic whole rather than as a collection of disparate parts. [68] Selections are entire pieces or large sections thereof. In my experience collections which permit an author to develop his ideas in full selections are of more value than those which, in attempting to embrace many ideas from many representative sources, use snippets. Finally, preference is given to Bushnell's sermons and occasional writings rather than to his more discursive works. This preference seems advisable in a collection of readings designed to express Bushnell's views of spirituality, since he sought as a speaker, preacher and essayist to stimulate as well as explain Christianity as a life process.

Conrad Cherry
Summer 1984

---

68. "Dissertation on Language," *God in Christ*, 85.

I.

INSPIRATION

Fundamental to Bushnell's view of the human spirit is his conviction that every person is religious in the sense that a yearning for God burns within each human breast. Yet equally basic is Bushnell's belief that that yearning, or "religious nature," is by no means the same as being inspired by God, or "religious character." In the sermon "Religious Nature, and Religious Character," Bushnell describes the role of the general religious nature in preparing one to relish the character-transforming encounter with God, but he also differentiates between that encounter and the idolatrous, aimless searching which precedes it.

In 1875 Bushnell began a tract on the Holy Spirit which he never completed, but what he did manage to finish elevated "inspirableness" as the supreme human faculty. In "Inspiration by the Holy Spirit" Bushnell summarizes the work of God in moving the person from searching to finding, from inspirableness to inspiration, from promise to fulfillment. And he affirms in the selection many of the motifs of his entire view of Christian spirituality: inspiration by the Spirit of God, the freedom of the person to respond to the inspiration, and the meaning of growth into God's spirit over time.

This section of selections concludes with "Christ the Form of the Soul," the sermon which Bushnell preached immediately following his critical spiritual turning point in 1848. Flush with the religious experience which changed his existence into one marked by free, easy access to God, Bushnell elucidates what it means to be inhabited by Christ and launched on a life of growth into the likeness of God.

RELIGIOUS NATURE, AND RELIGIOUS CHARACTER[1]

"That they should seek the Lord, if haply they might feel after him, and find him, though he be not far from every one of us."—Acts 17:27.

Sometimes a truth or distinction of the greatest consequence will come into expression in a writer's language, when he does not notice it, or is not particularly aware of it himself. Thus Paul, in his notable speech here to the men of Athens, drops out, unawares to himself, in the form of his language, a most accurately drawn distinction that is of the highest possible consequence. In passing through their city, and beholding their devotions, he had been strangely affected by finding, among others, an altar to the *Unknown God*. That was the type, in a sense, of all their idolatries. In them all, impelled by a natural instinct for religion, they were ignorantly worshiping; wanting a God, and feeling after him, but not able to find him. And yet he is not hidden, wants to be found, orders every thing to bring them to himself.

This expression, "feel after," has a mental reference plainly enough to what they, as God's blind offspring, were doing; and the expression, "find him," to what God, never afar off, wants to have them do. In one, the deep longing of a nature made for God and religion is recognized; in the other, a satisfied state of holy discovery and rest in God.

What I propose, accordingly, at the present time, is to unfold, if I can, the profoundly real and practically wide distinction here suggested, *between having a religious nature, and being in a religious life;* or, what in fact is the same, *between feeling after God, and finding him.*

In proposing this distinction, it may be important to say, that I do it with deliberate reference to what appears to be a great religious danger of our time. It used to be the common doctrine of sermons, as many of you will remember, that mankind, under sin, have really no affinity for God left. Total depravity was made total, in such a sense as to leave in the soul no receptivity for God whatever. Human

---

1. From *Sermons on Living Subjects* (New York: Scribner, Armstrong & Co., 1872), 129–47. Date of delivery unknown; first published in 1872.

nature itself, it was declared, is opposition to God; able, therefore, only to be the more exasperated in its opposition, the nearer God is brought. Instead of having still a religious nature, it seemed to be supposed that we have rather an anti-religious nature, and that nothing can be done for us or by us till a new nature is given.

All which now is virtually gone by. We familiarly recognize now the fact of a religious nature still left, hungering and heaving in us, and beginning oft to be in want; longings after the divine, however suppressed by the overmastering tides of evil and vain desire. The soul, we believe and acknowledge, has a sensibility to good and to God, able to be drawn by Christ lifted up, capable thus of being recovered to holiness without being literally new-created in it. And the result is what might well enough be expected. Where before, the soul, heaving and hungering and often much disturbed, was battered and beaten down by the huge impossibility of religion,—dumbed even to prayer, and kept in stern dead-lock, waiting for the arrival of God's omnipotence to remove the opposition of nature, and give the new heart of grace—we are passing out rather now into a kind of holiday freedom, talking piety as a natural taste, enjoying our fine sentiments of reverence to God, and protesting our great admiration of Christ and his beautiful lessons,—all in the plane of nature itself. Multitudes of us, and especially of the young, congratulate ourselves that we are about as good Christians, on the ground of mere natural sentiment, as need be. Nay, we are somewhat better Christians than there used to be, because we are more philanthropic, better reformers, and in that are so easily up to the level of Christianity, in a fashion of piety so much more intelligent. Our doctrine of the gospel grows flashy, to a large extent, in the same manner. High sentiments, beautiful aspirations, are taken, sometimes wittingly and sometimes unwittingly, as amounting to at least so much of religious character. Where we shall be landed, or stranded rather, in this shallowing process, is too evident. Christianity will be coming to be more and more nearly a lost fact. A vapid and soulless naturalism will be all that is left, and we shall keep the gospel only as a something in divine figure and form, on which to play our natural sentiments. In this view it is that I propose the distinction stated, between having a religious nature, and being in a religious life. That we may unfold and verify this distinction, consider,—

1. What it is, accurately understood, to have a religious nature.

It is neither more nor less than to be a man, a being made for God and religion; so far, and in such sense, a religious being. It implies, in other words, that we are so made as to want God, just as a child's nature wants a mother and a father. It does not follow, that the child ever knew, or, practically speaking, ever had either one or the other. And yet the want is none the less real on that account; for when it feels itself an orphan, out on the broad world alone, it only sighs the more bitterly, it may be, for the solitary lot it is in: and, when it notes the tender love and faithful sympathy in which other children are sheltered in their homes, how sadly does it grieve and weep many times for that unknown, unremembered parentage it can never look to or behold! So it is with our religious nature. It may not consciously pine after God, as an orphan for his lost parents; and yet God is the necessary complement of all its feelings, hopes, satisfactions, and endeavors. Without God, all it is becomes abortion. It wants God as its completest, almost only want; feeling instinctively after him even in its voluntary neglect of him, and consciously or unconsciously, willingly or unwillingly, longing and hungering for the bread of his fatherly relationship. And it hungers none the less truly that it stays aloof from him, refuses to seek him in prayer, tries to forget him and be hidden from him, or even fights against all terms of duty towards him; even as the starving madman is none the less hungry, or fevered by hunger, that he refuses to eat.

Now this natural something in the soul, which makes God its principal and first want, includes very nearly its natural every thing. It has not a faculty that is not somehow related to God. It feels the beauty of God, even his moral beauty. All its bosom sentiments would play around him, and bask in his goodness. Considering who God is, it has the feeling of admiration towards him, rising sometimes even up to the pitch of sublimity. God's creating strength and all-dominating sovereignty in good, are just that in the soul, without which he would not be sufficiently great. His omnipresence, thought of it may be with dread, is yet thought of also as the needed qualification of a complete world-care and government. Reason gets at no limit of rest and satisfaction till it culminates in God. The imagination flies through solitary worlds of vacancy and cold, till it feels the brightness of God's light on its wings, and meets him shining everywhere. Even fear wants to come and hide in his bosom; and guilt, withering under his frown, would only frown upon him if he were not exactly just, or less just than he is.

There is a kind of incipient feeling after the state of piety thus, in what we call the religious nature. It has great sentiments swelling in its depths, honors waiting there for truth, glad emotions waiting to spring up and meet the face of God's beauty, aspirations climbing after his recognition, dependencies of feeling running out their tendrils to lay hold of him in trust.

Nor let any one imagine that these things are at all the less true, under the perverse and perverting effects of human depravity. Human nature as created is upright, as born or propagated, a corrupted and damaged nature. But however corrupted and damaged, however fallen, it has the original divine impress on it, everywhere discernible. It has the same feelings, sentiments, powers of thought and affection, the same longings and aspirations, only choked in their volume, and crazed by the stormy battle of internal discord and passion in which they have their element. The most sad fact—fact and also evidence— of human depravity is, that the religious nature stands a temple still for God, only scarred and blackened by the brimstone fires of evil; more majestic possibly as a ruin, than it would be if it did not prove its grandeur by the desolations it withstands.

Denying therefore, as we must, that human nature is less really religious because it is depraved, or damaged by sin,—as on mere physiological principles it must be—denying also that it is made incapable of approving or admiring God, or being drawn by his beauty, it is not to be denied that there are times or moods, when it will even be exasperated by his very perfections; that is, when it is tormented by its own guiltiness, and resolved on courses of life which God is known, with all his might of sovereignty, to oppose. At such times, there will flame up a horrible fire of malignity; and the better he is, the more dislike of him will be felt. But these are only moods. The same persons, in a different mood, when they are not thinking of themselves, and not pressed by the sense of conflict with him, will think of him admiringly, and almost lovingly; as it were, feel after him, to know him more perfectly. The religious nature in them is more constant than their moods of perversity, and is reaching after God in a certain way of natural desire all the while. Holding fast now these conceptions of the religious nature, let us pass on,

2. To inquire what it is to be in the practically religious life; or, what is the same, to be in religious character. There is nothing practical in having a merely religious nature. A very bad man has it as truly as a good: the most confirmed atheist has it. Mere natural desire, want, sentiment God-ward, do not make a religious character. They are even compatible and consistent often with a character most profoundly irreligious. What does it signify that the nature is feeling after God, when the life is utterly against him? If a man has a natural sense of honor, does it make him an honorable man, when he betrays every trust and violates every bond of friendship? If a man has a fine natural sensibility to truth, does it make him a true man, when he is a sophist or a liar in all the practice of his life? Where there is naturally a fine sense of moral beauty, and a capacity to draw the picture of it even with admirable justice and artistic skill, does it make the man a morally beautiful character, when his life, as will not seldom happen, is a life in utter disorder and deformity? Even a thief may have a good sentiment of justice, and be only the more consciously guilty because of it. There may even be a wondrously tender sensibility in the heart of a robber or assassin; such, that in his family, or among his clan, he will be abundant in the most gentle and kindest offices. And in just the same way a man may have the finest feeling of natural reverence to God, the highest sentiments of admiration for God's character, the grandest rational convictions of his value to the world, as its moral Governor[2] and providential Keeper, and yet not have so much as a trace of genuine piety in the life. He may even go so far as to enjoy the greatness and beauty of God, and have the finest things to say of him, and have no trace of a genuinely religious character, any more than if he were enjoying or praising a landscape. He will do the two things, in fact, in exactly the same manner; and one will have just as much to do for his piety as the other.

What, then, is it to be a practically religious man? When is it and how, that a man begins to be religious in the sense of religious character? To conceive this matter distinctly, two things need to be understood beforehand. First, that religious character is more than

---

2. Many New England theologians, including Bushnell's teacher at Yale, Nathaniel Taylor, made God's moral government of the world the center of their interpretations of Christianity. Here and elsewhere Bushnell challenges the centrality of that doctrine.

mere natural character, and different from it, as what we are by con-
stitution is different from what we do, and practically seek, and freely
become. It is that which lies in choice, and for which we are thus
responsible. It is made by what the soul's liberty goes after, with a
reigning devotion,—what it chooses and lives for as its end. If the
man, therefore, lives for himself, or for the world, as all men do in
the way of sin, he is without God, without religious character, and is
all the more guilty in it, that his nature is feeling after God in throes
of disappointed longing. Then again, secondly, it must be understood
that souls are made for God, to have him always present in them, and
working in their liberty itself, even as gravity is in matter, impelling
its motions. They are to know God and be conscious of him, even as
they know and are conscious of themselves. They are to live and move
and have their being in him,—not as omnipresence only, but as inward revelation. Inspiration is to be their life, and their freedom is to
be complete in the freedom and sovereignty of God. As they are God's
offspring, they are to live in his Fatherhood, and have their finite
being complemented in the sense of his infinite greatness and perfection inwardly discovered.

Assuming these two points, it follows that a man is never in
religious character till he has found God; and that he will never find
him, till his whole voluntary nature goes after him, and chimes with
him in his principles and ends. Whatever ends he has had of his own
must be given up, as being his own, and God's must be enthroned in
him by a supreme devotion. "Ye shall seek for me and find me, if
ye search for me with all your heart." God can not have room to
spread himself in the soul, and fill it with his inspirations, when it is
hugging itself, and is habitually set on having its own ways. A great
revolution is so far needed, therefore, if it is to find God; for God can
not be revealed in it, or born into it, save when it comes away from
all its lower ends to be in God's. No movings of mere natural sentiment reach this point. Nothing but a voluntary surrender of the whole
life to his will prepares it to be set in this open relation to God. And
just here it is, accordingly, that religious character begins. The soul,
as a nature, feeling instinctively after him, baffled still and kept back
by self-devotion, has in fact no trace of piety. It is only when God is
moving into it, and living in it, that the true piety begins: this is the
root and life of the religious character. Now it communes knowingly
with God, receives of God, walks with God, and lives by a hidden

life from him. Now, for the first time, the religious nature is fulfilled, and all its longings rest in the divine fullness. It has found God. Observe now,—

3. How easily, and in how many ways, the workings of the mere religious nature may be confounded with the workings of religious character, and, as successful counterfeits, take their place. The admiration of God's beauty—what is it, some will say, but love? Do we not, then, all of us, love God? The sentimental pleasure felt in God's qualities,—what is it but the real joy of religion? and how satisfactory it is to think so! Even the soul's deep throbs of want,—what are they but its hungerings after righteousness? and that void of hunger must be filled, even though it refuses to be. So they think. In short, there is a vast religious poetry in the soul's nature; and what is it all but a religious character begun? Is any thing more certain, as we look on man, than that he is a religious being; and what is this, by a straight inference, but to say that he has a naturally religious character? And so it comes to pass, that religion is the same thing as mere natural sentiment; and the feeling after God—poor, flashy delusion!—substitutes the finding God altogether. And this it is thought, by alas how many, is the more intelligent kind of religion! They love to hear of it, because it plays on their natural sentiment so finely. It is almost a modern discovery, and they love to be religious in this way. It will not organize a church, or raise a mission, or instigate a prayer, or help any one to bear an enemy, and even quite dispenses with finding God; the Spirit of God bearing witness with our spirit is not in it; but, for all this, it seems to be a more superlative kind of religion!

We can hardly think it possible that a feeble imposture like this should beguile the most common understanding; and yet we have had a most eloquent teacher[3] of this religion vaunting himself in it, here in our New England, as if it were the true Christianity! He finds a natural reverence for God in souls, sentiments of adoration towards him, longings that feel after him; and that he calls religion. All men have it; no man, even the worst, wants it. And the true doctrine is, that, living in the plane of nature, we are to cultivate ourselves in it, and grow better always—certain always of being religious because of it. And this kind of mock gospel is infusing itself, by a subtle con-

---

3. This "teacher" could be any one of a number of American transcendentalists or Unitarians, but Bushnell likely has in mind Ralph Waldo Emerson.

tagion, into the general mind of our times; appearing and reappearing in our literature, sometimes in our sermons, and turning our youth quite away from every thing most vital and solid in the supernatural, soul-renewing doctrine of Christ.

It is exactly the religion of Herod, who did many things under John's preaching, and heard him gladly, and then took off his head to please a dancing woman. He had all the sentiments of religion, and loved to have them brought into play; but the graceful trip of dancing feet pleased him a great deal more! Pilate, the Roman, had the same religious nature, felt the greatness, quivered in sublimest awe of Jesus, and devoutly washed his hands to be clear of the blood, and ended by giving up the glorious and majestic victim to his murderers. Felix had the same religion; so had Agrippa; so had Balaam; and the world is full of it,—sensibility to God, truth, right, coupled with a practical non-reception of all.

It results, accordingly, just as we should expect, that there are always two kinds or classes of religion in the world; those which are the product of a religious sentiment more or less blind, and those which look to the regeneration of character; religions that are feeling after God, and a true religion that finds him, and discovers him inwardly to the soul. The religion of the Athenians was of the former class, and all the idolatrous religions of the world are of the same kind. What a sublime and almost appalling proof of the religious nature of man, feeling dimly, groping blindly after God, imagining that he is somewhere and everywhere; in the sun, in the moon, in the snakes of the ground, the beetles of the air, the poor tame vegetables of the garden, the many-headed monsters carved in wood or stone, that never were any where but in the crazy fancy of superstition! Look on these, and see how man feels after God: does he therefore find him? And if we speak of character, truth, love, mercy, purity, in what do those blind struggles of our almost divine nature issue, but in a defect of every thing heavenly, and even comely? What but hells of character are these idolatrous religions?

Under the guise of Christianity, too, we may distinguish at least two kinds of religion, that are corrupted in a greater or less degree by infusions of the same error. One is the religion of forms, where the soul is taken by them as a matter of taste; loves to play reverence under them; has a great delight in their beauty, antiquity, order; and takes the mere sentimental pleasure it has in them, and the hope of being buried in them, for the certain reality of religious character. The other is a religion of sentiment throughout, and fed by reason; feeling after God in the beautiful and grand objects of nature; pleased to have such high sentiments towards him; taking hold of these sentiments to cultivate them more and more; delighted with Christ's beautiful lessons of natural virtue; and praising him even as the finest of all the great men of the world! It is not intended, under either of these mistaken forms of worship, to renounce Christianity; and the mischiefs they propagate in their adherents are in all degrees. Sometimes the infusion of sentimentality is slight, sometimes it quite takes the place of piety, and there is no room left for so much as a vestige to grow. Now, the true gospel is that which brings a regenerative power, and creates the soul anew in God's image. Any religion that has not this is so far a mock religion. The true test question, therefore, by which every man is to try his religion is this,—have I found God in it? Has it more than pleased me? has it pierced me, brought me to the light, given me to know God? If it has not done this for you, too little can not be made of it. And the sooner it is cast behind you, with all its fine sentiments, in a total turning of your heart to God himself, the better. *The life of God in the soul of man,*—that is religious character, and beside that there is none. And that is salvation, without which there is no salvation. For this it is that makes salvation; that the soul, before without God alienated from the life of God, is won back to a real God-welcome, and has him revealed inwardly in holy Fatherhood, as the life of its life. Hungry as the prodigal, it has come back from its wanderings in shameful penitence, to be greeted with a kiss, and clothed again, and feasted, and hear its Father say, "O dead, thou art alive again!"

Having endeavored, in this manner, to impress the wide distinction between a religious nature and a religious character, between feeling after God and finding him, I must bring my illustrations to a close.

The sum of the whole matter is this,—understand, have it never to be disguised from you, that your salvation lies in finding God, and that you may know your salvation only as you know that you have found him,—know that you have found him as the graciously felt preserver, the conductor, guide, peace, joy of your heart. You will not know him outwardly, but within by the secret flood of his movement in your life. You will be consciously configured to his character as once you were not; raised, exalted, married to his ends, one with him. Count yourself no Christian, because you like thoughts and discourses about God. Be jealous of any gospel that merely pleases you, and puts your natural sentiments aglow. See God in the flowers, if you will; but ask no gospel made up of flowers. Look after a sinner's gospel, one that brings you God himself. Doubtless you are hungry; therefore you want bread, and not any mere feeling after it. Understand the tragic perils of your sin, and think nothing strong enough for you but a tragic salvation. Require a transforming religion, not a pleasing. Be enticed by no flattering sentimentalities, which the children of nature are everywhere taking for a religion. Refuse to sail in the shallows of the sea; strike out into the deep waters where the surges roll heavily, as in God's majesty, and the gales of the Spirit blow. Man your piety as a great expedition against God's enemies and yours, and hope for no delicate salvation, not to be won by great sacrifices and perils.

Let me add in this connection, also, a word of necessary caution respecting a particular form of unbelief that is now common. How many are beginning to say, and have it for a fine discovery, that there is no such thing as a distinction of kind among men; nothing to hang a distinction of worlds upon; nothing to make that distinction better than a superstitious moonshine of the past ages! Saints, and not saints; born of God, and not born; sons of God, and aliens,—these are all a kind of fiction that has come to an end. Are we not all religious, all good?—some a little, some more, and some very good? Even where there is no pretense of piety, where there is great wrong, corruption, brutality of life, is there not still a little sense of God that only wants to be increased; some tender yearnings after God, however suppressed? What have we, then, but distinctions of degrees, and no distinction of kind? Where, then, is the footing for heaven and hell? Let this fiction go: it is time now to be clear of it. I have shown you here, I think, where the true distinction lies, and the profound reality of it. No great gulf fixed was ever thought of that is wider or deeper, or more absolute. It is the distinction between a religious nature and a religious character. We all have such a nature, feeling after God; but we have not all found him. We all have religious sentiments, desires, yearnings; but how many never choose a religious end! how many, in fact, never did any thing in the practical life, but trample the sentiments, desires, yearnings of their nature, in lives of disobedience, and a fight of rejection against God and every holy thing! No, my friends, the gospel distinctions are not gone by; the heaven and hell of the Scripture are not yet antiquated. Here they stand, based in the everlasting distinction of kind: darkness and light, chaos and order, falsehood and truth, are not more opposite, more impossible to be reconciled. A religious nature signifies nothing where there is no religious character; nothing, I mean, but the greater wrong and wrath the more deserved.

Once more, it must strike you all alike, the most unreligious as truly as the others, that it is a very great thing, in such a view as that now presented, to have a religious nature. Oh, if you had any true sense of it, you would even begin to tremble at the thought of yourselves! See, the whole world over, in all ages and times, men shaping their strange religions: they are groping all and feeling after God, to them the unknown God. And you, it may be, are doing the same. Your great nature, made in his image, answers to him, reaches after him in suppressed longings. A sublime uneasiness keeps you astir, and you know not what it means. You think of it often, perhaps, or even speak of it complainingly, that God has made your life so strangely barren. The secret of it is, that you are empty, hungry, shivering in the cold, for want of God; and that because you seek him not. Always feeling after what you always have not, and even refuse to have: how can it be otherwise? And what is to become of this great, almost divine nature, that is heaving thus in your bosom? This will become of it, and nothing else. It will grope and writhe and sigh, only tasting now and then little admirations of God, till finally its lofty affinities will all go out and die. All faculties that can not have their use grow stunted and thin and withered, as inevitably even as an arm or a leg. How much more the godlike powers and affinities of the religious nature, when for years and years they can not have their God,—receptivities all, yet never allowed to receive.

So God understands himself; and therefore keeps himself near, wanting to be found. Even as the apostle told those groping, blind men of Athens, "Though he be not far from any one of us." They were all feeling after him instinctively, even in their vices and grim idolatries; and still he was nigh, ready, behind their thinnest veils of thought, to break through into the discovery of their heart. God was pronounced, in fact, upon their whole nature, in every faculty and fibre. And yet they could not find him. Therefore, also, he became at last incarnate in his Son, and put himself before their senses, and took society with them, and showed them what they might have thought impossible, that the unseen, infinite Being has a suffering concern for just those hungry natures that in sin are groping after him. And this Christ is for us all,—"the light of the knowledge of the glory of God." The veil is taken away. To come unto Jesus now, and believe in him as one come out from God is really to find him. No one can earnestly seek him now, and miss of him. Mere feeling after him by dim instinct will not find him, but earnest, honest, prayerful seeking will. And therefore he declared himself, in his first sermon, when he took up his ministry,—would that all ye hungering and groping souls could hear the promise!—"Ask, and ye shall receive; seek and ye shall find; knock, and it shall be opened unto you. For every one that asketh receiveth, and he that seeketh findeth, and to him that knocketh it shall be opened." What an opening is that which opens the discovery of God! and what a finding is that which finds him!

INSPIRATION BY THE HOLY SPIRIT[4]

I. Inspirability

Inspirableness, or the faculty of inspiration, is the supreme faculty of man. It is the faculty of being permeated or interiorly and receptively visited by the higher nature of God, communicating somewhat of his own quality. A window-pane is permeable by the light, but having no receptive quality it retains nothing. The whole body of natural substance in what is called the creation is permeable by the divine omnipresence or the all-ruling Spirit of God, but this mere going through of power lodges no quality where it goes, save that so much of inert substance is thereby modulated in terms of coun-

---

4. From *The Spirit in Man. Sermons and Selections* (New York: Charles Scribner's Sons, 1903), 7–33. The first section of an uncompleted treatise on the Holy Spirit, begun in January 1875.

sel and constituent harmony. The permeating Spirit of God, as Holy Spirit, is a different matter. We call it inspiration, because it inbreathes something of a divine quality and configures the subject in some way to itself. The sun has been shooting its beams for many thousands of years through the illimitable spaces of the sky and has not raised their heat even by a degree, because it has not encountered anything there that has a receptivity for heat. Whereas the beams of the Holy Spirit shine to beget heat, and to lodge a divine property in moral natures that is akin to itself. Job saw a great many things long ages ago that were never taught him save by his own self-discovery, and this, I think, was one: "There is a spirit in man; and the inspiration of the Almighty giveth them understanding." There was never a conception of man and of the Holy Spirit as related to man that was more exact or more complete. (1) The spirit in man is spirit not a solid too impenetrable or a vapor too fugitive to be taken possession of, but a grand receptivity of life. And then (2) the Spirit of the Almighty is like to it, to be inbreathed and interfused, and to make internal lodgement in it of his divine properties. Which is called (3) the "giving understanding." That is, wisdom is given, and good and great thoughts, and love and truth and energy—a nature, in short, so contempered to God and conformed to his counsel as to have a natural and free working with his. Man was made for this, from this sin took him away, and the Holy Spirit as a quickening and regenerative force is to beget him anew, and make his life a recovered inspiration, fuller and wiser and more indestructible than it could have been but for the double experience passed through.

It is hardly necessary to say again that this faculty of inspiration is the summit of our human nature. By it we have or may have the inhabitation of God. In a sense, God inhabits the world, and as we just now said turns all the mechanical powers and substances of things to work in harmony with his plan; but in this inhabitation of his Spirit he temples himself socially and morally in our human nature, working it responsively toward himself, imparting his own thought and the very habit in which he lives. In the completest and truly inmost sense, without putting any strain upon the figure, he makes us partakers of his divine nature. It really seems impossible that any human creature, however dulled or besotted by sin, should be inattentive to so great opportunity, undesiring or unexpectant of an honor and footing of life so transcendent. O, what other promontory that we pass over is fanned by such breezes of health and life-invigorating purity!

II. *Personality of the Spirit*

In the communication to us or lodgement in us of personal qualities, the supposition is involved that the Holy Spirit is a person. He cannot ingenerate or inbreathe sentiments that are personal, affections that put us in social and reciprocal relation with God, confidences that belong to a personal faith in God, if he be not himself a person. He might be Spirit to us in a certain pantheistic way, as when God is conceived to be the eternal run of causes; and might be just as really operative in what part of our nature belongs to the sphere of causes as he is to all mere things in the domain of nature, that is, no-wise operative save as all unintelligence may be; but he cannot waken love answering to love, nor move any sentiment that is to have society with sentiment in himself. In order to do this he must be a person; for without personality the thing is inconceivable or even impossible. That class of teachers who reject the Trinity very commonly resolve the Holy Spirit into a mere influence; and another class, who do not reject the Trinity but are overintent on saving the integrity of the will, that it may seem not to be taken away by the irruption of the Spirit in his converting efficacy, call him also an influence, denying that he ever operates save as by influence. But if we insist on reducing his work to a mere influence, supposing no direct agency of personal will, how is he to refashion the personal sentiments, as in regeneration, and set us chiming with God in the closest adaptations of character and the most intricate subtleties of his personal nature? A carpenter makes a tight joint by making it, and not by an influence on the timber. In like manner a power that can inwardly configure a soul to God, and conjoin it by living adaptations with his inmost nature, must be divinely personal itself, working more directly and less vaguely than by any mere influence.

But there is another and different kind of mistake at this point in over-asserting the personality. In preaching the Holy Spirit, a great many have it as their first point to insist on his personality, which, having duly established, they assume it in their simplicity to mean that he is, *more humano,* personal; so that when they meet the scripture figures of the Spirit, they assert and use them with a most unquestioning emphasis of literality which robs them of their true value, and throws them into a confused medley that is virtual distraction. How large a part of the disciples of our time are incommoded by this kind of distraction, I do not know.

Thus we have given us for epithets or instrumental conceptions of the Spirit the terms: "sent, sent down, poured out, descends, comes, withdraws, departs, present, absent, taken away, restored." Indeed, we can hardly pretend to recite the whole roll of the Scripture words and phrases thus applied, only never applied save in the tacit assumption of their figurative nature and their need of attentive qualification. The Holy Spirit is a person only in the sense that the Father and the Word are persons. Omnipresence is predicable of him as of them. But the epithets just recited suppose, every one of them in the list as far as the natural form is concerned, a lack of omnipresence. For it will be seen when the eye is run over the list that they are all words which imply motion in space, and a nature of course that does not measure space save by motion in it. They do not signify a being omnipresent or infinite. And yet they are all the better, if we can so understand, in that they handle truths concerning the Spirit by instrumentations of language that are finite. Thus when it is said that the Spirit is sent or sent down, the truth signified is not that he was locally absent or that he comes in a horizontal or a downward motion, but only that being inherently and always present he comes into a mode of power or of felt action. And then the word "sent" has another value, viz., that the Spirit is not conceived as omnipresence, beginning from itself to act, but as beginning from the Father and the Son, showing the whole circle of constitutive and redemptive agency concurrent. A great many persons indulge what they suppose to be their wit on these terminologies of Scripture language, asking how many Gods there are in the personal three of trinity? If the Holy Spirit is poured out, from what vessel, by what hand? If he comes down, why he might not as well have come up? Probably some really serious disciples get tangled in this net and know not how to clear their way. But the discovery should not be difficult that these figures of Scripture have an overplus of form besides the meaning, as all figures have, which overplus after it has served as vehicle for the meaning is then to be held of no account. So taken, they serve the uses of intelligence and cumber its processes by no distractions caused by residues of form that cannot be reduced. Thus when a man can pray: "Send down thy power," "Pour out thy Spirit," "Breathe upon us, O Breath," "Blow upon us, O Wind," "Come and be present with us," "Leave us not afar off," "Return upon us, Holy One of God," knowing perfectly that these lines of motion in space have nothing to do with his prayer save as machineries of language, how greatly is he helped in his endeavor and how perfectly clear of distraction is he! But suppose that, dropping out all these instrumentations, he were to begin at the omnipresence of the Spirit and word a prayer for these same gifts or bestowments, how very soon will he be instructed as to their necessity? "Come down"—No, that certainly is not what is wanted. "Draw near"—No, he is near enough already. "Grant us thy presence"—No, we have his presence before we ask it. "Return, O thou departed"—No, we must not ask it, for he is not departed. And so the prayer that was going to be worded without these finite epithets and figures fails and leaves us dumb, just because we have no vehicle. But how beautiful and simple and almost wonderful in the wisdom of its machinery is the prayer that can be wise enough to lay hold of the figures that are given, and use them as they are meant; for they are not meant to set the Spirit moving in space according to their forms, but simply to obtain a consciousness of his presence, who before was unconsciously or less consciously present.

III. By the Spirit God Communicates Himself

We may assume it without rashness to be the supreme object of God as the creator and governor of men to bestow himself upon them or be inwardly communicated to them. For this men are constituently made, even as an eye is made for the light. In a certain first view of things, observing chiefly the bounties of the world, one might guess that God's prime object here is the preparing of growths and fruitages that will grow men, growing animals for their sake; but in deeper second thought it will be seen that he is building and ruling for mind, to make himself the light of intelligence, the friend of guidance, the supreme joy of love. Physical production plainly enough is no main purpose with him. He glasses himself on every side in objects and forms related to mind. By music and fragrance and color he wakens the sense of his beauty. By unnumbered and persistent ways of discipline he trains experimentally to the knowledge of himself. So far, in things without, self-communication visibly engages him. To which, inwardly correspondent, we have the all-permeating Spirit engaged to fulfil the self-communicating purpose and become, what that purpose implies, a universal inspiration. What else or less can he be, as a Spirit omnipresent in all God's dispositions? As he is a universal Spirit, he must have a universal working. Gravity in matter can as well keep itself back and refuse to be more than a half principle, ruling it by half a law. The Holy Spirit carries the heart of God with him, and the heart of God is universal. To say that he ministers the love of God puts him in a like paternal relation to all mind, even as gravity to all matter.

So we reason, but where is the fact? someone will answer. Of course it will not be understood, when I speak in this unrestricted manner, that I imagine no kind of limitation such as will accord with the facts of observation. The term inspiration has been largely used in past times—almost solely applied—to denote a certain special infallibility in the Scripture writings and writers. That particular kind of inspiration, it is generally admitted, has fallen upon no mortal of the race for an almost geologic era—a subject that will be discussed at a future stage in my argument. I only suggest here that inspirable conditions are sometimes wanting or uninspirable conditions present, by which the ranges of inspiration are partially restricted. The universal inspiration of which I wished to speak is that which is grounded or supposed in the natural relation of God to souls; that which Job affirms, with a great deal more, when he says: "For there is a spirit in man; the inspiration of the Almighty giveth them understanding." By this we are to understand, first, a nutritive inspiration that unfolds the natural and moral powers, and secondly, a corrective inspiration. The former is absolute, entering without leave into all the growths of sentiment and intelligence. The latter is distinguishable in two degrees, either as act or as fact. As act, it is to God the permeation of his will in corrective and restorative impulse, while to the subject it is either a grace unobserved, or a grace resisted, or a grace accepted in true welcome. Wherein it becomes a grace as in fact, having found true lodgement and become the seed of a true character, a living, everlasting inspiration. This inspiration of fact is a great deal more, it will be seen, than a mere intromission of God, as in act; adding to the kind first-named the nutritive inspiration, what respects both character and the staple of the man, what is grown in him or what he grows

to be in the scope of his intelligence, the health of his moral sentiments, the beauty of his disposition, the generosity of his temperament. Raising these distinctions of inspiration, it will not be
surprising or extravagant to anyone that I assert the doctrine of a universal inspiration; for there will be room enough after that for any
kind of denial that will seem necessary to be made.

It is a pleasant evidence, here to be cited, that Mr. Emerson
appears to come as near asserting the fact of a universal inspiration
as he well can under his particular mode of conceiving such kind of
subjects. I refer to his chapter entitled "The Oversoul," where he
reports and represents the true inspiration better than he does in most
of his writings. By the Oversoul, he means in fact the Holy Spirit,
writing as one who is captivated by the beauty of his character and
office. He conceives him to be a kind of all-infolding Soul, communicating God and life to man and filling the office of an all-cher-
ishing all-correcting nurture in the race. He has no questions to raise
concerning the universality of the conception. Its beauty proves it,
he would say, to be true.

At this point two particular facts ask as it were to be named,
which as far as I know are never connected with the doctrine of the
Spirit at all. I speak of his inspirations in the time of infancy, and in
times of lapsed consciousness in the dying. Infancy has no Bible, no
language, no capacity for a time of representative instruction. All the
form-world of the mind is vacant or empty. But it is a world open to
the Spirit and the dear inspirations of God, where, going through as
living bible in the sweet effusions of love and gentleness, he may
lodge all most beautiful germs of character, probably sometimes
never to be effaced. He is completely beforehand here; milk before
the mother's, we may almost say; counsel infused before counsel
given. Hence the wondrous and almost divine beauty of childish un-
consciousness and guilelessness. It is the sole gift and grace of the
spirit. We call it angelic, finding flavors in it that we cannot impute
to any purest motherhood, or to anything but some celestial nutrition.

When the Spirit helps the dying it is in a different manner, but
sometimes in a manner scarcely less affecting. He has carried the
soldier through his war, and now he sleeps. For whole hours or possibly days he has been wholly unconscious and speechless. Is he
alone? or is his divine friend with him? How very often are we permitted to see! As, when he opens suddenly his eyes to say, looking

up and round: "Beautiful angels," "Lord Jesus, I come," "The gates, thank God, are open," "Good-by all." What is it now that puts it in the soul, shut up for so many hours in the supineness of a block, to break out thus perceptibly into second life and a second world, unless it be the Spirit of God, who has finished his charge and is by, as the second world's Lord also, to open the gates and usher him in? As he came to the infant, bible before Bible, so here he comes to the servant lapsing in death as a bible revelation within when the word without is gone by, to put him on thoughts not spoken outwardly, and to open discoveries that can be witnessed only by their own light.

IV. Promise of the Spirit as Paraclete

Just before the departure of Christ from the world, when gathering in his ministry for the close, he added a chapter promising a kind of new beginning to be inaugurated shortly before his departure, and to be carried on by a different executive agency. It is to be a dispensation of the Spirit called by the special name, Paraclete, a name designed to suggest his more official connection with the new economy now organized, to replace the old in which as Spirit he had hitherto held a less conspicuous place. This Greek name, Paraclete, is badly translated in our English version by the name Comforter.* Not that he is never a dispenser of comfort, but that this is never distinctively his office. The two elements of the word, Para and Clete—Near and Caller—are probably to have a meaning that is cast in that mould, indicating that the Spirit will have it for his office to call or draw or bring men to the new salvation provided. If the name Paraclete were translated Inductor, it would probably be as closely represented in the name as it well can be in English.

It is not the conception of Christ that the Holy Spirit as Paraclete is a new agent or a new fact promised. That kind of interpretation is one that is possible only to a certain want of culture. It imagines in fact that a new God or new Divine Person is now sent to undertake the world—a conclusion that will not be readily accepted. He comes, it is true, by promise, and so far there is an air of newness; but the

---

* The whole passage concerning the Comforter, John xvi. 7–14, is fully discussed in Part I., chapter 3, of my Vicarious Sacrifice, vol. 1.

newness consists in the fact that he before was more especially the illuminator of prophets and the counsellor and guide of magistrates, imparting a divine energy and capacity to the institutional men of the state or state church; whereas he is now to be, and be understood as appointed to be, the monitor and quickener of souls, dispensing to them life and salvation from the world's Messiah. That is, he drops out his more peculiar charge in the old semi-political economy, and takes up a charge that is more personal and experimental, and respects the propagation of life in all the people of mankind.

We distinguish in the form of the promise two points that Christ appears to have in mind, as points of advantage now to be served by the Spirit. Thus he tells his disciples, giving it as the occasion for a new administration, that the time has now come when the cause he is in will be more easily advanced if he, himself, retires. And he speaks in a way which shows that he is apprehending no mere fatality such as may befall him at the hands of his enemies, but is thinking rather of some prior condition that even requires him to be removed. "I tell you the truth, it is expedient for you that I go away." And if we begin to ask, why expedient and how? it is not difficult, I think, to hit upon the answer. Such a ministry as that of Christ in the world plainly enough could not be perpetual, or be continued for any but a short period of time. He is a visible and audible teacher, acting only where he is and when he is somewhere present; that is, under conditions of locality. He can traverse a small country; he can pass on foot back and forth between Jerusalem and Jericho, or between Jerusalem and Galilee. It is not reported, I think, that he ever went as far south as Hebron, or more than once as far north as Dan. He did once cross the border into the coast of Tyre and Sidon, but never found his way over to Damascus. Now consider that he is come into the great world to be the teacher and Saviour of the world, and it will be seen at a glance that he is capable in body of no such transitional velocity as permits the fulfilment of such an office. Besides, it is not enough that he should some time reach a given place or people; he must be with them every week all round the world. Considered thus as a bodily nature, which was to be the great point of the incarnation, his incarnation would thus be in another view his chain of detention, holding him back from everything most necessary to be done. Taken thus, in the large view of nations and peoples and in the long view of the times without limit, his bodily nature is adapted in fact to nothing which belongs to his undertaking. In fact nothing Christian can be done with Christianity till the visible head, the embodied Christ, is taken quite away and substituted by some other mode or machinery of action set in his place. No being can do the work that is undertaken but one who is not under conditions of locality and brings to it an attribute of universal presence. The incarnation is a means to an end only for a certain time. After that time it must be ended. The incarnate person, living in the form of God and revealing the beauty and tragic love of God, will have prepared the necessary power to engage the feeling and make up the staple of a regenerative gospel.

But he must not stay long enough to raise the question: How much longer? Three years of a merely cursitating pedestrian ministry are probably long enough to lodge this gospel in the world; and when that is done it is quite expedient that he go away. And when he goes, it is even required by the supposed conditions of the question that some unlocalized Inductor and Disseminator take his place, and minister his ministry without limit or travel or exhaustion. He requires too, it will be seen, to be omnipresent, not only as related to space but as related to mind—all mind that is concerned to know and receive the salvation provided. How sublime the transition, and how manifestly squared and appointed by the regulative wisdom of God! That the new Inductor thus to be established must be a Spirit divine is just as clear as that he must be inexhaustible, never to be wearied by his multiplicities or staled by time.

But there was another reason which Christ had in mind when he asserted the expediency of his removal and the introduction of a successor working by another method, viz., that his gospel, gotten into language by his incarnate ministry and teaching, lacked altogether when taken by itself the efficiency needed to make it a great converting power. It does not appear that Christ gained many converts by his preaching; partly for the reason, I suppose, that he was always too much of a problem to be a proper word of salvation. His miracles begot a state of questioning and of idle wonder too curious to be convincingly serious; much as we see now in the levitations and aërial transportations and ghostly oracles of our wizard practitioners. For the time, in the first stages of the development of his mission the promulgations bore a look of extravagance; for what could be the impression first made by the assertion of a descent from heaven and of a nature mysteriously akin to God, but that Christ in such pretences exceeded all bounds of nature and rational credibility? The material he was building thus into a history could never form to itself a state of settled conviction till after his withdrawment, when the disturbances of sight and sense were gone by. And not even then would there be any converting power in the revelation-story prepared.

Mere revelation, or a word of truth that has gotten form as in language, has by itself no effectually quickening or regenerative power in character. It stands before the mind, glassing truth in a way to act upon it, but it can accomplish nothing save as another kind of power acting in the mind makes it impressible under and by the truth. Hence the necessity of the Paraclete and the new dispensation, promised to complete the full organization of the saving plan. The gospel ended off in Christ or his personal story and set before the world would do little, save as another kind of power invisible is prepared in the world to raise a new sensibility for it and toward it. Christ himself describes the initiating function of the Spirit by saying: "When he the Spirit of truth is come, he will guide you into all truth. He shall glorify me, for he shall receive of mine and shall show it unto you." That is, he will set you in a state of sensibility toward the truth that will be its glorification, and bring you into it as a new life. What follows is to be taken more popularly, not as indicating that the Holy Spirit is to receive and pass and show the truth, as it were, by literally acting on the truth and with it, but that, by a divine acting on the man, he will give it a power to enter and possess and lodge itself and be inwardly appropriated.

It has sometimes been a seriously debated question whether the Holy Spirit operates by divine efficiency—that is, by the absolute sway of omnipotence—or, what is conceived to be the better alternative, by mere influence or persuasion. The former conception is certainly not true; for why should so great pains be taken to prepare a gospel of life when there is really nothing to be done with it? when, in fact, new character is to be struck out after all as by lightning, wholly one side of the word and the prayers of the faithful and even the prayers of the subject himself? But if we say that the Spirit carries all effect by influence, what does it mean? Influence we cannot imagine to be some third thing between the Spirit and the souls to be renewed which, by acting upon it, he can turn persuasively. The true

Christian idea appears to be that the Spirit operates efficiently in the subject to prepare him to the word, convincing him of sin, raising him up, for the time and more or less always, to a state of just sensibility, so that he may apprehend the divine things of Christ in a lively manner, and there stops short, as he must, laying no hand of force on the man that shall break his natural or thrust him out of his chosen liberty. Three kinds of agency must in this view always be concurrent in the change: first, the agency of the force-principle, uplifting the man to be swayed by his better sensibilities; secondly, the agency of the gospel or word-principle, prepared to work regeneratively in and through his sensibilities; and thirdly, the assenting faith and concurrent yielding of the man's own liberty.

It will appear from the outline thus far given that the Holy Spirit could not be conjunctively at work in his office at the same time that Christ was at work in his personal ministry. So heavy a disturbance in the senses took away of necessity all inwardness and power of meditational reception, requiring his particular saving work to be for the time suspended. He was not, of course, sent out of the world, but was present in all mind as before. But there was a kind of pause in the inspirations, as we ourselves feel, and it could not be otherwise till after Christ should be taken away. It may be that there had never been a time for hundreds of years when the tides of inspiration ran lower than when Christ was fulfilling his outward ministry. And then, when that was ended and everything was ready, as in gospel outfit, the new Christian era of the Spirit is inaugurated in the scene of the Pentecost, and his great inductorship is verified by the ingathering of converted thousands in a day.

V. *The Inaugural of the Spirit*

Assembled with the disciples after his resurrection, he commanded them not to depart from Jerusalem, but to wait there for the promise of the Father, "which," saith he, "ye have heard of me; for ye shall be baptized with the Holy Ghost not many days hence." They waited accordingly for the unknown something of the promise, continuing all with one accord in prayer and supplication for the unknown gift. It may not be, most strictly speaking, a gift unknown. He had called it himself their induement with power from on high and also, as we just now saw, their being baptized with the Holy Ghost. And this latter expression was yet further explained when he said, shortly after: ''Ye shall receive power after that the Holy Ghost is come upon you, and ye shall be witnesses unto me both in Jerusalem, in all Judea, and in Samaria, and unto the uttermost parts of the earth.'' They understand by a certain inchoate way of apprehension what it must signify to have power come upon them from above, what to have the Holy Ghost descend upon them; for there were desultory and sporadic manifestations of the Spirit all along down the Old Testament history; besides, they could hardly miss of some enthusiastic meaning in their own designation to be witnesses, the wide world through, to their Master and his truth. I do not say, observe, that they closely understood for what they waited and prayed. How many of the very best, most fruitful Christian prayers never come into their own full meaning till their answer is born. They are, in fact, prayers for the Unknown, lifting as it were by their upward pressure the veil of mystery that shuts them in, till such time as they break through into God's revelation of their meaning in their answer. As it was in the prayers for a Messiah to come, so it is to be in these prayers for the new forthcoming of the Spirit.

But the hour of the promise is now arrived. Suddenly there is a sound from heaven as of a rushing, mighty wind. What else, or less, should represent the invisible waft of the Spirit, the Pneuma or Life-Breath of God? And it filled and shook the place where they were sitting. Connected also with the wind-symbol, there were manifested lambent tips of fire sitting on the heads of the assembly; for this designation by flame was also needed to represent, as only fire can do it, the purifying touch and search of the Spirit. By these two symbols, breath and fire, added here as tokens, the virtual incarnation of the Spirit is also accomplished; for his revelation required his coming into sense just as truly as did that of Christ, and for the same reasons. Another fact is added as first effect, viz., the speaking with tongues; which shows the Spirit making discourse and playing out intelligence in words, a living proof that he is at the seat of intelligence within. So that here again the Spirit is got more nearly incarnated in that he is seen to be the occupant, if not of body, yet of mind.

Taking now all these externalities together as tokens of manifestation, how impressive and wonderfully apt is the inaugural of the

e

Spirit that is given. Without the first two, the wind-movement and the tips of flame, the tongues breaking out of silence in the little assembly would scarcely have been a sufficiently distinct announcement of the Spirit waited for, and without the tongues the other two signs would have signified nothing as regards a Spirit of grace for mind. Indeed, all three of the outward signs would have failed of their significance if they had not been followed by the very work of the Spirit itself, in a degree of power and cogency corresponding with the energetic vigor of the signs. And what do we see, but that these poor heart-broken disciples, who had been waiting here so many days for they knew not what, and had been disciples so far of a gospel whose meaning and future they as little understood as they did the future story of the seven stars, have their minds suddenly opened, and one of them begins forthwith to preach directly out the whole Christ-mystery of a new salvation for the world. Conviction by the Spirit goes with the word, and multitudes crowding in from all the streets are converted to God, three thousand in a day. And this makes up the true inaugural of the Spirit. Of course, he is not to be inaugurated as God. I only mean that, as the gospel is to be a personal grace for the world, the way of the Spirit in the old time is to be replaced by his all-diffusive and personal agency. I do not find that, before this, any distinct and generally prevalent impression was held of his practical relation to sin and the implanting of a new life-principle in character, unless it be in the fifty-first Psalm already referred to. This henceforth is to be distinctly seen, and the whole new ministry of the Spirit is to be cast in this mould.

It appears in at least two cases reported in the Acts of the Apostles (viii. 16, and xix. 5) that conversions, or what were so accounted, were made where the agency of the Spirit was for a time not understood; also, that when the sign of the Spirit was given in the laying on of hands or in baptism, the subjects immediately began to speak with tongues and to prophesy. Hence it has been imagined that these signs were considered to be and in fact were a fixed accompaniment of the Spirit. They may have been for a time, but after a time they certainly were not. The real question appears to be whether they belonged as casual demonstration to the inaugural of the Spirit, or whether they belonged to the appointed products and fruits of the Spirit for all coming time. There was certainly something casual in the demonstrations of the inaugural scene, and something not casual, something pertaining to what is most inherent in the gospel plan itself. Certain English teachers have gone so far as to maintain that the demonstrations of conversion in the scene of the Pentecost were themselves casual and extraordinary, having to do with nothing but the inauguration by the Spirit of a new Church order. Men, it is said, are not to be converted in this sudden, almost indecorous, way hereafter, but more gradually, in a more sacramental fashion. All these and other like questions will be discussed hereafter when we come to speak of miracles and supernatural manifestations, and are therefore passed for the present.

VI. *Ways and Modes of the Spirit*

When we undertake a doctrine of the Spirit, we begin at once to question about his line of approach, his point of contact, whether he works without contact and by what kind of power. But the better way is to conceive him as arrived without approach, at his point of contact without contact, working by no power physically representable. For all these are but figures of speech that undertake to dominate our conceptions, and if they are allowed to be accepted literally are sure to breed mistake. The better way is to seize on a word of description that is not under conditions of matter and space, and say that the Spirit is *immediately* present and works *immediately*—so and not otherwise. In this mode of statement we drop out a great many questions that are not to be answered, and obtain a so much closer footing of doctrine.

Starting now at this point of our immediate agency, is it so far immediate or in such a sense that it cannot be resisted? Many of the high Calvinistic school accept this conclusion without difficulty, and have it as a rather favorite form of doctrine to assert the resistless agency of the Spirit. The Spirit, they conceive, goes through to his mark like all the decretal forces and absolute determinations of God, and the agency is immediate in the sense that he does it as and when he pleases. He does not ask consent, but takes it without asking. This kind of teaching was never Scriptural, and is really a very great hindrance to any fair conception of the Spirit. The immediate agency of the Spirit supposes no such thing. We call it immediate because it is able without consultation or notification to raise a conviction, stir a feeling, turn the soul's currents of thought by a simply acted presence. But we need to observe that the agency of the Spirit, immediate though it be, is in two degrees, which carry a large distinction of idea, viz., the preparative or quickening agency, and the transforming or assimilative. We conceive it in the first stage as a power that wakens the religious nature out of sleep, makes the man attent, perceptive, receptive, and prepares him to be a susceptible receiver of God's revelations. By this mere quickening agency the man is prepared to the still more advanced kind of agency, for there is no such distinction of kind that the one may not pass forward into and be merged in the other. As a preparative and quickening agency, it offers the subject to God's love and beauty and truth in such a manner as to be most effectively drawn by their attractions. There he has it for his right to stand all his life long, and make good his resistance to the last. But the address of the Spirit to his conscience, which is made by the opening of his heart to the love and beauty of God, ought to win a lodgement for inspiration in the character when, of course, he is born of God by the opening of the heart, that is, by a preparative and quickening agency. For this is the way of the Spirit, who does not present the truth to the subject as filling the office of a preacher, but the subject to the truth, erect in the spirit of attention, quick in perception, tender in sensibility. He gives the truth advantage, not by adding a projectile force, but by setting all the windows of access open to its convincing and glad messages. His power as regards the new-born inspiration will be wholly in the man, never in the book.

It becomes a matter therefore of some consequence, in adjusting our conceptions of the Spirit, that we rightly construct our notions of his relation to us at the particular point of resistance. If he were out upon us in creative force, using omnipotence not merely at the point of quickening but in the very issue of conversion itself, it would be very difficult to adjust any moral conception at all of his agency. But we are abundantly authorized by many passages of Scripture to exclude any such idea. Thus it is declared by Stephen: ''Ye do always resist the Holy Ghost,'' which, of course, means that they resist in some measurable way and degree. The style of the accusation is hyperbolical, and is plainly meant to be. It is a charge sent home by rhetorical emphasis, which does not consider qualifications. Another passage supposes the possibility of resistance even to the extent of victory, at least for the time. The subject moved by the Spirit may turn himself away in such levity or neglect of manner as virtually to quench God's fire. "Quench not the Spirit," therefore, is the Apostle's very heavily accented charge.

Again, we have a very different case where the Apostle, speaking of such as have been graciously accepted and born of God, says: "Grieve not the Holy Spirit of God, whereby ye are sealed unto the day of redemption." Imputing grief to God is, to say the least, a figure of divine sensibility most remarkable. If there is anything tender in the world beyond all human comparison, it is this simple appeal to spare the grief of God.

Thus far we encounter no Scripture that regards the Holy Ghost as being so far offended by a course of resistance and bold transgression as to be finally and fatally irreconcilable. A single passage is often quoted as to that effect; that, I mean, which denounces the unpardonable sin, the sin of blasphemy against the Holy Ghost. Precisely what that sin is or was conceived to be I do not know, but words of blasphemy are words of wrath and desecration, words that are meant to mock the sanctities of the subject and trample him in contempt. Supposing an act committed of so great presumption, the consequences may follow in two degrees, or in one or the other of two degrees. The nature of the man may receive so heavy a shock as to be virtually paralyzed and be henceforth the end of all his religious sensibilities. The scorch of his sin has burned out his susceptible life. I have seen a great many persons who imagined themselves to be in this condition. But the remarkable thing in every case has been that, instead of being more inert and dead, they were lifted into virtual frenzy by the impetuosity of their self-accusations. If they are in such a state as they assume to be they ought even to care nothing for it, but think it a thing supremely ridiculous and laugh it away.

Another way to use this Scripture is to handle it in a way more loose and accommodating. Consider it, for example, as intended to be a very cogent warning—overstated, not exactly measured—bidding the disciples make a very serious matter of their relations to the Holy Spirit, lest they some time wake to the discovery that they have trespassed too far. Perhaps they will not be certainly forsaken of God, and perhaps they will. It would be a very hard way of treatment for disciples so little practised in divine things to be absolutely shut away from God, for the simple neglect of misimprovement of his Spirit on this or that or even many occasions. A great many of the Scripture threatenings are left in just this way.

CHRIST THE FORM OF THE SOUL[5]

Until Christ be formed in you.—Galatians iv. 19.

What form is to body, character is to spirit. For as all material bodies are shaped by the outline or boundary which contains them, so the soul has its working and life contained within the limits or laws of the character. Indeed, we can give no better definition of character than to say that it is the form of the spirit, that habit or mould into which the feelings, principles, aims, thoughts and choices have settled.

And as all material objects have their beauty in their forms, so the soul has her beauty in the character, that lovely shape of goodness and truth in which she appears to men. It is on the ground of this analogy between form and character that the word *image* is so frequently used in Scripture with a spiritual sense. Other kindred words are used in a similar manner. Thus it is that Christ, the divine Word, is spoken of as being in the form of God, the image of God, the image of the invisible God, the express image of his person. In the same way man is said to be created in the image of God, the design being not only to affirm a resemblance between his nature and God's, but also that his character is in the form or likeness of God.

It is under the same analogy also that we call sin, deformity. We conceive the feelings passing into ugly and perverse shapes, the temper growing angular and crabbed, the thoughts limping by the judgment-seat of the conscience as a troop of foul and half-disabled phantoms, the soul herself, in fact, becoming a shrivelled and withered form, a base and haggish spectre of guilt. Sin takes away the image or form of God, and makes the soul a truly deformed creature. Such is everywhere the representation of Scripture.

---

5. From *The Spirit in Man,* 39–51. An abbreviated version of the sermon preached in North Church, Hartford, in February 1848. Brackets in the text indicate the condensation of sentences and are part of the 1903 edition.

These remarks will prepare us to understand the real intent of Paul in my text. He is addressing the Galatian disciples, who have lost in a degree their spirituality, and he is afflicted by the deepest anxiety on their account. He longs to see them restored to the liberty they once had, to see them fixed in this liberty, and rising to a pitch of character that is high above their previous attainments. In a word, he desires their sanctification. And this he beautifully conceives to be the same as having Christ formed within them. "My little children, of whom I travail in birth again until Christ be formed in you." He imagines Christ dwelling in their soul or spirit, and giving it a form out of his own. This we may say is the grand object of the gospel plan. For this Christ is incarnated in the world. Being in the form of God, the eternal Word assumes humanity, that he may bring into humanity the form of a divine character. By the incarnation he descends to our level, and makes the closest approach possible to our human feeling. He lives with us and among us. He tastes all our sorrows and becomes a partaker in our adversities. He even bows himself to the burden of our sins and drinks the cup of shame and ignominy for us. In a word, he is as perfectly one with us as he can be and not be a sinner with us. Meantime he is the clear image of the divine beauty and goodness, the express image of God. We behold his glory, as of the only begotten of the Father, full of grace and truth. In his life all the depths of divine purity, mercy and goodness are unbosomed to us. We see, too, in his divine modes of carriage and conduct that which is the essential form of God's perfect character.

If now we embrace him, we embrace the divine Word. He becomes united to us and habited within us. Our love gives him a welcome in our soul and entertains him there. This we may call repentance, faith, conversion, regeneration, or by whatever name. The sublime reality is that the divine has made a junction with our nature, and Christ has begun to be formed within us—only begun. Henceforth the great object and aim of the Christian life is to have what is begun completed. Whether we speak now of growth, of sanctification, of complete renovation, or redemption, everything is included in this, the having Christ formed within us. This measures all our attainments, this is the mark of our high calling, the end or consummation in attaining which we are complete in all good. God seeks nothing else. We have nothing else to seek.

In this we see a beautiful correspondence with what we just now said of sin as a cause of deformity. The deformity is removed when Christ is formed in us. And how manifest is it that nothing short of this can truly restore our nature. Some persons imagine that nothing is wanting in us, save to do what we may in and upon ourselves by self-reformation, self-culture, a life of duty and good works and a faithful endeavor to polish and beautify ourselves. As if we could put ourselves on a footing with God without any gift from him, or participation of his divine nature! And what can be a more dreary and cheerless faith than this, which leaves a man only to his own will-works, to be forever at work upon his own soul and toiling at a self-perfecting process, without any sense of union to God or hope of a derivative grace from him. What a joy and relief it should be to the soul to find the incarnate Word descending to its aid, to go out of herself and rest herself in a love not her own, and thus to form herself unto a new and noble life by adherence to another!

When Christ says: "Come unto me," how deep is the meaning, if we understand that Christ formed within us is the very good he comes to yield us! And so, when he says: "I am the vine, ye are the branches," it is as if the divine life passing into the human were the hidden sap of the vine passing into the branches, to unfold the leaves and color the fruit. In like manner did the apostle, setting forth the whole scope of the gospel as a renovating power, say: "But we all, with open face beholding as in a glass the glory of the Lord, are changed into the same image from glory to glory." If, then, we are to succeed [in the effort to complete our Christian life] we must succeed in God's way, and take the method he himself has chosen. The main difficulty with us is to entertain a thought so high as that he is concerned to have Christ formed in us. Inspiring and glorious thought, if we can only receive it and believe in it! Open your soul to it and give it welcome. Consider and know that the divine Word, being himself in the form of God, has descended to you and become the foundation power of a new life in you. He comes to impart the divine. And this alone is your sanctification. It moves from him and not from you. It is no vague struggle to ascend some height you cannot see, no wearisome, legal drill of duty and self-cultivating discipline. It is simply and only to have your being filled and occupied and transformed by Christ. Consider what you would be if the divine Word had rested in you, instead of in Jesus the Son of Mary. What you would thus become, you are really and truly to be. Viewed in this light, sanctification is the brightest and sublimest thought ever offered to a rational creature. If you had thought otherwise before, if before the work seemed forbidding or dry, everything repulsive or uninviting now disappears.

Or if you have looked despairingly upon this work, believe in God, and your despair will give way to courage and hope. Doubtless your sins are strong and you are weak, but Christ is here, and Christ is not weak. Had you looked upon the vast abyss of chaos, without form and void and covered with the pall of darkness, you might well have despaired, considering only what powers chaos had in itself wherewith to pass into form, fill itself with light and clothe itself in beauty. But when you behold the divine Spirit hovering over it, and the divine Word by whom the worlds were made descending into it, to form it into shapes that dwell in the eternal mind, then surely there is hope even for chaos. So also in the wilder chaos of sin that reigns within you. There is nothing, in fact, that you can undertake with so great hopefulness and assurance as a victory over yourselves, if only you can believe in God. It is nothing then but to have Christ formed in you, and that is a work to be done not as much by you as by him.

Still there is something for you to do. And here we may sum up all in one comprehensive rule, viz., that you are to present yourselves to Christ in just that way that will most facilitate his power over you and in you. If you are truly his disciple and united to him by faith, then he has already begun the transforming process of which we speak, and nothing is wanted but to remove all hindrances out of his way and offer yourself to him in every manner, active and passive, that will most expedite his gracious designs. Make this your constant rule of proceeding, shape your life by it, observe it with religious fidelity. Let all your plans and works and questions be determined by this one law—so to conduct your life that Christ will have the greatest power over you and in you, and you will find all difficulties melting away before his gracious power. Live to Christ, and Christ will live and reign in you. Your mind will grow clear, your affections pure, you will ascend into liberty and the bondage of sin under which you now groan will be left behind you.

[What, then, is it to live to Christ?] Remember that he said: "Whosoever he be of you that forsaketh not all that he hath, cannot be my disciple." And in another place he says: "Deny thyself, take up thy cross and follow me." Now the object of these requirements is to empty the soul, so that Christ may find room in it. Therefore you must die to the world and to selfishness in all its forms, and here is the hardest struggle you have anywhere to encounter. The power of the world is great, and you are accustomed to bow to it and love it. The forms of selfishness are so many and so cunningly hidden that you will need to make the most searching scrutiny to detect them. The opinions and fashions of the world will crowd upon you. Your industry will tempt you, your idleness will tempt you. Flattery, money, ambition, society, the lust of the eye, appetite indulged so as to stifle your feelings and clog your spirit, carnal lusts, anger, pride, vanity, envy will all be trying their seductions, and stealing back into your heart as often as they are thrust away. You may even seek religion for the luxury of feeling there is in it or the joy it may yield.

Selfishness and self-love must be crucified. You must be willing to bear the cross. If you are to behold in Christ as in a glass the glory of the Lord and be changed into the same image, you must look with open face. Every veil must be torn away that his unobstructed beauty may shine directly into your heart. Having made sure that all hindrances are removed, you must draw yourself as closely to Christ as possible and receive as fully as you can his spirit. You must have the closest intimacy and be, as it were, one spirit with him. You will need to make his character and life a perpetual study, and dwell on them till your intellectual life is filled with Christ-like thoughts and images of divine beauty drawn from his person. Your good and Christ-like affections will help your understanding, and the truths that fill your understanding will feed your affections.

More will depend on a right use of prayer than on any other kind of exercise. This will keep your soul open to Christ and pliant to all divine dispositions. Offer your prayers in his name. Love the exercise, because it draws you so closely to him. Live in prayer, by prayer and upon it. Pray always, let your life itself be an aspiration after Christ, an earnest and holy longing for society with him. Bringing yourself thus into the most intimate and closest possible union of spirit with Christ, you will find that he grows dearer to you and holds a more complete and blessed power over you, and thus you will have a growing confidence that he is being formed in you.

You are called meantime to make your life an imitation of Christ; for though you are to be changed only by his power dwelling in you, still you will never offer yourself so completely to his power as when you are actively concerned to be like him. The Scriptures seem to me to set it before us to live the very life of Christ himself. Of course, there is something in the office and divine relation of Christ to men that requires a difference. But with this reserve, and regarding Christ in his human life and relations, we are called to be as like him in character as one human being ever can be to another. We have all diversities of natural character. We are men and women, young and old, different in our powers, callings, duties and spheres. This diversity is one of God's appointments and cannot be done away. It is beautiful in itself and will continue, I doubt not, forever. Still we may receive the very spirit and beauty of Christ himself. We are to partake even the divine through him, and live a life that is fashioned by the divine Word living in us. The Saviour himself says: "Learn of me." Discovering the spirit of ambition in his disciples, he requires of them to forsake such thoughts and to receive another spirit from their Master. "Whosoever will be chief among you let him be your servant, even as the Son of Man came not to be ministered unto but to minister." That is to say: "Your calling is mine. You are not in the world to gratify yourselves, but you are here to minister as truly as I am." And if all his disciples had it as the object of their lives to minister and communicate good, what a transforming power would they find in such a life! How visibly to others, how consciously to themselves would Christ be formed in them!

Again, in that beautiful scene where he washes the disciples' feet, what does he teach? What he does is nothing in itself, it communicates no good and relieves no misery, it is intended simply as a spiritual lesson to their hearts. "If I then, your Lord and Master, have washed your feet, ye ought also to wash one another's feet. The servant is not greater than his Lord, neither he that is sent greater than he that sent him." He thus lays it upon them to follow him in his self-oblivion, his unambitious and pure life of love, to be willing to do or to suffer anything, in a word, to be wholly unselfish as he himself is. But, on the other hand, and as if showing where their true ambition should be, he said in his last prayer: "The glory which thou hast given me I have given them." What could he give us more than a participation of the divine glory? And again he says: "My peace I give unto you." And once again: "These things I have spoken unto you that my joy might remain in you and that your joy might be full.'' Glory, peace, joy—Christ's own glory, joy and peace! What more could be offered us, what higher participation of the divine?

I have thus endeavored to set before you that which is the highest and sublimest hope ever offered to man, and the manner also in which this hope may be attained to. The great design of God in the incarnation of his Son is to form a divine life in you. It is to produce a Christ in the image of your soul, and to set you on the footing of a brother with the divine Word himself. ''This is the will of God, even your sanctification,'' and upon this Christly character formed in you rests the fellowship and glory of the redeemed world. He will raise the human even to the divine, for it is only in the pure divine that God can have complacence and hold communion. To entertain such a thought seems a kind of daring, but faith is a daring exercise. We must be daring, to ascend high enough to meet God's thoughts concerning us and his purposes toward us. Paul in one of his utterances seems to go farther than we have done. He speaks of the divine Lord himself as coming to be glorified in his saints and ''be admired in all them that believe,'' as if some glory were to accrue, some admiration come unto Christ himself, from those whom he has formed to the image of his own likeness and glory.

If now, my brethren, your hearts have been longing after some more advanced state, but have not seen how you can rise to it, if your soul has been discouraged and depressed and the struggle has seemed insupportable, here is relief. The work is not yours only. God is in it, cherishing higher designs for you probably than you have ever conceived. God's plan for you all is to have Christ formed in you. And the only question for you is whether you will suffer it. Can you put away your hindrances? Can you present your soul to the divine occupancy of Christ so as to favor his power in you? Can you draw your life into the active imitation of Jesus? Suppose it were offered you today as your calling to go forth and be to men, to yourself and to God all that Christ was in his human walk, to be sent into the world as he was, to minister as he ministered, to carry his light, his peace, his joy, his glory to men, to reveal his purity, to suffer with his patience! And what but this is the calling and mission of the gospel? That wonderful beauty with which Christ has irradiated the world it is his very purpose to form in you. Such a thought, it would almost seem, were enough to inspire the dead.

And if this hope may not be instantly fulfilled or completed in you, enough that it may begin and every day add something of progress toward it. What progress has been made by apostles and other holy men, you have seen in their lives. The same is possible to you, possible to all. Christ may be formed in you, in the same manner as he has been in them. O, what rest may such a confidence impart to every sinner on earth who will truly give himself to God! If we speak of struggles, Christ was himself a living struggle with evil, but he had his joy and peace, and so will you. And when life and struggle is over, then you will discover the divine filling your nature, all that is human in you transformed by the renewing of Christ, and your vile body itself fashioned like unto his glorious body. This is redemption. Then you are pure indeed, even as Christ is pure. You have borne the image of the earthy, now you bear the image of the heavenly. You discern in yourself, and all others discern in you, the perfect lineaments of Christ. Christ is formed in you. The work is done.

Canst thou suffer such a work as this? Wilt thou let it enter thy bosom and reign there? Canst thou deny thyself for it? Canst thou cast away the dull pleasures and the dross of this world's good for it? Shall it be thy pleasure to live in the imitation of Jesus and to offer thy soul to his gracious indwelling and power? This, O man! is life, and to this I delight to assure thee to-day thy Saviour calls thee, saying: "Take my yoke upon thee and learn of me, and thou shalt find rest unto thy soul." The fulness of Christ's fulness shall be in thee. His glory and peace shall rest upon thee.

II.

FREEDOM

*"Freedom," according to Bushnell, is another name for "superna-
ture" or the ability of persons to transcend the closed natural system of cause
and effect. Freedom so defined is constitutive of the human being and is
enhanced by the Christian religion. In a sermon revealingly entitled "Personality Developed by Religion," Bushnell takes the story of Jacob's wrestling with the angel as a parable of religious freedom: "instead of seeking
to reduce our individuality or the assertion of our will-force in religion, God
rather designs to intensify it and bring it into greater power."*

*The theme of freedom, and most especially Christian freedom, is de-
veloped at length in "Work and Play," the Phi Beta Kappa address which
Bushnell delivered at Harvard in 1848. As playful in its style as in its content,
the address deals with a wide range of human ventures illustrative of the
manner in which play is "the highest and complete state of man" and concludes with a depiction of Christian liberty as "pure spiritual play."*

*Bushnell suggests in his essay on play that Christian liberty frees the
human heart to love without ambition and the human mind to pursue truth
as an end in itself. In the sermon "The Eternity of Love," Bushnell elab-
orates on the meaning of liberated love: a love that is not an emotion but a
motion which flows toward the object of what is loved. And in an essay,
"Our Gospel a Gift to the Imagination," Bushnell analyses what it means
to pursue religious truth imaginatively through its "fact-forms" or symbols.
Such imaginative knowledge is liberation from all types of religious dogmatism and rationalism.*

PERSONALITY DEVELOPED BY RELIGION[1]

And he said, Thy name shall be called no more Jacob, but
Israel: for as a prince hast thou power with God and with
men, and hast prevailed.—Gen. xxxii. 28.

The story of Jacob wrestling with the angel is too familiar to
need recital. It is what may be called a parable acted, a case where
the matter in hand is taught not by words but by something done. We
have many such examples in the scriptures, as in Abraham's offering
of Isaac, the prophet's girdle, and the sale commanded of the young
ruler's property. Jacob had no manual of prayer and had probably
received no very explicit teaching concerning it, but he is put to the
lesson to learn it by a pull of muscular exertion. And so beautifully
is the wrestling with the Jehovah Angel adjusted in the analogies of
prayer, that we can find no teaching in the matter of prayer more
explicit or more instructive.

He has wrestled all night with the angel. His thigh is out of joint,
but he will not loosen his hold. With a pertinacity that seems even
presumptuous he still protests, saying, "I will not let thee go except
thou bless me." So he finally prevails, and is honored on the spot
with a new and princely name, in commendation of his persistency.
"Thy name shall be called no more Jacob, but Israel; for as a prince
hast thou power with God and with men, and hast prevailed." The
truth or principle here discovered, and which it will be the object of
my present discourse to illustrate is this: that, instead of seeking to
reduce our individuality or the assertion of our will-force in religion,
God rather designs to intensify it and bring it into greater power.

It makes a very great difference, for example, in the matter of
prayer, and so in everything else pertaining to religion, whether we
act in the vein of mere surrender and self-resignation to God or in that
of personal desire and preference, that is, from a will or choice of our
own. Faith in one method becomes little, if at all, different from an
act of submission; and indeed it is very frequently presented as a state
of mere self-surrender to God, becoming in that manner a very tame

---

1. From *The Spirit in Man. Sermons and Selections* (New York: Charles
Scribner's Sons, 1903), 185–98. Preached in North Church, Hartford in January
1854.

and really weak sort of pietism. In the other method, it is but a more complete manning of the man. He is lifted into energy, made positive and heroic. Knowing God, he knows how to be more completely, boldly himself, for he has the confidence begotten by his acquaintance with God, and so is able to assert himself in a higher, nobler key. It results that in all matters of duty or obligation the will-force of the man is increased, not diminished. He is no mere straw, floating on the currents of God, but he is a man stemming all currents where the call of duty requires. He has no thought of merely basking in the pious luxury of nothingness, but he has his objects and is always on the lookout for something to be done. He deliberates, forms his plans, chooses his objects, and is only more resolute in his way than other men. His quiet is not quietism. It is in him to drive, but never to drivel; for to many, alas! drivelling in mere self-surrender is the same thing as piety. Therefore there is no indolent Oriental sentimentality in his piety, as if it were a state of absorption in God, but it is a girded state of personal energy and devout heroism.

In this contrast you perceive my object, which is to conduct you if possible into the true idea and state of Christian power, showing by what method God designs to exalt the personality of his servants and give them power in their individual life and action, power with him in prayer, power with men in what they do for the world.

To clear the subject or to bring it forward into a position where the truth may be rightly conceived, let us glance over some of the representations of scripture. How it was with Jacob is plain. In the first place, he gets everything ready himself, puts his ingenuity to the task in arranging the droves, and acts as if everything were to be carried by his own mere will and contrivance. He has his own point to carry, and he does not mean to fail of it. Then follows the suit, in which he is perfectly resolute, and we hear him protesting when the day dawns after wrestling all night: "I will not let thee go except thou bless me." Had it been the true idea of prayer that there is nothing to be done but to come into God's will and be resigned to it, to lose one's personal desires, renounce and die to all personal preferences, how different would have been the scene! How different also the close! Instead of the new name given to signalize the wrestler and his power with God for all coming ages, instead of being raised to honor as a prince, the man would have been signalized as a devotee, who mistook impotence for merit and could not imagine a God high enough to maintain his eminence, save as he is complimented by the self-annihilation of his worshippers.

So in like manner, when Moses finds a riotous spirit springing up in the people because of the lack of suitable supplies of food, he goes to God in the boldness of a prince, demanding almost as a right some deliverance from his personal burdens. "Whence should I have flesh to give unto all this people. I am not able to bear all this people alone, because it is too heavy for me. And if thou deal thus with me, kill me, I pray thee, out of thy hand." On another occasion he came in also between the people and God's destroying anger, protesting and saying: "Wherefore should the Egyptians say that thou hast brought them out among the mountains to slay them?" urging boldly also God's covenant promise and oath to Abraham as a bar to his judgment. In the whole history of Moses, his acts and works and prayers, you find a man girded up to the intensest individuality of choice and charge and feeling, bearing as it were the whole nation of his people on his own shoulders. The will of Pharaoh in rejecting God is not a whit more conspicuous than the personal choice and determination of Moses in executing the call of God.

So in all the strong characters both of the Old and New Testament, as Samuel, David, Nehemiah, Paul. They are men that act and plan and preach and pray as if they had their people and times in their own personal keeping and disposal. They are princes, all, of God, bearing their institutions, their temple, their whole race and nation on their shoulders. Probably the most efficient Christian by far that ever lived was the apostle Paul, and you see this in him everywhere as a distinction most of all conspicuous, that while he is intensely conscious always of his own insufficiency he is at the same time most intensely personal in all his responsibilities, having on his soul the care of all the churches, asserting, or, as he himself calls it, boasting, his own spiritual fatherhood and dignity against the teachers that have sought to undermine his influence and let down the value of his teachings, having continual heaviness and sorrow of heart for his brethren and kinsmen according to the flesh. It is never in his thought just to bow down like a bulrush and let the torrents of divine will roll over him, but he is out in the flood, standing fast, fighting it out on this line for the whole campaign of his ministry. His personal desires, feelings, preferences, purposes, plans, responsibilities are all as conspicuous in his work as if he had even the care of the world on himself.

Not that he is ignorant of all resignation or submission to God, but
that he is perfectly resigned, perfectly submitted; for precisely here
is the distinction between a half resignation and one that is complete,—the half resignation is passive, ending there, and the other is
a resignation to being active, personally responsible, personally efficient for God. The former is the resignation of a Brahmin, the latter
of an apostle.

The same thing appears in regard to all that is said in the scriptures of our own personal charge and choice in the matter of prayer
itself. The very call to prayer: "Ask and ye shall receive," is a call
to the expression of our personal wants and preferences, and the design is to let every disciple see that he has power with God. It is very
true that all prayer rightly ordered is in a sense from the divine Spirit,
who works in the secret springs of every man's feeling to guide him
into the best desires and the worthiest objects, even such as are according to the will of God. But the Spirit does not undertake to get
us into God's will by repression. He stirs up the soul, rather, to greater
eagerness, so that it is heaving out groans of desire and prayer that
pull on God and that draw it up into God's very mind; and there it is
to hang, refusing to let go till its very groanings become an argument
and reason for God's will.

In the parable of the unjust judge we have the wrestling scene
of Jacob over again. The whole intent of it is to throw the praying
man upon his personality and encourage him in adherence to his personal desires, even up to the point of pertinacity. It is not the design
of the parable to say that there can be no mistake or error on this side,
for it is very plain that we may have selfish desires, and such as God
can never grant. But the particular design is to correct another and
opposite error, namely, the having or daring to have no desires, the
being so passively, indolently, selfishly resigned to God, that we are
too nearly indifferent as regards our objects. The very greatest temp-
tation of many Christian souls is that they submit and give up too
easily. Therefore, it is a great point with God to maintain the will-
force of our personality and he does it by training us even to wrestle
with him.

You may also discover how he loves to put this kind of honor
on his servants, when he calls for them, as it were, to come in with
their petitions and be intercessors before him. "And I sought for a
man among them that should make up the hedge and stand in the gap

before me for the land, that I should not destroy it, but I found none.'' So, again, he says: ''I will be inquired of by the house of Israel to do it for them.'' In which you see that, so far from wishing to carry out his own will by itself, he invites and waits for intervening wills and intercessory desires, because it is possible when these are before him to bestow blessings which he otherwise could not.

Such everywhere is the manner of scripture. It proposes no destruction or demolition of our personality, but rather seeks to invigorate and embolden it, saying: ''Let us enter the holiest with boldness.'' Nowhere does it seek to make us the mere channels of a divine agency, but always to make us agents ourselves in a more complete and free sense than before, ''co-workers with God.'' ''We then,'' says an apostle, ''as workers together with him, beseech you.'' ''For we are laborers together with God.'' The apostle has no thought, you perceive, of ceasing to be, as a distinct centre of choice, feeling and life; but he has come, rather, to be more really, distinctly, gloriously and powerfully personal, more consciously exalted and empowered by his faith in Jesus.

It will be seen at a glance that the very problem of God in our training and redemption is to raise and perfect our personality, not to demolish it. Were it possible to bring all our desires, choices, wills into a perfect, everlasting and silent resignation to God, it would answer none of the purposes of God in our spiritual education under the gospel of Christ. For it is not our perfection that we may be absorbed as into Brahma, and lost in the abysses of his sleep; it is not that we may be schooled into the harmless dulness of an eternal inefficiency or undesiring impotence, but the word is: ''Remember this, and show yourselves men.'' The plan is to raise us out of a condition of weakness and spiritual incapacity, restoring us to love and a sound mind. It is not more true that a university is designed to raise the power and strengthen the exercise of the pupils, than that Christianity is designed to liberate the will, clear and fortify the affections, and restore the coordinate harmony of choice and reason. Instead of reducing, levelling, demolishing, absorbing our personality, the design is to fill it out and to complete and glorify it. Raising us out of sin and the bondage of sin, which is itself a load of slavish weakness and depression, it sets us on a higher plane of choice and liberty, there to be empowered as sons of God and co-workers with him.

And in just this manner it was that so many low-minded, uneducated fishermen, such as Peter and John, were raised into such eminence and power as apostles. It was not the annihilation of their personality but the associating of it with a higher life, even that of Christ, that wrought so great a change. And so it was with Paul. He was not a very remarkable man before his conversion. It was in his conversion that his glorious personality was liberated from its weakness and endued with true power. He had will enough before, but it was such will as passion instigates, and passion is weakness. He was violent, and violence is weakness. God therefore will have vehemence but not violence, and vehemence is will-force itself. And this it is which the prophet represents when he declares in God's name: "Behold, I will make thee a new, sharp threshing instrument, having teeth; thou shalt thresh the mountains and beat them small and shalt make the hills as chaff." How many of these tremendous threshing instruments, such as Moses and Paul and Luther and Cromwell, has God raised up to thresh down the mountains of perverse hindrance and make them chaff before his cause! A genuine faith has never any other kind of effect. It sharpens the personality, and tunes it to a higher key. And God will have it so. To make an eleventh chapter of Hebrews as long as the world's history is the very object of his training, that he may open the shining roll and say: "Who through faith subdued kingdoms, wrought righteousness, obtained promises, stopped the mouths of lions, quenched the violence of fire, out of weakness were made strong, waxed valiant in fight, turned to flight the armies of the aliens." These are the princes, or Israels, that have power with God and with men and so prevail, heroes of the faith whom God is raising up into a glorious and transcendent personality, to make them kings and priests unto God, that they may reign forever.

But, you may object, we are required to be little children, to put on meekness and suppress the passions that flame up out of our individual feeling and the instigations of our evil will; and what is this but to make a surrender of our force and cease in so far from all pertinacity? Was then Christ, I would ask, less completely a person, less distinct, less eminent in the grandeur of his personal attitude, that he consented to bear his enemies and be a lamb before his persecutors? Where else does he rise to a more truly incomprehensible greatness, becoming a personality more transcendently divine, a will more resistless, than here?

But we are placed, it will be said, under conditions of repression and required to let "every thought be brought into captivity to the obedience of Christ." Even so, for just there we are raised into the very highest force of our personality. Until then what we call our life is unregulated force, which in religion, as in doings with nature, is but another name for all defeat and impotence. But when every thought of our soul is brought into the harmony of Christ, which is the harmony of thought and impulse with all order and truth and reason, then it becomes a regulated force, and the personality, almost wrecked under the discords and disorders of sin, is restored to its native energy, to be a prince having power with God and with men. Real power is but another name for regulated power.

Again, the doctrine of faith is sometimes held as being only a doctrine of resignation to God, and he is supposed to have the most faith who can be stillest, least in exercise, most completely hushed in desire and care under the will of God. But there is no such will of God as wants or will accept any such faith. It is a mock faith, not a true. The true faith believes a great deal more. Instead of lying down before God as a clod to be disposed of by him, it believes that God will reason with it, and that he calls it to come and reason with him; that God will give heed to its desires, suffer its importunities, justify it in the pursuit of its chosen ends and objects, come over to it in favor, as the angel to Jacob, and cover it with princely honors. This is faith, and nothing less can be. It believes that God will so far acknowledge its desires, arguments, and prayers as to give it power even with himself.

I have a most particular satisfaction in the conclusion to which these thoughts bring us, viz., to the fact that no man is required, in coming to Christ, to make any sacrifice that will at all diminish or infringe on the distinctive will-force of his personality. He will be just so much more of a man as he is more of a Christian. His unregulated force, becoming regulated force, will be weakness raised into power. His will, which we say in one view is now all-dominant, will yet be manifold stronger than it is now. His command of himself will be greater, his thoughts higher, his vision clearer, his affections broader and more full, and there will be a certain divine inspiration in him that will lift him into a higher range of consciousness, and empower him for greater works and undertakings. And here in great part is the joy of a Christian life. It is the sense of personal enlargement found in a love that comprehends the world. He who has received this love is surprised at the breadth revealed in his nature. He thought, looking on the life of religion from without, that it would very nearly be the end of him to become a Christian, that after renouncing so much there would be nothing left but a few slender vestiges of existence. But he finds, instead, that in the loss of himself he has found himself, and has now in fact but just begun to be. O, this new sense of freedom! this living life! this fulness! this confidence of power! Do not think, my friends, that when we call you to Christ we call you away from existence, to be nothing and cease. If you ever find him, you will make a very different discovery from that. Your greatest wonder and surprise will be that God has been able to make so much out of a spirit so shrivelled and dulled by the dryness, the littleness and meanness of a selfish life.

Hence it is the feeling of all true saints of God that they have a princely rank, that God is not jealous of power in his people. He stirs them up to pertinacity. He exasperates their desires. He groans in their compassions. He lets them come and wrestle that they may be strong. He calls them to ''stand in the gap'' as intercessors before him; and when they prevail, he crowns them as belonging to his own divine nobility. And he saith: ''Thy name shall be called no more Jacob but Israel, for as a prince hast thou power with God and with men, and hast prevailed.''

Observe, too, that he speaks not only of power with him, but of power with men; for the design is to give us power in every direction, with God as with men, with men as with God. That is, he will have us take upon us points to be carried with our fellowmen, just as we do points to be carried with him. And he will have us say to them, as to him: ''I will not let you go.'' As you have desires to be urged in prayer, so you will have objects, charges, responsibilities, works, and you will adhere also to these under the same conditions as you do to your prayers. Slight hindrances will not discourage you. Opposition or seeming defeat will not be taken as an excuse from your work; but you will follow it and adhere to it and press it onward till it is carried. For if you go into any such engagement under the leading of God's spirit, you will be endued with power for it. A power will be developed in you, the power heretofore unknown of your own mysterious personality. All things are possible to one who is girded in this manner by the divine Spirit and his call.

And here is the new type of character that is wanted in our day.

For this the world is waiting, and for this also God, as the king and redeemer of the world. Before the great day of Christ shall come there must be a new development of the Christian life. And it will be when all the pietistic, artificial, dogmatically enfeebled and emasculated forms of piety give place to the heroic life of faith and a Christian personality, girded by the Spirit. This, in fact, is the very coming of the Lord. Come, Lord Jesus, come quickly!

WORK AND PLAY[2]

Mr. President, and Brethren of the Society,

There are many subjects or truths, and sometimes those of the greatest moment, which can not well be formally announced. They require to be offered rather by suggestion. They will enter the mind and be in it only as they are of it, generated by the fertile activity of a meditative spirit. This is frequently true even in matters of scientific discovery, where also it is often remarked, that the best suggestives are the humblest instances; such as the mind can play itself upon with the greatest facility, because it is not occupied by their magnitude or oppressed by their grandeur. Some lamp is seen swinging on its chain, some apple falling from the tree, and then, perchance, the thoughtful looker-on, taking the hint that nature gives, will be able also to look in; thus to uncover truths not measured by their instances,—laws of the universe.

More true is this, if possible, of moral subjects; for there are many of these which the soul will not suffer to be thrust upon her. She must ask for them, catch the note of them in some humble suggestive, entertain them thoughtfully, take them into her feeling, and there, encouraging, as it were, their modesty, tempt them to speak. So especially it is with the subject in which I desire to engage you on the present occasion. No formal announcement will probably do more for it, than just to thrust it on your disrespect.

Let me call to my aid, then, some thoughtful spirit in my audience; not a poet, of necessity, or a man of genius, but a man of large

---

2. From *Work and Play* (New York: Charles Scribner, 1984), 9–42. Delivered before the Society of Phi Beta Kappa at Harvard on August 24, 1848.

meditation, one who is accustomed to observe, and, by virtue of the warm affinities of a living heart, to draw out the meanings that are hid so often in the humblest things. Returning into the bosom of his family, in some interval of care and labor, he shall come upon the very unclassic and certainly unimposing scene,—his children and a kitten playing on the floor together; and just there, possibly, shall meet him suggestions more fresh, and thoughts of higher reach concerning himself and his race, than the announcement of a new-discovered planet, or the revolution of an empire would incite. He surveys, with a meditative feeling, this beautiful scene of muscular play,—the unconscious activity, the exuberant life, the spirit of glee,—and there rises in his heart the conception, that possibly he is here to see the prophecy or symbol of another and higher kind of play, which is the noblest exercise and last end of man himself. Worn by the toils of years, perceiving, with a sigh, that the unconscious joy of motion here displayed is spent in himself, and that now he is effectually tamed to the doom of a working creature, he may yet discover, in the lively sympathy with play that bathes his inward feeling, that his soul is playing now,—enjoying, without the motions, all it could do in them; manifold more than it could, if he were down upon the floor himself, in the unconscious activity and lively frolic of childhood. Saddened he may be to note how time and work have changed his spirit and dried away the playful springs of animal life in his being; yet he will find, or ought, a joy playing internally over the face of his working nature, which is fuller and richer as it is more tranquil; which is to the other as fulfillment to prophecy, and is, in fact, the prophecy of a better and far more glorious fulfillment still.

Having struck, in this manner, the great world-problem of WORK AND PLAY, his thoughts kindle under the theme and he pursues it. The living races are seen, at a glance, to be offering in their history, everywhere, a faithful type of his own. They show him what he himself is doing and preparing,—all that he finds in the manifold experience of his own higher life. They have, all, their gambols, all, their sober cares and labors. The lambs are sporting on the green knoll; the anxious dams are bleating to recall them to their side. The citizen beaver is building his house by a laborious carpentry; the squirrel is lifting his sail to the wind on the swinging top of the tree. In the music of the morning, he hears the birds playing with their voices, and, when the day is up, sees them sailing round in circles on the upper air, as skaters on a lake, folding their wings, dropping and rebounding, as if to see what sport they can make of the solemn laws that hold the upper and lower worlds together. And yet these play-children of the air he sees again descending to be carriers and drudges; fluttering and screaming anxiously about their nest, and confessing by that sign that not even wings can bear them clear of the stern doom of work. Or passing to some quiet shade, meditating still on this careworn life, playing still internally with ideal fancies and desires unrealized, there returns upon him there, in the manifold and spontaneous mimicry of nature, a living show of all that is transpiring in his own bosom; in every flower, some bee humming over his laborious chemistry and loading his body with the fruits of his toil; in the slant sunbeam, populous nations of motes quivering with animated joy, and catching, as in play, at the golden particles of the light with their tiny fingers. Work and play, in short, are the universal ordinance of God for the living races; in which they symbolize the fortune and interpret the errand of man. No creature lives that must not work and may not play.

Returning now to himself and to man, and meditating yet more deeply, as he is thus prepared to do, on work and play, and play and work, as blended in the compound of our human life; asking again what is work and what is play, what are the relations of one to the other, and which is the final end of all, he discovers, in what he was observing round him, a sublimity of import, a solemnity even, that is deep as the shadow of eternity.

To proceed intelligently with our subject, we need, first of all, to resolve or set forth the precise philosophic distinction between work and play; for upon this distinction all our illustrations will depend. That, in practical life, we have any hesitancy in making the distinction, I by no means intimate. At least, there are many youths in the universities, not specially advanced in philosophy, who are able to make their election with the greatest facility, be the distinction itself clear or not. But as I propose, on the present occasion, to speak of the state of play in a manner that involves a philosophic extension of the idea, I am required to distinguish the idea by a careful analysis.

You will discover, at once, that work and play, taken as modes of mere outward, muscular activity, can not be distinguished. There is motion in both, there is an exercise of force in both, both are under the will as acting on the muscular system; so that, taken outwardly, they both fall into the same category. Indeed, they can not be discriminated till we pass within, to view them metaphysically, considering their springs of action, their impulse, aim, and object.

Here the distinction becomes evident at once; namely, that work is activity *for* an end; play, activity *as* an end. One prepares the fund or resources of enjoyment, the other is enjoyment itself. Thus, when a man goes into agriculture, trade, or the shop, he consents to undergo a certain expenditure of care and labor, which is only a form of painstaking rightly named, in order to obtain some ulterior good which is to be his reward. But when the child goes to his play, it is no painstaking, no means to an end; it is itself rather both end and joy. Accordingly, it is a part of the distinction I state, that work suffers a feeling of aversion, and play excludes aversion. For the moment any play becomes wearisome or distasteful, then it is work; an activity that is kept up, not as being its own joy, but for some ulterior end, or under some kind of constraint.

Another form of the distinction is made out, and one that is more accurately adapted to philosophic uses, by saying that work is done by a conscious effort of will, and that play is impulsive, having its spring in some inspiration, or some exuberant fund of life back of the will. So that one is something which we require of ourselves, the other something that we must control ourselves not to do. We work because we must, because prudence impels. We play because we have in us a fund of life that wants to expend itself.

But man is not a muscular creature only; he does not consist of mere bones and integuments. He is a creature also of thought, feeling, intelligence, and character. And what we see of him in the muscular life he is, or should be, in the higher domain of spirit. Regarding the child as a creature full of life and spontaneous motion, thus and therefore a playing creature, we are to see in him, not the measure, but the sign, of that which shall be. For as the race began with an outward paradise, which, being lost, may yet offer the type of a higher paradise to be gained, so each life begins with muscular play, that, passing through the hard struggles of work, it may carry its ideal with it, and emerge, at last, into a state of inspired liberty and spontaneous beauty. In short, we are to conceive that the highest and complete state of man, that which his nature endeavors after and in which only it fulfills its sublime instinct, is the state of play.

In this view, study is to be regarded as work, until the disciple gets beyond voluntary attention, application constrained by prudence, rivalry, ambitious preparations for life, and begins to dwell in beauty and truth as inspirations. For then he passes into another and more perfect kind of activity, an activity that is spontaneous or impulsive, and is to itself both reward and end.

And this kind of activity, call it enthusiastic or inspired, or by whatever name, we shall discover is commonly regarded as a higher and nobler—in fact the only perfect activity conceivable. In the article of memory, for example, we regard a spontaneous memory, that which mirrors all the past before us without any effort of recollection, as the only perfect memory. But a reflective memory, supported by mnemonic contrivances, and assisted by recollective efforts, is so far in the nature of work; and the necessity of work argues the imperfection of the instrument. Our idea of a perfect or complete memory is, that it reports the past spontaneously, or in play.

When we ascend to the higher modes of action, such as involve the inventive exercises of reason, fancy, imagination, or the sentimental exercises of feeling, passion, humor, we find that we are even offended by the signs of work; or, if not offended, we are unsatisfied, just in proportion to the evidence of work or effort obtruded on our attention. For work, we allow, argues defect or insufficiency, and to say that the man *labors* is the same as to say that he fails. Nothing is sufficient or great, nothing fires or exalts us, but to feel the divine energy and the inspiring liberty of play.

Then, again, as we ascend still higher, to modes of activity that are moral and religious, we become quite intolerant of any thing in the nature of work. To be good or true, for the sake of some ulterior end, is the same as to value goodness and truth second to that end; which is the same as to have no sense of either. So, if some benefit or gift is bestowed upon us by constraint, and not from any compassion for our lot or interest in our welfare, we deem the gift itself an insult, and call the charity hypocrisy. In like manner purity, forced by self-restraint or maintained by mere prudence, argues impurity. True purity, that which answers the perfect ideal, is spontaneous; unfolding its artless, unaffected spotlessness in the natural freedom of a flower. It could not defile itself without an effort. Nay, it is supposable that perfect purity could not even blush. In like manner, self-denial is never a complete virtue till it becomes a kind of self-indulgence. It must bathe itself in the fountains of a self-oblivious charity. Forgetting fame and reward, rising above the constraints of prudence, and losing the nature of work, it must become the spontaneous impulse of our being, a joyous overflow of the soul's liberty.

It follows, in this view, that work is in its very nature temporary, or should be, having for its end the realization of a state of play. Passing through activity *for* an end, we are to come into activity *as* an end; beyond which, of course, there is nothing higher. As we rest in the one, we are to cease from the other. And might we not have said as much beforehand? Who that considers the ethereal nature of a soul can conceive that the doom of work is any thing more than a temporary expedient, introduced or suffered to perfect our discipline? To imagine a human creature dragged along, or dragging himself along, under the perpetual friction of work, never to ascend above it; a creature in God's image, aching for God's liberty, beating ever vainly and with crippled wings, that he may lift himself into some freer, more congenial element—this, I say, were no better than to quite despair of man. Nay, it were to confess that all which is most akin to God in his human instincts is only semblance without reality. Do we not all find within us some dim ideal, at least, of a state unrealized, where action is its own impulse; where the struggles of birth are over, and the friction of interest and care is no longer felt; where all that is best and highest is freest, and joyous because it is free; where to be is to be great, because the inspiration of the soul is full, and to do is easy as to conceive; where action is itself sublime, because it is the play of ease and the equilibrium of rest?

Let no one imagine that I derogate thus from the dignity of work. Rather do I dignify it the more, that I represent it as the preparative to a state so exalted. Possibly our modern writers, in their zeal to dignify work, have sometimes excluded or omitted the notice of this, which is its only dignity. Indeed, some of our poets seem to have worked harder to change the world's work into poetry, than the world need have done to finish it in prose. Work is transitional, having its good in its end. The design is, that, by a fixed law of nature, it shall pass into play. This is its proper honor and joy.

Let us notice, then, for a moment, in what manner work becomes the preparative or necessary condition of play. Observe the child as a playing creature in the muscular life. Full of animated glee, unable to contain the brimming life that is in him, he must needs expend himself in action. He leaps about the ground, climbs into the trees, screams among his fellows in notes that tingle on the air; not because he will, or has any ulterior end, but because the play-fund is in him, and he must. But we do not always note that a period of trial answering to work was necessary to prepare this liberty of motion; that the child had first to practice eye, voice, ear, hand, foot, putting forth carefully by little and little, and gradually getting possession of the bodily machinery that now plays so nimbly. Every muscle in his body had, in fact, to be graduated in the little university of motion, before he was ready for play. He had many falls to suffer, in order to get the balance of his members; much crying to do, to get possession of his voice; and this, I suppose, must be taken for work. By the same kind of necessity is mental and spiritual work necessary to the play-state of the soul. The man must go into experiment, through experiment or study get possession of his soul, so that he can turn every faculty whithersoever he will, and have the whole internal machinery in the exactest play. I speak not here of the discipline merely of schools and colleges, but, as much, of the struggles we encounter and the scenes through which we pass in this great school of life—its objects, relations, and duties; its sturdy trials, fears, falls, crosses; its works, and wars, and woes; all discovering to us, and thus helping us to possess, ourselves. We get the helm thus of our thoughts, tempers, passions, aspirations, and wants. And if a vigorous training in the school be added, our capacities of taste, fancy, observation, and reason are also discovered, and limbered for the free activity of spiritual play.

It will also be seen that this free state of man involves a moral experience, and possibly somewhat of a bad or selfish experience, whereby his choices may be settled in permanent love of goodness. For this, in fact, is the greatness of all greatness, that it is of the man himself—the measure of his own free aims and aspirations. And if so much depends on the soul's choices, it needs to be made wise that it may choose wisely, and possibly to choose unwisely in order that it may be wise. Thus it descends into selfishness and evil, which are only forms of work, there to learn the wisdom of goodness in the contrasts of distaste, weariness, and hunger. And this, I suppose, is the solution of the various travail that is given to the sons of men to be exercised therewith. Some men work to get money; others, quite as hard to spend it. Some men work to get reputation; others, who have it by accident, work harder in seeing it go by a law. There is a laborious ease, and even a laborious idleness. What we call pleasure is commonly but another name for work; a strenuous joy, a laboriously prepared and therefore wearisome happiness. We all go to our self-serving and work, till at last we learn, it may be, to cease from ourselves, and then—we play.

But there is yet another office served by work, without which the state of play is never complete. The man must find inspiring forces, objects that exalt the feeling, ideals to embrace that will beget a spontaneous greatness in him. But he is ignorant, at first, even of facts; and how shall he find his ideals, unless they are discovered in the practical throes of experience, labor, and study? How shall he turn himself to things that shine with their own brightness, ideal objects born of the soul's own thought, and luminous by a divine quality hid in themselves, unless he has sweltered for a time in self-exercise and the dust of labor? Then, at last, he conceives and embraces in his love sublimity, beauty, honor, truth, charity, God; and the inspiration he feels imparts to him somewhat of a higher nature, spontaneously good, wise, great,—joyous of necessity.

Thus it is that work prepares the state of play. Passing over now to this latter, observe the intense longing of the race for some such higher and freer state of being. They call it by no name. Probably most of them have but dimly conceived what they are after. The more evident will it be that they are after this, when we find them covering over the whole ground of life, and filling up the contents of history, with their counterfeits or misconceived attempts. If the hidden fire is seen bursting up on every side, to vent itself in flame, we may certainly know that the ground is full.

Let it not surprise you, if I name, as a first illustration here, the general devotion of our race to money. This passion for money is allowed to be a sordid passion, one that is rankest in the least generous and most selfish of mankind; and yet a conviction has always been felt, that it must have its heat in the most central fires and divinest affinities of our nature. Thus the poet calls it the *auri sacra fames—sacra*, as being a curse, and that in the divine life of the race. Childhood being passed, and the play-fund of motion so far spent that running on foot no longer appears to be the joy it was, the older child, now called a man, fancies that it will make him happy to ride! Or he imagines, which is much the same, some loftier state of being—call it rest, retirement, competence, independence—no matter by what name, only be it a condition of use, ease, liberty, and pure enjoyment. And so we find the whole race at work to get rid of work: drudging themselves to-day, in the hope of play to-morrow. This is that *sacra fames*, which, misconceiving its own unutterable longings after spiritual play, proposes to itself the dull felicity of cessation, and drives the world to madness in pursuit of a counterfeit, which it is work to obtain, work also to keep, and yet harder work oftentimes to enjoy.

Here, too, is the secret of that profound passion for the drama, which has been so conspicuous in the cultivated nations. We love to see life in its feeling and activity, separated from its labors and historic results. Could we see all human changes transpire poetically or creatively, that is, in play, letting our soul play with them as they pass, then it were only poetry to live. Then to admire, love, laugh; then to abhor, pity, weep,—all were alike grateful to us; for the view of suffering separated from all reality, save what it has to feeling, only yields a painful joy, which is the deeper joy because of the pain. Hence the written drama, offering to view in its impersonations a life one side of life, a life in which all the actings appear without the ends and simply as in play, becomes to the cultivated reader a spring of the intensest and most captivating spiritual incitement. He beholds the creative genius of a man playing out impersonated groups and societies of men, clothing each with life, passion, individuality, and character, by the fertile activity of his own inspired feeling. Meantime the writer himself is hidden, and can not even suggest his existence. Hence egotism, which also is a form of work, the dullest, most insipid, least inspiring of all kinds of endeavor, is nowhere allowed to obtrude itself. The reader himself, too, has no ends to think of or to fear,—nothing to do, but to play the characters into his feeling as creatures existing for his sake. In this view, the drama, as a product of genius, is, within a certain narrow limit, the realization of play.

But far less effectively, or more faintly, when it is acted. Then the counterfeit, as it is more remote, is more feeble. In the reading, we invent our own sceneries, clothe into form and expression each one of the characters, and play out our own liberty in them as freely, and sometimes as divinely, as they. Whatever reader, therefore, has a soul of true life and fire within him, finds all expectation balked, when he becomes an auditor and spectator. The scenery is tawdry and flat; the characters, definitely measured, have lost their infinity, so to speak, and thus their freedom; and what before was play descends to nothing better or more inspired than work. It is called going to the play, but it should rather be called going to the work; that is, to see a play worked, (yes, an *opera* ! that is it)—men and women inspired through their memory, and acting their inspirations by rote; panting into love, pumping at the fountains of grief, whipping out the passions into fury, and dying to fulfill the contract of the evening, by a forced holding of the breath. And yet this feeble counterfeit of play, which some of us would call only "very tragical mirth," has a power to the multitude. They are moved, thrilled it may be, with a strange delight. It is as if a something in their nature, higher than they themselves know, were quickened into power,—namely, that divine instinct of play, in which the summit of our nature is most clearly revealed.

In like manner, the passion of our race for war, and the eager admiration yielded to warlike exploits, are resolvable principally into the same fundamental cause. Mere ends and uses do not satisfy us. We must get above prudence and economy, into something that partakes of inspiration, be the cost what it may. Hence war, another and yet more magnificent counterfeit of play. Thus there is a great and lofty virtue that we call *cour-age*, taking our name from the heart. It is the greatness of a great heart; the repose and confidence of a man whose soul is rested in truth and principle. Such a man has no ends ulterior to his duty, duty itself is his end. He is in it therefore as in play, lives it as an inspiration. Lifted thus out of mere prudence and contrivance, he is also lifted above fear. Life to him is the outgoing of his great heart,—*heart-age*, action from the heart. And because he now can die, without being shaken or perturbed by any of the dastardly feelings that belong to self-seeking and work, because he partakes of the impassibility of his principles, we call him a hero, regarding him as a kind of god—a man who has gone up into the sphere of the divine.

Then, since courage is a joy so high, a virtue of so great majesty, what could happen but that many will covet both the internal exaltation and the outward repute of it? Thus comes bravery, which is the counterfeit, or mock virtue. Courage is of the heart, as we have said; bravery is of the will. One is the spontaneous joy and repose of a truly great soul; the other, bravery, is after an end ulterior to itself, and in that view, is but a form of work,—about the hardest work, too, I fancy, that some men undertake. What can be harder, in fact, than to act a great heart, when one has nothing but a will wherewith to do it?

Thus you will see that courage is above danger; bravery in it, doing battle on a level with it. One is secure and tranquil, the other suppresses agitation or conceals it. A right mind fortifies one, shame stimulates the other. Faith is the nerve of one, risk the plague and tremor of the other. For if I may tell you just here a very important secret, there be many that are called heroes who are yet without courage. They brave danger by their will, when their heart trembles. They make up in violence what they want in tranquillity, and drown the tumult of their fears in the rage of their passions. Enter the heart and you shall find, too often, a dastard spirit lurking in your hero. Call him still a brave man, if you will, only remember that he lacks courage.

No, the true hero is the great, wise man of duty; he whose soul is armed by truth and supported by the smile of God; he who meets life's perils with a cautious but tranquil spirit, gathers strength by facing its storms, and dies, if he is called to die, as a Christian victor at the post of duty. And if we must have heroes, and wars wherein to make them, there is no so brilliant war as a war with wrong, no hero so fit to be sung as he who has gained the bloodless victory of truth and mercy.

But if bravery be not the same as courage, still it is a very imposing and plausible counterfeit. The man himself is told, after the occasion is passed, how heroically he bore himself, and when once his nerves have become tranquillized, he begins even to believe it. And since we can not stay content in the dull, uninspired world of economy and work, we are as ready to see a hero as he to be one. Nay, we must have our heroes, as I just said, and we are ready to harness ourselves, by the million, to any man who will let us fight him out the name. Thus we find out occasions for war—wrongs to be redressed, revenges to be taken, such as we may feign inspiration and play the great heart under. We collect armies, and dress up leaders in gold and high colors, meaning, by the brave look, to inspire some notion of a hero beforehand. Then we set the men in phalanxes and squadrons, where the personality itself is taken away, and a vast impersonal person called an army, a magnanimous and brave monster, is all that remains. The masses of fierce color, the glitter of steel, the dancing plumes, the waving flags, the deep throb of the music lifting every foot—under these the living acres of men, possessed by the one thought of playing brave to-day, are rolled on to battle. Thunder, fire, dust, blood, groans—what of these? nobody thinks of these, for nobody dares to think till the day is over, and then the world rejoices to behold a new batch of heroes!

And this is the Devil's play, that we call war. We have had it going on ever since the old geologic era was finished. We are sick enough of the matter of it. We understand well enough that it is not good economy. But we can not live on work. We must have courage, inspiration, greatness, play. Even the moral of our nature, that which is to weave us into social union with our kind before God, is itself thirsting after play; and if we can not have it in good, why then let us have it in as good as we can. It is at least some comfort, that we do not mean quite as badly in these wars as some men say. We are not in love with murder, we are not simple tigers in feeling, and some of us come out of battle with kind and gentle qualities left. We only must have our play.

Note also this, that, since the metaphysics of fighting have been investigated, we have learned to make much of what we call the *moral* of the army; by which we mean the feeling that wants to play brave. Only it is a little sad to remember that this same moral, as it is called, is the true, eternal, moral nature of the man thus terribly perverted,— that which was designed to link him to his God and his kind, and ought to be the spring of his immortal inspirations.

There has been much of speculation among the learned concerning the origin of chivalry; nor has it always been clear to what human elements this singular institution is to be referred. But when we look on man, not as a creature of mere understanding and reason, but as a creature also of play, essentially a poet in that which constitutes his higher life, we seem to have a solution of the origin of chivalry, which is sufficient, whether it be true or not. In the forswearing of labor, in the brave adventures of a life in arms, in the intense ideal devotion to woman as her protector and avenger, in the self-renouncing and almost self-oblivious worship of honor—what do we see in these but the mock-moral doings of a creature who is to escape self-love and the service of ends, in a free, spontaneous life of goodness; in whom courage, delicacy, honor, disinterested deeds, are themselves to be the inspiration, as they are the end, of his being?

I might also show, passing into the sphere of religion, how legal obedience, which is work, always descends into superstition, and thus that religion must, in its very nature and life, be a form of play— a worship offered, a devotion paid, not for some ulterior end, but as being its own end and joy. I might also show, in the same manner, that all the enthusiastic, fanatical, and properly quietistic modes of religion are as many distinct counterfeits, and, in that manner, illustrations of my subject. But this you will see at a glance, without illustration. Only observe how vast a field our illustrations cover. In the infatuated zeal of our race for the acquisition of money, in the drama, in war, in chivalry, in perverted religion—in all these forms, covering almost the whole ground of humanity with counterfeits of play, that are themselves the deepest movements of the race, I show you the boundless sweep of this divine instinct, and how surely we may know that the perfected state of man is a state of beauty, truth, and love, where life is its own end and joy.

Passing now into the life of letters, we may carry with us a light that will make intelligible and clear some important distinctions that are not always apprehended.

Here is the distinction between genius and talent, which some of our youthful scholars are curious to settle. Genius is that which is good for play, talent that which is good for work. The genius is an inspired man, a man whose action is liberty, whose creations are their own end and joy. Therefore we speak, not of the man's doing this or that, but of the man's genius as doing it; as if there were some second spirit attendant, yielding him thoughts, senses, imaginations, fires of emotion, that are above his measure—lifting him thus into exaltations of freedom and power that partake of a certain divine quality. His distinction is, in fact, that he is a demonized or demonizable man. Talent, on the other hand, we conceive to be of the man himself, a capacity that is valuable as related to ends and uses, such as the acquisition of knowledge or money, to build, cultivate, teach, frame polities, manage causes, fill magistracies.

But we need to add that talent, in every sphere, passes into genius through exercise; for if geniuses are born, as we sometimes hear, they must yet be born again of study, struggle, and work. First the man comes into action, gets possession of himself, fills out the tone of his energies by efforts and struggles that are of the will. If then ideas find him, when he is ploughing in uses, and drop their mantle on him, he

becomes a prophet. I say, if they find him; for he is little likely to
find them, by going after them. Inspiration sought is inspiration hind-
ered. It must be a call. No man makes a breeze for his vessel by
blowing in the sail himself. Neither is any man to act the genius willfully, or to have it for a question, previous to study and work, whether
possibly he is born to the life of genius. To preconceive the life is, in
fact, not to suffer it. The most any mortal can do in this matter is to
do nothing, —save to offer a pure, industrious, lively nature to all
beauty and good, and be willing to serve them, till he is permitted to
reign with them. If then there fall into his bosom, as it were out of
heaven, thoughts, truths, feelings, acts of good to be done, all of
which are joy and reward in their own nature, and the man, taking
fire in these, as with something divine, rises into play, that is the kind
of activity we mean by the word *genius*. For if there be an example,
now and then, of some precocious fondling, who appears to be born
to inspiration, and begins to play in the lap, as it were, of mere nature—plays in the university as a poet, too divinely gifted for the
tough discipline of study—if possibly he is reckoned a genius, he will
yet turn out to be a genius of the small order, and it will be wonderful,
if, as lambs and kittens are sobered by the graver habit of their ma-
jority, the growth of his beard does not exhaust his inspiration. However this may be, all the heavy and massive forms of genius, all the
giants of inspiration, are sons of work.

Such being the distinction between talent and genius, we shall
look for a like distinction in their demonstrations; the distinction,
namely, of work and play, activity for an end and activity as an end,
that of the empty and that of the full, the acquisitive and the creative,
the ascent of the ladder and the ascent of fire.

Here lies the distinction between wit and humor, a distinction
which the rhetoricians have not always distinctly traced, though well
aware of some real and very wide difference in their effects. Wit is
work, humor is play. One is the dry labor of intention or design,
ambition eager to provoke applause, malignity biting at an adversary,
envy letting down the good or the exalted. The other, humor, is the
soul reeking with its own moisture, laughing because it is full of
laughter, as ready to weep as to laugh; for the copious shower it holds
is good for either. And then, when it has set the tree a dripping,

"And hung a pearl in very cowslip's ear,"

the pure sun shining after will reveal no color of intention in the spar-kling drop, but will leave you doubting still whether it be a drop let fall by laughter, or—a tear.

The rhetoricians have also labored much to make out some ex-ternal definition by which prose may be distinguished from poetry. No such distinction is possible, till we pass into the mind of the writer, and contemplate his subjective state. If he writes for some use or end ulterior to the writing, and of course superior as a motive, or if we read with a feeling produced that the writing is only means to an end, that is prose. On the other hand, every sort of writing which is its own end, an utterance made because the soul is full of feeling, beauty, and truth, and wants to behold her own joy, is poetry. She sings be-cause the music is in her heart. Her divine thought burns, and words flock round about, fanning the fire with their wings, till she goes up in flame, unable to stay.

Poetry, therefore, is play, as distinguished from prose, which is work. Hence, too, poetry is distinguished from prose by a certain quality that we call rhythm. For when a man thinks or acts for an end ulterior, suggested by self-love, then the drag of his end, being to-wards himself, makes a specialty of him,—he is a mote in the great universe, centered in itself and not in the sun, and pulling to get some-thing to or in itself; therefore he is out of rhythm in his feeling, and the music of the stars will not chime with him. But when he lets go his private want or end to play, then he is part of the great universe under God, and consciously one with it, and then he falls into the rhythmic dance of the worlds, giving utterance, in beat and number, to a feeling that is itself played into beat and number, weaving and waving with those graces that circle the throne of all beauty, and chiming with the choirs of light in their universal, but, to the most of mankind, inaudible, hymn. Or, to bring an instance from below the stars, where no fiction may be suspected; as the mountains of the world, having a certain secret law of rhythm in their moulds and gran-ite masses, take up the discordant sounds of horns or screaming voices, part the discords, toss the silvering harmonies about in re-duplicating beats of echo, and fine away the notes till they seem vi-brations of spirit, pulsing still, after the air is silent; so, when a man falls under inspiration from God and his worlds, and begins to play, his soul forthwith becomes a tuneful creature; his thoughts submit to the universal rhythmic laws, and when he speaks he sings.

If in verse, then, the number is cast by the feeling or inspiration; all is of the feeling, and the words are gathered into their places, not by choice, but by a certain instinct which they themselves feel after; as when birds of passage hook themselves to each other in waving lines of propagated action, all feeling all, and chiming in the beat of their wings. If the writing be in the form of prose, and yet be truly in play, still it will be felt that some higher law than choice has called the words into their places. We have still a feeling of number and rhythm, and certain mystic junctures and cadences, born, as it were, of music, remind us that the son of song is here.

The same may be said of the orator; for there is no definite line of distinction, as many imagine, between the true orator and the poet,—unless we say that the orator is the poet in action, the impersonation of rhythm and play. For though the speaker begins with a cause which he is charged to gain, yet as he kindles with his theme and rises into inspired action, his men become gods, his cause is lifted out of the particular into the universal, or into such a height that speaking for it becomes an end in itself, and his advocacy, raised above the mere prose level, becomes a lofty, energetic improvising. What he began with a purpose hurries him on now as a passion. His look changes. His voice takes a modulation not of the will. His words and cadences seem rather to make use of him than to be used by him. His action, being no longer voluntary, but spontaneous, falls into the rhythm of play, where you distinguish the sharp, invective iambic, the solemn, religious spondee, the swift trochaic run of eagerness or fear, the heavy molossic tread of grief or sorrow. He becomes, in fact, a free lyric in his own living person, the most animated and divinest embodiment of play,—thus and therefore a power sublime above all others possible to man.

Pursuing the same method, I might also exhibit a similar distinction of work and play between rhetorical beauty, labored by the rules of the professors, and the free beauty of original creation. Criticism holds a like relation to all the productive energies of genius; logic also a like relation to the spiritual insight of reason; understanding a like relation to the realizations of faith.

There is yet another topic which requires to be illustrated, in order to complete my subject, but which I can touch only in the briefest manner. I speak of philosophic method, or the true method of scientific discovery. The inductive method, sometimes called the Baconian, is commonly represented in a manner that would make the philosopher the dullest of beings, and philosophy the dullest of all drudgeries. It is merely to classify facts on a basis of comparison or abstraction; that is, to arrange a show-box and call it philosophy! No, the first and really divine work of philosophy is to generate ideas, which are then to be verified by facts or experiments. Therefore we shall find that a certain capacity of elevation or poetic ardor is the most fruitful source of discovery. The man is raised to a pitch of insight and becomes a seer, entering into things through God's constitutive ideas, to read them as from God. For what are laws of science but ideas of God,—those regulative types of thought by which God created, moves, and rules the worlds? Thus it is that the geometrical and mathematical truths become the prime sources of scientific inspiration; for these are the pure intellectualities of being, and have their life in God. Accordingly, an eloquent modern writer says,—"I am persuaded that many a problem of analysis of Kepler, Galileo, Newton and Euler, and the solution of many an equation, suppose as much intuition and inspiration as the finest ode of Pindar. Those pure and incorruptible formulas which already were before the world was, that will be after it, governing throughout all time and space, being, as it were, an integral part of God, put the mathematician in profound communion with the Divine Thought. In those immutable truths, he savors what is purest in the creation. He says to the worlds, like the ancient,—'Let us be silent, we shall hear the murmuring of the Gods.' "

Accordingly we find, as a matter of historic fact, that the singular and truly wonderful man who first broke into the ordinances of heaven and got a foothold there for definite science was inflamed and led on by the inspirations of geometry. "Figures pleased me," he says, "as being quantities, and as having existed before the heavens." Therefore he expected to find the heavens included under geometric figures. Half mad with prophetic feeling, and astrologically possessed also by the stars, he goes up among them praying and joking and experimenting together, trying on, as it were, his geometric figures to see how they will fit, and scolding the obstinacy of heaven when they will not; doubting then whether "perhaps the gibbous moon, in the bright constellation of the Bull's forehead, is not filling his mind with

fantastic images;'' returning again to make another trial, and enduring
labors which, if done in the spirit of work, would have crushed any
mortal,—till, at last, behold! his prophetic formula settles into place!
the heavens acknowledge it! And he breaks out in holy frenzy,
crying,—"What I prophesied two-and-twenty years ago, as soon as
I discovered the five solids among the heavenly orbits; what I believed
before I had seen Ptolemy's Harmonics; what I had promised my
friends; that for which I joined Tycho Brahe, I have brought to light!
It is now eighteen months since I got the first glimpse of light; three
months since the dawn; very few days since the unveiled sun, most
admirable to gaze on, burst out upon me. Nothing holds me; I indulge
my sacred fury! I triumph over mankind! The die is cast; the book is
written,—to be read, either now, or by posterity, I care not which. It
may well wait a century for a reader, as God has been waiting six
thousand years for an observer!''

And yet this man was no philosopher, some will say; he did not
proceed by induction and the classification of facts, he only made a
lucky guess! Be it so, it was yet such a guess as must be made before
science could get any firm hold of the sky; such a guess as none but
this most enthusiastic and divinely gifted mortal, trying at every gate
of knowledge there, could ever have made.

So too it is now, always has been, always will be,—boast of our
Baconian method as we may, misconceive the real method of philosophy as we certainly do,—all great discoveries, not purely acci-
dental, will be gifts to insight, and the true man of science will be he
who can best ascend into the thoughts of God, he who burns before
the throne in the clearest, purest, mildest light of reason.

Thus, also, it was that Linnaeus, when the mystic and almost
thinking laws of vegetable life began to open upon him, cried,—
*"Deum sempiternum, omniscium, omnipotentem, a tergo transeun-
tem, vidi, et obstupui!"*[3]

So, too, when the animate races are to open their wondrous history, you yourselves have seen the hand of play, or of scientific genius, dashing out, stroke by stroke, in a few free lines, those creative
types of God in which the living orders had their spring; and have

---

3. ''I saw God eternal, omniscient, omnipotent passing by, and I was stupe-
fied.''

seemed, in the chalk formation of the lecture-room, to see those creatures leaping into life, which the other and older chalk formation under ground has garnered there, as the cabinet of Jehovah.

But it is time to bring these illustrations to a close, and it is scarcely for me to choose the manner. They have their own proper close, towards which they have all the way been drawing us, and that we must now accept; namely, this,—that, as childhood begins with play, so the last end of man, the pure ideal in which his being is consummated, is a state of play. And if we look for this perfected state, we shall find it nowhere, save in religion. Here at last man is truly and completely man. Here the dry world of work and the scarcely less dry counterfeits of play are left behind. Partial inspirations no longer suffice. The man ascends into a state of free beauty, where well-doing is its own end and joy, where life is the simple flow of love, and thought, no longer colored in the prismatic hues of prejudice and sin, rejoices ever in the clear white light of truth. Exactly this we mean, when we say that Christianity brings an offer of liberty to man; for the Christian liberty is only pure spiritual play. Delivered of self-love, fear, contrivance, legal constraints, termagant passions, in a word, of all ulterior ends not found in goodness itself, the man ascends into power, and reveals, for the first time, the real greatness of his nature.

I speak thus, not professionally, but as any one, who is simply a man of letters, should. I am well aware that Christianity has hitherto failed to realize the noble consummation of which I speak. We have been too much in opinions to receive inspirations; occupied too much with fires and anathemas, to be filled with this pure love; too conversant with mock virtues and uncharitable sanctities, to receive this beauty or be kindled by this heavenly flame. And yet how evident is it that religion is the only element of perfected freedom and greatness to a soul! for here alone does it finally escape from self, and come into the perfect life of play. For just as the matter of the worlds wants a law to settle its motions and be its element of order, so all intelligences want their element of light, rest, beauty, and play in God. Hence we are to look, as the world rises out of its barbaric fires and baptized animosities into the simple and free life of love, to see a beauty unfolded in human thought and feeling, as much more graceful as it is freer and closer to God. Christian love is demonstrably the only true ground of a perfect aesthetic culture. Indeed, there is no perfect culture of any kind, which does not carry the man out of himself, and kindle in his human spirit those free aspirations that shall bear him up, as in flame, to God's own person.

Therefore I believe in a future age, yet to be revealed, which is to be distinguished from all others as the godly or godlike age,—an age not of universal education simply, or universal philanthropy, or external freedom, or political well-being, but a day of reciprocity and free intimacy between all souls and God. Learning and religion, the scholar and the Christian, will not be divided as they have been. The universities will be filled with a profound spirit of religion, and the *bene orâsse* will be a fountain of inspiration to all the investigations of study and the creations of genius.

I raise this expectation of the future, not because some prophet of old time has spoken of a day to come, when ''the streets of the city shall be full of boys and girls playing in the streets thereof,'' (for I know not that he meant to be so interpreted,) but because I find a prophecy of play in our nature itself, which it were a violation of all insight not to believe will some time be fulfilled. And when it is fulfilled, it will be found that Christianity has, at last, developed a new literary era, the era of religious love.

Hitherto, the love of passion has been the central fire of the world's literature. The dramas, epics, odes, novels, and even histories, have spoken to the world's heart chiefly through this passion, and through this have been able to get their answer. For this passion is a state of play, wherein the man loses himself, in the ardor of a devotion regardless of interest, fear, care, prudence, and even of life itself. Hence there gathers round the lover a tragic interest, and we hang upon his destiny, as if some natural charm or spell were in it. Now this passion of love, which has hitherto been the staple of literature, is only a crude symbol in the life of nature, by which God designs to interpret, and also to foreshadow, the higher love of religion,—nature's gentle Beatrice, who puts her image in the youthful Dante, by that to attend him afterwards in the spirit-flight of song, and be his guide up through the wards of Paradise to the shining mount of God. What, then, are we to think, but that God will some time bring us up out of the literature of the lower love, into that of the higher?—that as the age of passion yields to the age of reason, so the crude love of instinct will give place to the loftier, finer, more impelling love of God? And then, around that nobler love, or out of it, shall arise a new body of literature, as much more gifted as the inspiration is purer and more intellectual. Beauty, truth, and worship; song, science, and duty, will all be unfolded together in this common love.

Society must of course receive a correspondent beauty into its character and feeling, such as can be satisfied no longer with the old barbaric themes of war and passion. To be a scholar and not to be a Christian, to produce the fruits of genius without a Christian inspiration, will no longer be thought of; and religion, heretofore looked upon as a ghostly constraint upon life, it will now be acknowledged, is the only sufficient fertilizer of genius, as it is the only real emancipator of man.

If now it be doubted whether a hope of so great beauty is ever to be realized here on earth; whether, indeed, the visions of the Christian seers that look this way are more than rhapsodies of their poetic mood, it must be enough that just such rhapsodies of promise are chanted by the world's own order. Let no expectation seem romantic because it wears the air of poetry; for religion is itself the elemental force of all free beauty, and thus of a life essentially poetic. Its inspired seers and prophets are the poets of God. Its glorious future bursts up ever into song, and pictures itself to the view in poetic sceneries and visions. Even the occupations and felicities of the good beyond life are representable only in the play of choirs and chimes of poetic joy. Music and rhythm are the natural powers, indeed, of order and crystallization, in the social life of all moral natures; as we see in the fact that the ancient laws of the race were framed in verse, and sung into authority, as the *carmen necessarium* of the state. Therefore I can easily persuade myself, that, if the world were free,—free, I mean, of themselves,—brought up, all, out of work into the pure inspiration of truth and charity, new forms of personal and intellectual beauty would appear, and society itself reveal the Orphic movement. No more will it be imagined that poetry and rhythm are accidents or figments of the race, one side of all ingredient or ground in nature. But we shall know that poetry is the real and true state of man, the proper and last ideal of souls, the free beauty they long for, and the rhythmic flow of that universal play in which all life would live.

THE ETERNITY OF LOVE[4]

Charity never faileth.—1 Cor. xiii. 8.

[My subject is] the durable and ceaseless character, the essential eternity of love, considered as a fixed passion of the eternal soul.

And it ought to have this enduring character for reasons that are obvious:

1. Because it has a permanent source—Jesus Christ, the same yesterday, to-day and forever, unchangeable in his love and so an abiding and fixed root of love in his followers. "For love is of God;" whence it follows that if God is the source, the love kindled in us from his central heat ought to be permanent as its source.

2. The joy of love is inexhaustible. No one tires of love. No power exercised by it demands a respite. All the springs of the soul are full to overflowing when it is in God's love. It lubricates the play of thought, feeling, purpose, every faculty, and keeps it fresh forever. It makes a state eternally and completely luminous. "He that loveth his brother abideth in the light."

3. There would be no use in the new creating grace of love, no good reason why it should be regenerated in us, if it were a fitful and frail power, like the transitory, momentary impulses it has to contend with in us. It can finally regenerate all bad impulse only as it has a lasting and durable hold of us. It must be the love that never faileth, else it might as well not be at all.

4. This love must be enduring because it proposes for its end a mission to organize an eternal society, knitting souls to souls, men to angels, angels to men and all to God in a grand fraternity of blessedness. It gives to each a property in all, to enjoy all as being enjoyed and loved by all. In a word, it organizes *heaven,* and must therefore be a bond as durable as heaven, else it is unreliable and worthless. God, therefore, stakes even the eternal order of his empire on the essentially indestructible basis of love, calling it the charity that never faileth. The stars may fall, gravity may let go of matter, matter itself may lapse, the everlasting hills dissolve and be no more; but love

---

4. From *The Spirit in Man,* 240–45. An abbreviated version of a sermon preached in North Church, Hartford in March 1859. Brackets indicate the condensation of sentences and are part of the 1903 edition.

which is of God and durable as God, this he makes the foundation of his throne, the constitutive bond and law that is to organize, conserve and sustain the eternity of blessing in which his counsel turns.

Christian love is, properly speaking, neither an emotion nor a sentiment. These are excitements or movements of the soul that affect only some particular sensibility at a particular time; but love is a power that occupies and moves the whole man. Pity, for example, is a movement of the sensibility at one particular point and by reason of some special occasion. Love is no such partial, limited affection. It is the longing of one's whole nature, the ruling and fixed passion of the man. As contrasted with an emotion, it is a kind of *all-motion,* the bent, the polar force of a durable attraction fastened in the man. Another and stronger contrast between emotions or sentiments on one side and love on the other is to be seen in their merely transitional, momentary character. They cease with their occasion, while love is abiding and fixed. Thus the word *emotion* means a *moving out* of feeling into the foreground of the moment, elicited by some object or appeal. The cries of orphans, the wants of starving families, any sort of woe, distress or wrong, any sort of great action or beautiful conduct excites emotion. The theatre is the place of emotions, emotions are the luxury of theatres. Men go there to buy the luxury and count themselves repaid if they get the hour-long bliss expected. But such emotions do not wake again the next morning with the theatre-goer when he wakes. They even die out and cease before he reaches home. All emotions cease with their occasions. But it is not so with the state or fixed passion of love. It abides, stays with the man all day, wakes with him in the morning when he wakes, and he has even slept his sleep as a loving man. His heart is drawn by the magnetism of a divine polarity, settled thus to its pole of eternal aspiration, even as the needle itself. Thus when David says: "My heart is fixed, O God, my heart is fixed," he describes the true reality of love without using the word. He means that he is settled by a divine love, which is the fixed passion of his nature.

Again, it will be seen that emotions and sentiments pass into no practical results. Sometimes the momentary impulse will beget a single momentary act, the giving of a charity for example, but generally the impulse dies in the bosom, issuing in no results of action at all. On the other hand, every sort of love actuates the man practically, settles the ends, determines the doing of his life. And the true Christian love will in this way set a man to a life of charity, seeking after objects and occasions and works to be done. It bends the soul practically to its objects. It is itself the soul of action, and so it grows into greatness, proves itself real and true and fashions thus a Christly man. There is no pretence, no cheat in it, for it is no idling play of the heart, but a real, honest, fixed passion of doing the good that wants to be done. Again, the emotions and sentiments create no fixed aspirations; whereas it is in the nature of all love to be an aspiration after its object. All fixed passions, such as avarice, the lust of power, the thirst for revenge, the love of a person, are in their very nature aspirations. Accordingly some of the most emotional, most sentimental people are such as have really no fixed aspirations at all. They will luxuriate in all beautiful sentiments respecting God and his character and works. They will weep under sermons, melt under Christ's passion with all finest sympathy, swell into loftiest admiration of God's majesty and greatness, and yet will never truly come to God or set themselves practically with him, because they have no aspirations. Love in their hearts would be a fixed passion, tending ever toward him. ''Whom have I in heaven but thee,'' is the language of it, and it puts the soul on sacrifice, labor, love, persistent prayer and faithful striving, that they may come unto him and find his friendship.

Every man's love determines what he will be in character. He is as his love, and not otherwise. If he loves the bad, the low, the false, the selfish, his love is the fixed affinity of his soul with what he loves. If he loves what is honorable, right, true, good, God and Christ and heaven, his love will mould his character to its object. Hence it is declared that ''every one that loveth is born of God,'' that the changing of a man's ruling love changes the man, makes him a new man, because the love of God into which he has come must needs be the root of a character in him which is God-like. Love, in short, is not emotion, but motion rather; not some jet of feeling raised by objects and occasions, but the practical drift and current of the man.

It is a love which takes one off his own centre and makes him cease from the minding of his own things. The prime example of it is in Christ himself and his life and death of sacrifice. It is such a kind of love as takes on itself as a burden the wrongs and woes and wants and spiritual undoing of others. It puts the subject in a vicarious position, like even to that of Christ himself, to bear other men's burdens, to be willingly afflicted and sacrificed for them, to forgive their wrongs, to cling to them mercifully even in their unrighteous enmities. Call such love as this an emotion, a sentiment! class it with these firefly gleams of natural feeling! What have they in common with it? What has it with them? Why, it is divine, the God-power fallen upon man! By what bridge will any of these natural emotions or sentiments pass over into this love of enemies, this passion of self-sacrifice, this devotion to the evil and shameful and low? Christ only, Christ revealed in the man,—he is the soul of this love; it is supernatural and divine. This love is of God, it comes down as Christ and with him from above, and fashions a supernal character wholly by itself. The various human loves we talk of are only the natural types of it, generating words by which to speak of it, images by which to conceive it, but are as different from it in kind as flesh and spirit, matter and God.

O, this Charity that never faileth, soul of God's beauty, bond of all perfectness! Length, breadth, depth, height! Love of God that passeth knowledge! On this deep sea of God's fulness the ages of eternity navigate and the tides of eternity swing. Hither, mortals, come and hear the sounding of the many waters, beating out their hymn eternal on the tremulous shores. This is love's grand world of order and life, full and free and deep and strong, the empowered and organized bliss, the settled state of glorified society in God. O, God of love, mercifully grant that we may none of us come short of this thy fulness!

OUR GOSPEL A GIFT TO THE IMAGINATION[5]

The most unilluminated and least valuable of the Bampton Lecture volumes has been recently published by Mr. Garbett,[6] under the title, "The Dogmatic Faith;" a title which does about equal violence to both the terms of which it is compounded. For the Gospel is no dogma, and if it were, could not be a faith. The word dogma indicates

---

5. From *Building Eras in Religion* (New York: Charles Scribner's Sons, 1881), 249–85. An essay originally appearing in the magazine *Hours at Home* in 1869.
    6. Edward Garbett, whose *The Dogmatic Faith* appeared in 1867.

in its etymology and supposes in its common uses, a something thought; it is opinion offered to opinion as having a standard right; whereas the gospel is a revelation made up of fact and form and figure, and offered as a presentation to faith. It calls itself indeed "the faith," and he infers at once that, since it is an "authoritative faith," it must be dogmatic. Whereas all truth has this attribute of authority, though it does not follow that it has such kind of authority as allows it to be no faith at all, viz., dogma. What is given to faith is put forth in some fact-form or symbol to be interpreted by imaginative insight, or the discerning power of faith. What is given to opinion is given to the notional understanding. One imports liberty, and the other a certain dictational right as respects thinking. In one there is a perceiving by trust and the soul-welcome of trust; the other is a notional perceiving or thinking, without perhaps any soul-welcome at all. In his treatise therefore on the Dogmatic Faith, we are not surprised to find that Mr. G. is rather mixing ideas than clearing them, confounding also things to be spiritually discerned with things logically reasoned, or ecclesiastically determined.

His argument is principally concerned in removing "six" opposing claims, or points maintained. Whether he succeeds or not is a matter of small consequence, for he would not prove his doctrine if he should. Just that after all may be a fact, which, by a certain remarkable fatality, he assumes is not; for he ventures strangely on the affirmation, that the opposers of theoretic dogmatism in our day "do not rest on any allegation of inaccuracy in the process of formulating truth, but on objections against the existence and certainty of the truth itself." Exactly contrary to which, it will be seen that, on this question of a possible "accuracy in formulating truth," in distinction from "the existence and certainty of truth," everything, in the issue he makes, most emphatically depends. He supposes himself that there is to be a formulating process; which is a virtual concession that the gospel is not the complete dogma. And the precise difficulty here to be encountered is that no such process of accuracy in "formulating" the dogma, as permits a possible hope of success, is provided by human language. As he himself conceives, dogma is "the settled and positive truth stated in words sharply defined;" or again, more exactly still, "a settled and certain truth, an attained resting-place for belief, from which, as from the maxims of mathematical science, we may confidently argue," —just what everybody knows has never yet been found. And could he simply call it opinion, he would see at once that there has been no end to opinions under it and against it. Dogma has been always going to be, or just about to be settled, by some new school or teacher, yet in fact never is. If we could possibly think out a gospel, we could not frame it and phrase it in language, so as to make a finality of what we think. For we have no language for opinions in moral and religious matters that is not compounded in forms and figures, which are only images, and not exact notations for what they represent. They are good for the uses of faith and, in fact, more wondrously significant and sufficient in that manner, but they have no such determinate property as permits them to serve the uses of dogma.

I propose, in these suggestions, no formal controversy with Mr. Garbett's book. I only refer to it in the way of introducing a presentation as nearly opposite as may be at the point here stated. What I am going to advance will hold equally well in all matters of philosophic speculation; but, to simplify the argument, I propose to confine my illustrations within the ranges, for the most part, of the Christian truth.

I shall endeavor to exhibit, as far as I can in the restricted limits of this article, the fact that our Christian Gospel is a Gift more especially to the Human Imagination. It offers itself first of all and principally to the interpretative imaginings and discernings of faith, never, save in that manner, to the constructive processes of logic and speculative opinion. It is, in one sense, pictorial; its every line or lineament is traced in some image or metaphor, and by no possible ingenuity can it be gotten away from metaphor; for as certainly as one metaphoric image is escaped by a definition, another will be taken up, and must be, to fill its place in the definition itself. Mathematical language is a scheme of exact notation. All words that are names of mere physical acts and objects are literal, and even animals can, so far, learn their own names and the meaning of many acts done or commanded. But no animal ever understood a metaphor: that belongs to intelligence, and to man as a creature of intelligence; being a power to see, in all images, the faces of truth, and take their sense, or read [*intuslego*] their meaning, when thrown up in language before the imagination.

Every word is a figure called in to serve a metaphoric use, in virtue of the fact that it has a physical base naturally significant of the spiritual truth or meaning it is used metaphorically to express. Physical bases are the timber, in this manner, of all mental language, and are generally traced in the etymologies of the dictionaries; though sometimes they are lost and cannot be traced. And it is not merely the verbs, nouns, adjectives, that carry these metaphoric uses, but their very grammar of relationship, as they are found originally in space themselves, is also framed in terms of space by the little words called prepositions, which show their spatial images in their faces, *up, down, by, through, to, under, from, beyond* and the like. The whole web of speech is curiously woven metaphor, and we are able to talk out our thoughts in it,—never one of them visible,—by throwing out metaphoric images in metaphoric grammar so as to give them expression.

Let us go back now and take our lesson at the type history of the Scriptures. The temple and the whole temple service,—the sacrifices, lustrations of blood, purifyings, and the like,—was a figure, an apostle declares, for the time then present. His word here is παραβολη [*parable*]. Sometimes he uses the word *image,* sometimes *ensample,* and oftener the word *type;* but they all mean nearly the same thing. And here it is that we come upon the curiously fantastic type-learning, which figures so conspicuously in the sermons, commentaries, and theologic treatises of the former time. It is only fit subject of mirth, when it assumes that the types were given to signify to the ages that received them the great living truths of Christianity, and not to be vehicle and metaphor, afterward, for them when they should arrive. These types, patterns, shadows, images, parables, ensamples, or whatever else they were called, are simply bases of words prepared to serve as metaphors of the new salvation when it should come. And for this purpose, in part, the altar service was instituted; for the gospel grace was to be a grace supernatural, and there were no types, no bases of words in nature, that could serve the necessary metaphoric uses. All the natural metaphors were in a lower field of significance, and all mere natural language fell short of the mark.

It may occur to some as an objection, that the apostle says: "a figure for the time then present." But he means "for the time then present," only in the sense that in using the altar-rites or rites of sacrifice, for their liturgy of worship, the men of old were brought into faiths, repentances and tempers analogical to those of the gospel grace. He does not mean that they saw Christianity and the gospel grace typified and foreshadowed in their rites. Not even the prophets themselves understood any such thing, but ''were searching *what,* and what manner of time, the Spirit of Christ which was in them did signify.'' These men of old were in the patterns of the heavenly things, not in the heavenly things themselves. Their rites were the bases of words some time to be used as metaphors of the Christian grace, but they did not see, as yet, what things the metaphors were going to express. They lived in the shadow of good things to come, but not in the very import of them.

But we must look into language itself and see how the great revelation of God is coming and to come. First of all, it is impossible, as we have seen already, that any terms of language for mental notions, things of the spirit, unseen worlds, beings invisible, should ever exist, save as there are physical images found to serve as metaphoric bases of the necessary words; for we cannot show them to the eye and then name them, as we do acts or objects visible; we can only hint them by figures, or objects metaphorically significant of them. And so we see beforehand, that all the truths of religion are going to be given to men by images; so that all God's truth will come as to the imagination. Hence the necessity of the old physical religion to prepare draperies and figures for the new. Hence also, when we come to the new, we are constantly met, we perhaps know not why or how, by images taken from the old, in a way that seems half fanciful and curiously mystical. Adam is the figure of him that was to come, the second Adam, because he, Christ, was to be the head, correspondently, of a spiritual generation. Christ is David, Melchizedek, high priest, the spiritual Rock, a prophet like unto Moses and I know not what beside. John the Baptist is Elias that was to come. In the same manner, heaven is a paradise or garden, or a new Jerusalem, or a state of glorious city life in God; the new society of grace is to be the kingdom of God, or the kingdom of heaven; and Christ himself is Messiah, that is, king. All the past is taken up as metaphor for all the future. All these things, we are to say, ''happened unto them for ensamples,'' that is, types for the expression of our higher truth.

And so we are questioning often about the credibility of a double meaning in scripture; as if it were a thing fanciful beyond belief. Whereas the meanings double and redouble as often as new typologies are made ready. The spiritual comes out of the physical, and the more spiritual out of the less; just because one thing is ready for the expression of another and still another. There is nothing fantastical in it, but it comes to pass under a fixed law of language,—all language, even the most common,—even as a stalk of corn pushes out leaf from within leaf by a growth that is its unsheathing.

Every dictionary shows the unsheathing process always going on; meanings coming out of meanings, and second senses doubling upon first, and third upon second, and so every symbol breeding families of meanings on to the tenth or twentieth and saying always, in the scripture way: "that so it might be fulfilled." This fulfilling is no scripture conceit, but is the systematic fact of language itself.

We shall get further insight into this matter by just considering the state of mind a prophet is in when he writes. He is lifted by his inspiration into a state of high beholding, as regards some matter which is to be the particular subject of his testimony; and the divine perceptiveness thus quickened in him,—so far the particular matter he sees,—will be the specially God-given import of his message. Then he is to conceive, express, set forth in words for himself what is in his beholding. But he cannot testify any thing unknown, we see at once, save by images taken from the known. Suppose him to be set in some high *pose* of seership that really relates, if he could say it, to our new western world and the new day some time here to be seen. He cannot say, "America," for that is a name not known as Grecia was. If he says, "beyond the sea," it would only mean outside the pillars of Hercules or Gibraltar Rock. He cannot seize on images in the Gulf Stream, or the Mammoth Cave, or Niagara, or the great lakes, or the forests, or the prairies, or the rivers, or the fierce, wild warriors of the woods. He has not an image distinctly American in his whole stock. What then can he say? Manifestly nothing; because he has nothing in which to say it. Possibly some of Isaiah's pictures of the "Isles waiting for God," and "the ships of Tarshish bringing sons from far, their silver and their gold with them," may have a look this way, taking old Tarshish for a figure, but we can never know. Under this same law, we have the fact of creation, as given in the first chapter of Genesis, beautifully illustrated. No human spectator saw the creation, and the only way in which it could ever be reported was by a kind of prophecy backward. Some great prophet soul, we may imagine, coasting round the work of God in a power of holy insight, or divine beholding, framed, as it were, his own divine conception of the fact as progressive, drawing itself on by irregular, indefinite stages,—no matter how long or short, or even how many,—and to set the stages forth, he caught up the natural time-spacing symbol of days, and made up a chapter of progressions that took a week of days before it was finished. To conceive anything more pitiful than the grubbing literalism that cannot think of days going thus into metaphor because they are in the Almanac would, I think, be difficult. Was there ever a case for metaphor more easily discernible beforehand?

We perceive in these illustrations how every revelator and teacher of things spiritual or things future, gets and must get his power to express the unknown by drawing images and figures from the known. As he must portray the new world by some old image of a Tarshish in the sea, or by some other like symbol, if he does at all, or the creation by the spacing figure of days, or heaven by the image of a paradise, or a great city Jerusalem, so it must be with everything.

Thus if God is to be himself revealed, he has already thrown out symbols for it, filling the creation full of them, and these will all be played into metaphor. The day will be his image, the sea, the great rock's shadow, the earthquake, the dew, the fatherhood care of the child, and the raven and the feeble folk of the conies,—all that the creation is and contains, in all depths and heights and latitudes and longitudes of space,—everything expresses God by some image that is fit, as far as it goes. "Day unto day uttereth speech, and night unto night showeth knowledge." Metaphor on metaphor crowds the earth and the skies, bearing each a face that envisages the Eternal Mind, whose word or wording forth it is to be. Again he takes a particular people into covenant specially with himself, just in order to make their public history the Providential metaphor, so to speak, of his rulership and redeeming teachership, leading them on and about by his discipline, and raising light and shade as between them and the world-kingdoms of the false gods about them, to set himself in relief as the true Lord of all. And then, following still the same law of expression by outward fact and image, he crowns the revelation process by the incarnate life and life-story of his Son, erecting on earth a supernatural kingdom to govern the world in the interest of his supernatural redemption. And if we do not take the word in some light, frivolous, merely rhetorician way, we can say nothing of Christ so comprehensively adequate as to call him the metaphor of God; God's last metaphor! And when we have gotten all the metaphoric meanings of his life and death, all that is expressed and bodied in his person of God's saving help and new-creating, sin-forgiving, reconciling love, the sooner we dismiss all speculations on the literalities of his incarnate miracles, his derivation, the composition of his person, his suffering,—plainly transcendent as regards our possible understanding,— the wiser shall we be in our discipleship. We shall have him as the express image of God's person. We shall have "the light of the knowledge of the glory of God, in the face of Jesus Christ." Beholding in him as in a glass the glory of the Lord, we shall be changed into the same image. The metaphoric contents are ours, and beyond that nothing is given.

Going on then to matters of spiritual use and experience in what we call the doctrine of his gospel, we have these given also to the imagination in terms of metaphor. As far back as the days of Abraham and Moses, words and images for this kind of use were very scantily provided. Even prayer was best described as a wrestling match. The prophets found images more nearly sufficient. And when Christ came, great images were evoked that never had been used before. He was called a door to be entered, a bread from heaven to be fed upon, a water of life to quench the thirst, life, way, shepherd, healer, teacher, master, king, and rock. And when the very point of a new life begun is to be explained or expounded, he draws on the well-known fact of proselyte baptism and calls it regeneration: "Art thou a master in Israel and knowest not these things?" Have you not seen the Gentile proselyte, before unclean, washed by a baptism and so regenerated, born over, naturalized, as we say, in Israel? So the unclean soul of sin, born of water and the Spirit, is entered, as a spiritually new man, into the kingdom of God. The great experience wrought is imaged thus, how beautifully and comprehensively, as a change from the unclean to the clean; and so the soul that was alien from God is inducted into citizenship in God's everlasting kingdom. No finest words of analysis and psychologic statement could describe the great mystery of the Spirit half as effectively. So in the same chapter, the same thing is set forth under the image of the serpent lifted up in the wilderness. "Look unto me," says the Great Teacher now to be lifted up, "and, by that fixed beholding of your faith, the sin-plague in you shall be healed." That plague in its secret working, that healing in its secret cure, who shall describe it psychologically, even as this simple image does by its metaphoric use? Both these images, however, of regeneration and of spiritual healing were impossible before the ministry of Providence had prepared them. They came late because they could not come before.

The same again was true of the great reconciliation or atonement, in Christ's life and death. Plainly there was here no lamb, no fire, no altar, no literal sacrifice. There was a blood of murder, but no rite in blood, no sprinkling, no kind of lustral ceremony. And yet all these things are here as in metaphor, and are meant to be. One great object of the old ritual was to prepare these images and get them ready as a higher language for the supernatural truth. The people of the law were put in training under these patterns of the heavenly things, till the very mind of their nation should be stocked with images and metaphors thence derived for the heavenly things themselves. Who could ever have conceived the ministry and death of Jesus in these words of atonement, sacrifice, and cleansing, whose mind had not first been Judaized in the stock images of its thinking? Suppose, for example, that some gifted Greek, having a soul configured to Plato's methods and ideas, had been with Christ, as Peter was, all through his life, and then, after his death, had written his epistle to expound him and his religion to the world. What could he have said of him more adequate than to set him forth as a beautiful and wise character doing wonders by his power; a friend of the poor, a healer of the sick, patient of contradiction, submissive to enemies, meek, true, the ever good, the perfect fair? That he has done any thing which can be called his sacrifice, any thing to recompose the breach of sin or to reconcile the world to God, will not occur to him, and he has no words to speak of any such thing. Not one matter most distinctively prominent in Christ's work, as expounded by his apostles, filling out in metaphoric glory all the terms of the altar, could have been given, or even thought by him. All the better, many will now say; we shall gladly be rid of all such altar figures; for it is too late in the day to be making Hebrews of us now. But suppose it should happen to be true that the all-wise God made Hebrews partly for this very thing, to bring figures into speech that Greeks and Saxons had not; that so he might give to the world the perfectly transcendent, supernatural matter of a grace that reaches high enough to cover and compose the relations of men to his government, a grace of reconciliation. Call the words "old clothes" then of the Hebrews, putting what contempt we may upon them, still they are such types and metaphors of God's mercy as he has been

able to prepare, and Christ is in them as in "glorious apparel!" Why
to say: "Behold the Lamb of God, that taketh away the sin of the
world," signifies, in the heart's uses, more than whole volumes of
palaver in any possible words of natural language. No living disciple,
having once gotten the sense of these types of the altar, will ever try
to get his gospel out of them and preach it in the common terms of
language. Quite as certainly will he never try, having once gotten their
meaning, to hold them literally,—Christ made literally sin for us, a
literal Lamb, literal sacrifice, bleeding literally for the uses of his
blood. But he will want them as the dear interpreters and equivalents
of God's mercy in the cross, putting himself before them to read and
read again, and drink and drink again their full divine meanings into
his soul. Beholding more truths in their faces than all the contrived
theories and speculated propositions of schools, he will stay fast by
them, or in them, wanting never to get clear of them, or away from
the dear and still more dear impression of their power.

So far on our way in discovering the close relationship of God's
revelations and the inlet function of imagination to which they are
given, I cannot do more, in this part of the subject, than simply to
generalize the argument by just calling attention to the fact that so
great a part of our Bible is made up of compositions that are essentially
poetic,—nearly all of it, except the parts rigidly historic or didactic,
and even these have their prose largely sprinkled with poetry. History
itself, in fact, is but a kind of figure, having its greatest value, not in
what it is, but in what it signifies. Besides, the scripture books most
nearly theologic are handling truths every moment, as we see at a
glance, by their images. How didactic are the parables, and yet they
are only metaphors drawn out! In the same way the disciples are God's
living epistles, temples of the Holy Ghost, cities on hills, working as
servants, running as in races, beholding as in glasses,—every single
point of instruction comes out in some metaphor, so that we may
safely challenge the specification of one that does not. And when we
look into the argumentations we find them also hanging on figures of
speech, such as law, circumcision, heart, grace, kingdom, life, motions of sins, liberty, flesh. Take up the chapters of Paul that are most
closely reasoned, the fifth to the ninth, for example, of the Epistle to
the Romans, and the scholar's eye, if not the common reader's, will
discover some metaphor showing its face and turning the current of
meaning in every sentence and in almost every principal word. Nay,

it will be seen that even the little prepositions are struggling as hard in the metaphoric revelations as any of the other images concerned. Thus when we read: "*of* many offences *unto* justification;" "dead *to* the law *by* the body of Christ;" "*through* righteousness *unto* eternal life;" "*of* faith that it might be *by* grace;" we see the meanings hanging quite as visibly on these little words as on the more prominent, and we go back, as it were, to their spatial images, before we get the meanings hitched in fit relationship. In as many as two cases they occur in triads, where some of our subtlest interpreters discover, as they think, affinities that tally secretly with the higher relativities of trinity: "For *of* him and *through* him, and *to* him;" "One God and Father of all, who is *above* all, and *through* all, and *in* you all." So strikingly is it shown us, everywhere on the face of scripture, that it is a gift in metaphor to the world's imagination.

Only God forbid that, when we draw ourselves out on this conclusion, we be understood to mean by the imagination what the rhetoricians teach, in the girlish definitions of their criticism. They describe it as a kind of ornamental, mind's-milliner faculty, that excels in the tricking out of subjects in high-wrought metaphoric draperies, and such they call "imaginative writing." As I am speaking here, the imagination has nothing to do with ornament. It is that which dawns in beauty like the day because the day is in it; that power in human bosoms which reads the types of the creation, beholding the stamps of God's meanings in their faces; the power that distinguishes truths in their images, and seizes hold of images for the expression of truths. So that a free, great soul, when it is charged with thoughts so high, and fresh beholdings in such vigor of life, that it cannot find how to express itself otherwise, does it by images and metaphors in flame that somehow body the meaning to imaginative apprehension.

Holding now this view of truth as presenting itself always by images metaphorically significant, never by any other possible means or media, it is very clear that all our modes of use and processes of interpretation must be powerfully affected by such a discovery.

First of all it must follow, as a principal consequence, that truth is to be gotten by a right beholding of the forms or images by which it is expressed. Ingenuity will miss it by overdoing; mere industry will do scarcely more than muddle it; only candor, a graciously open, clean candor will find it. We can take the sense of its images, only by offering a perfectly receptive imagination to them, a plate to fall upon that is flavored by no partisanship, corrugated by no bigotry, blotched by no prejudice or passion, warped by no self-will. There is nothing we cannot make out of them, by a very little abuse, or perversity. They are innocent people who can never vindicate themselves when wronged, further than to simply stand and wait for a more ingenuous beholding. And it is to be a very great part of our honor and advantage in the truth, that we have it by the clean docility and noble reverence that make us capable of it. We shall not be afraid of worshiping its images; for they are not graven images, but faces that express the truth because they are faces of God. We want, in fact, as a first condition, a mind so given to truth that our love and reverence shall open all our sympathies to it and quite indispose us to any violent practice on its terms.

All mere logically constructive practice on them, twisting meanings into them, or out of them, that are only deducible from their forms and are no part of their real significance, must be jealously restrained. Nicodemus was falling straightway into this kind of mischief, when the words "born again" put him on asking, whether a man can be born of his mother a second time? It was in the form of the words, but how far off from their meaning! So, when it is declared that God is a rock and that God is a river, what follows, since things that are equal to the same things are, in strict logic, equal to one another, but that a rock is a river? Meantime God was not declared to be either rock or river, except in a very partial, metaphoric way. In the same way Christ is called a priest, and a sacrifice, and it follows in good logic that a priest is a sacrifice. Nobody happens, it is true, to have reasoned in just this manner, but how many do reason that, being called a priest and a sacrifice, he must be exactly both in the sense of the ritual; when, in fact, he is neither priest nor sacrifice, save in such a sense as these words, taken as metaphors, are able to convey. Nothing is to be gotten ever, by spinning conclusions out of the mere forms or images of truth, but mischief and delusion. And the record of religion is full of just this kind of delusion. All mere logical handlings are vicious, unless they are so far qualified by insight that insight gives the truth, and then, of course, they are not wanted. Indeed, there is nothing in which the world is so miserably cheated, as in the admiration it yields to what is most logically deductive concerning moral and religious questions. It is even the worst kind of fault, unless it be only meant, as it often is when we say it, that they are written with true intellectual insight, which is a very different matter.

But we must have a theology, some will say; how can religion or religious truth get body, or any firm hold of the world, without a theology? And what is theology? It is very commonly supposed to be a speculated system of doctrine, drawn out in propositions that are clear of all metaphor and are stated in terms that have finally obtained a literal and exact sense. But no such system is possible, for the very plain reason that we have no such terms. We have a great many words that have lost their roots or have come to be so far staled by use that the figures in their bases do not obtrude themselves on our notice. But if we suppose, as we very commonly do in all the logical uses of speculation, that they have become exact coins, or algebraic notations for the ideas represented by them, we are in a great mistake. When they are framed into propositions there is always some element of figure in the other words conjoined, or in the grammar of their prepositions, which makes a figure of the sentences constructed. If there is anything we miss in the really supreme merit of Professor Whitney's late book on language,[7] it is a chapter showing at what point the constructive processes of language leave it, as regards the possibilities of an exact notation, for the uses of moral and religious speculation. His beautiful analysis and fine critical perception would have shown us, I have no question, that theologic and moral science are about as deep in metaphor as prophecy and poetry themselves.

Some years ago one of our most brilliant, most esteemed teachers of theology[8] published a discourse on "The Theology of the Intellect and the Feeling," meaning, it will be seen, by the Feeling, that which feels, or takes the poetic sense of figures and images; the same that I am calling here the Imagination. But the Intellect, he conceives, comes in, after all such vague presences or presentations to the feeling, gathers up the varieties, eliminates the contrarieties, and puts down in the terms of an exact language the real Christian doctrine. Taking, for example, the manifold various terms and figures employed in the metaphoric draperies of scripture language relating to the beginning of a new life,—"repent," "believe," "make you

---

7. William D. Whitney, *Language and the Study of Language* (1867), an rgument for the mechanical invention of language.

8. Edwards Amasa Park of Andover Seminary.

a new heart," "be converted," "born again,"—"the intellect," he says, "educes light from the collision of these repugnant phrases, and then modifies and reconciles them into the doctrine,"—literal now, exact, full-made theology,—*"that the character of our race needs an essential transformation by an interposed influence from God."* It does not appear to be observed, that this very sentence, which affirms the great, inevitable, scientific truth of regeneration, is itself packed full of figures and images, and is, in fact, interpretable only with more difficulty and more ambiguity than any and all the figures proposed to be resolved by it. Thus, for a first metaphor, we have *"character:"* and what is character? Literally it is *mark* or *distinction*. Then naturally it is one thing, morally another, spiritually another. Is it external? Is it internal? Is it made up of acts and habits? Is it the general purpose of the man? Or is it a birth into good affections by the Spirit of God? Or is it both? There is almost nothing we conceive so variously, and unsteadily, and advance upon by so many rectifications, even to the end of life, as this matter of character. *"Needs:"* and by what kind of necessity? Is it in the sense that we have full capacity, which, in our perversity, we will not use? Or in the sense that we have no capacity? Or that we have a receptive, or a partly receptive and partly active capacity? Do we need the change before believing, or after believing, or by and through believing? *"Essential transformation."* Here we have two figures dead enough to be packed together, and which yet, if they were less dead, could hardly be joined at all. One relates to what is inmost, viz., to what is in the *essence* of a thing, and the other to what is outmost, the *form* of a thing. In what sense then essential? In what a transformation? In how many senses lighter and deeper can the words be taken? *"Interposed influence:"* first a word of *pose* or position; secondly, a word of motion, or *flow*. And what is the inflow or influence, and what is it posited between? The Gospel revelation by Christ's life and death is one mode of influence; the power of the Spirit is another; the power of sacraments another; the human example of Jesus another. The influence may be summed up in truth, or it may be God's direct agency one side of truth. Could we but settle this one word *influence* alone, about all the great church controversies of eighteen centuries would be settled. *"From":* in what sense from? Is it *by* God from without? Or *by* God within? Is it *by* God directly, or *by* God medially, as in the Gospel? Or is it only *from* God as the source in whatever manner?

Now I do not mean that, knowing who the author of this general proposition is, we have so many doubts about his meaning in it, but that, bringing to it all the beliefs and misbeliefs of the world and the age, we have all these and a full thousand other questions raised by it. In one view it may be true that it "educes light;" at any rate there may be uses in a proposition thus generalized; and yet it was possible to be made, only because the words were staled in so many ambiguities. And all the terms of theology are under the same conditions. We think we are coming down, perhaps, on exact statements, because we are coming down upon words that forget their figures, and yet the propositions are all woven up in figures, and cover ambiguities only the more subtle that we do not see them.

But we must have science, some will remember; is there any hope for theologic science left? None at all, I answer most unequivocally. Human language is a gift to the imagination so essentially metaphoric, warp and woof, that it has no exact blocks of meaning to build a science of. Who would ever think of building up a science of Homer, Shakespeare, Milton? And the Bible is not a whit less poetic, or a whit less metaphoric, or a particle less difficult to be propositionized in the terms of the understanding. Shall we then have nothing to answer, when the sweeping question is put, why philosophy and every other study should make advances, and theology be only spinning its old circles and revising and re-revising its old problems? It must be enough to answer that philosophy, metaphysical philosophy, having only metaphor to work in, is under exactly the same limitation; that it is always backing and filling, and turning and returning, in the same manner; that nobody can name a single question that has ever been settled by all the systems it has built and the newly contrived nomenclatures it has invented. Working always in metaphors and fooling itself, how commonly, by metaphor, it gets a valuable gymnastic in words, and prepares to a more full and many-sided conception of words. So far it is fruitful and good, and just so far also is the scientific labor of theology. After all it is simple insight in both, and not speculation, that has the true discernment. Words give up their deepest, truest meaning, only when they are read as images of the same.

But we must have definitions, it will be urged, else we cannot be sure what we mean by our words, and when we have the definitions, why can we not have science? But if we mean by definitions an exact literal measurement of ideas, no such thing is possible. In what we call our definitions, whether in theology, or moral philosophy, we only put one set of metaphors in place of another, and, if we understand ourselves, there may be a certain use in doing it, even as there is in shifting our weight upon the other leg; perhaps we make ourselves more intelligible by doing it. And yet there is a very great imposture lurking almost always in these definitions. Thus if I may define a definition, the very word shows it to be a bounding off; where it happens, not unlikely, that a whole heaven's breadth of meaning is bounded out and lost; where again, secondly, it results that the narrow part bounded in and cleared of all grand overplus of meaning, is just as much diminished as it is made more clear and certain; and thirdly, that what one has bounded out another will have bounded in, either in whole or in part; whereupon debates begin, and schools and sects arise, clinging to their several half-truths and doing fierce battle for them. And probably another and still worse result will appear; for the generous broad natures that were going to be captivated by truth's free images, having them now defined and set in propositional statements, will, how often, be offended by their narrow theologic look and reject them utterly. Nothing makes infidels more surely than the spinning, splitting, nerveless refinements of theology. This endeavor, always going on, to get the truths of religion away from the imagination, into propositions of the speculative understanding, makes a most dreary and sad history,—a history of divisions, recriminations, famishings, vanishings and general uncharitableness. Lively, full, fresh, free as they were, the definitions commonly cut off their wings and reduce them to mere pebbles of significance. Before they were plants alive and in flower, now the flavors are gone, the juices dried and the skeleton parts packed away and classified in the dry herbarium called theology.

We deplore, how often, with how great concern, and with prayers to God in which we wrestle heavily, our manifold sects and divisions. We turn the matter every way, contriving new platforms and better articles of dogma, and commonly find that, instead of gathering ourselves into a new and more complete unity, we have only raised new sects and aggravated the previous distractions. And yet many cannot conceive that the gospel is a faith, only in that way to be received, and so the bond of unity. They are going still to think out a gospel, assuming that the Church has no other hope as regards this matter but in the completing of a scientific theology; which will probably be accomplished about the same time that words are substituted by algebraic notations, and poetry reduced to the methods of the calculus or the logarithmic tables. There was never a hope wider of reason. The solar system will die before either that or the hope of a complete philosophy is accomplished. No, we must go back to words, and compose our differences in them as they are, exploring them more by our faith and less by our speculative thinking. Having them as a gift to the imagination, we must stay in them as such, and feel out our agreement there in a common trust, and love, and worship.

See how it is with our two great schools or sects called Calvinism and Arminianism. The points at issue in the propositional methods of their theology are forever unreconcilable. They stand over against each other like Gerizim and Ebal. And yet they have a perfect understanding when they pray together, because they pray their faith out through their imaginative forms, and drop the word-logic forms of the Babel they before were building.

Again, we have a grand fundamental and most practical truth that we call trinity; Father, Son, and Holy Ghost, one God. These three images are God as delivered to the imagination, and the grammatic threeness in which they stand is a truth in metaphor, even as the grammatic personalities are metaphoric and not literal persons; and the God-idea, figured under these relativities, obtains, in the resulting mystery, the largest, freshest, liveliest impression possible. In what manner, at what point, the unity and plurality meet, we may never know. We only know that the unity is absolute and eternal; and the threeness, either a necessary incident of God's revelations, or of his own self-conscious activities considered as the revelation of himself to himself; in either case eternal. We also know that using the three freely as the mind's necessary instrumentations, all speculation apart, we have God as he is, and coalesce in him as in perfect unity. But we cannot rest in this, we must be wiser; so we begin to speculate and make up a theology. Have we not three persons here represented by the personal pronouns of grammar? And what are persons but self-conscious, freewill beings, such as we know them to be and are in fact ourselves? Now we have gotten our three persons out of the metaphor-world into strict literality, and are landed of course in absolute tritheism; such as permits no unity at all. We have no unity even if we say we have, but only a three as absolutely plural as John, James, and Peter. Over opposite, seeing now the very evident absurdity we are in, comes out the Unitarian, using our same false method over again, so to make up another conclusion just as wide of the truth. Is not a person a person? If then God is declared to be one person, and again to be three persons in the same sense, how are we going to believe it? So rejecting the three that were three transcendently, as in metaphoric type and grammar, he falls back on the one, the Father: he alone is God, and reason is no more offended. In that one personality he is thus a person thought, a dogmatic one person, having, of course, the exact type of the human person. The disciple of the new speculation is greatly relieved and with much self-gratulation. But let him not be surprised to find, as he goes on to assert the Father, always the Father, under the type of a finite personality, that his God is gradually losing dimensions and growing smaller and smaller, even to worship itself. The three metaphoric persons were going, at once, to save God's personality and his magnitudes, by the maze and mystery created, but now they are gone, and the one finite personality left sinks everything with it to the ground; so that one, and another, and another of the great authors in this key begin, spontaneously, to make up size for their deity, by speaking of the gods, and what is due the gods. How plain is it now that, if we all could take the scripture one and three, as given to the imagination, pouring in at that free gate to get our broadest possible knowledge of God, we should neither starve in the one, nor be distracted in the three, nor worried by controversy with each other as regards either one or three.

So when we come to the person of Christ; what he is to the imagination, as the express image of God, God thus manifest in the flesh, is everything; what he is in his merely human personality, and how that personality is related to and unified with the divine nature, is nothing. All is easy when we take him for what of God is expressed in him; but when we raise our psychologic problem in his person, insisting on finding exactly what and how much is in it, and how it is compacted, we are out of our limit, and our speculation is only profane jangling.

Exactly the same thing is true in respect to the metaphors of the altar, when applied to signify Christ's saving work and sacrifice. Take them as they rise in the apostolic teachings, God's figures for the men of old, in the time then present, and for us in the time now present;

then as facts of atoning, now as metaphors of the same; and they will be full of God's meaning, we shall know ourselves atoned once for all by their power. But if we undertake to make a science out of them, and speculate them into a rational theory, it will be no gospel that we make, but a poor dry jargon rather; a righteousness that makes nobody righteous, a justice satisfied by injustice, a mercy on the basis of pay, a penal deliverance that keeps on foot all the penal liabilities. All attempts to think out the cross and have it in dogmatic statement have resulted only in disagreement and distraction. And yet there is a remarkable consent of utterance, we plainly discover, when the cross is preached, as for salvation's sake, in the simple use of the scripture symbols taken all as figures for the time then present.

Once more, even that most intractable and seemingly unreducible division, in which communion is broken across the mere form of Baptism, when there is an admitted agreement and even ready acknowledgment in the living truth of experience, will at once be rectified by simply consenting to make due account of metaphor. Nothing is more clear on the face of the rite than that it has its whole significance as a metaphor; even as the Supper is a metaphor of hospitality. As a mere touch of the elements too in the Supper signifies metaphorically more than the gorging of a full meal, so the mere touch of that most pure, pure element, water, signifies practically more of the cleansing than a bowl, or a barrel, or a full bath. A sprinkle of clean water makes clean, a washing of the feet makes clean every whit. Nothing then is wanted for communion here, but for every brother to know that every other holds and means a baptism in the figure of a cleansing by the Spirit. Peter the apostle was able to draw this matter of baptism to a still finer point. For as Noah's flood was the world's cleansing, he declares that "the like figure, even baptism [baptism was a *figure*, as we see, to him] doth also now save us." In that water voyage of Noah, there was baptism enough, in his view, to serve as the analogon of salvation, though the particular point of the story was that, while the ark was sufficiently deluged with rain, Noah and his household were kept dry. I make nothing here of the *burial* figure, save that the cleansing itself imports a consecration in which there is, of course, a death to the world. Burials in water are not among human events. Will not our Baptist brotherhood some time awake to their privilege, in the discovery, that they may rightly own as the baptized all such as have truly meant baptism, and signified the same faith with them in God's all-cleansing Spirit,—which is the all of baptism? Go back here to the metaphor and keep that good, and nothing more is wanted, or can, without wrong, be required as the gospel condition of acknowledgment and unity. Nothing more will be required when the day of promised brotherhood and liberty arrives.

Here then is the point on which all sects and divisions may be gravitating and coming into settled unity. What is wanted, above all things, for this end is not that we carefully compose our scientific theology, but that we properly observe, and are principally concerned to know God in his own appointed images and symbols. We must get our light by perusing the faces of his truth; we must behold him with reverent desire in the mirrors that reveal him, caring more to have our insight purged than to spin deductions and frame propositions that are in the modes of science or of system. We shall of course have opinions concerning it. A considerable activity in opinions is even desirable, because it will sharpen our perceptiveness of the symbols and draw us on, in that manner, towards a more general and perfect agreement. Only our opinions must be opinions, not laws, either to us or to anybody; perhaps they will change color somewhat even by to-morrow. We must also understand that our opinions or propositional statements are just as truly in metaphor as the scripture itself, only metaphor probably which is a good deal more covert and often as much more ambiguous. We may draw as many creeds as we please, the more the better, if we duly understand that they are standards only as being in metaphor, and not in terms of exact notation. None the less properly standard is the Nicene Creed, that it is given visibly to the imagination, and has even its highest merit at the point where it takes on figure up to the degree of paradox: "God of God, Light of Light, Very God of Very God." Visibly absurd, impossible, false to mere speculation, it is even the more sublimely, solidly true. There has never, in fact, been a dissent from it which did not take it away first from the imagination and give it to the notional understanding.

And yet there will be many who can see no possibility, taking this view of the Christian truth, of any thing solid left. We set every thing afloat, they will say; nothing definite and fixed remains to be the base-work of a firm-set, stanchly effective gospel. What is the Christian truth but a dissolving view of something to be known only by its shadows? But we are easily imposed upon here by what has no such value as we think. We commence our thinking process at some point, we analyze, we deduce, we define, we construct, and when we have gotten the given truth out of its scripture images into our own, and made an opinion or definited thing of it, we think we have touched bottom in it and feel a certain confidence of having so much now established. But the reason is, not that we have made the truth more true, but that we have entered our own self-assertion into it in making an opinion or dogma of it, and have so far given a positivity to it that is from ourselves. And yet, the real fact is exactly contrary; viz., that there is just as much less of solidity in it as there is more that is from ourselves. We take up, for example, the doctrine so-called of repentance, and we find a certain word representing it which means thinking over, changing the mind, and then we lay it down as the positive doctrine that repentance is forming a new governing purpose. That sounds very definite, quite scientific; something we have now found that is clear and determinate. But it turns out, after a few years of preaching in this strain, that the truth we thought so solid is so inadequately true after all as not to have the value we supposed. As a merely one-figure doctrine it is of the lean-kine order, and we get no sense of breadth and body in the change defined, till we bring in all the other figures, the "godly sorrow," the "carefulness," the "self-clearing," the "indignation," the "fear," the "vehement desire," the "zeal," the "revenge," conceiving all these fruits to be from God's inward cogency working thus in us to will and to do. Now we take broad hold; these are the solidities of a completely, roundly adequate conception.

We never so utterly mistake as when we attempt to build up in terms of opinion something more solid and decisively controlling, than what comes to us in the terms of the imagination; that is, by metaphor. The Scriptures, we repeat how often, commend us to "sound doctrine," and assuming this to be the same as doctrine well speculated, we begin to magnify and breed sound doctrine after that fashion; whereas, they only mean sound-making, health-restoring [hygeian] doctrine; which is sure enough indeed to keep good, because it is sure to be wanted, having always in it the spirit of power, and of love, and of a sound mind. The most food-full doctrine is, in this view, the soundest. Is there any theologic article or church confession more solid and fixedly standard-like in its ideas than the Psalms and the Prophets? The parables of Christ,—what are they but images and figures visible given to the imagination? We turn them a thousand ways in our interpretations, it may be, but we revere them none the less and hold them none the less firmly, that they are rich enough to justify this liberty. A particular one of them in fact, the parable of the prodigal son, is even a kind of pole-star in the sky of the gospel, about which formulas, and creeds, and confessions, are always revolving in ephemeral changes, while that abides and shines. Again there is nothing, as we all are wont to feel, that is more solid than our heavenly state, and we call it, in that view, the city that hath foundations. And yet we have no formula that defines it, and no single word of description for it that is not confessedly a figure. It is a garden, a tabernacle, a bosom of Abraham, a new Jerusalem, a city of God cubically built on stones that are gems. If then, nothing is solid, as some will be ready to judge, that is representable only in terms of the imagination, our hopes are all afloat in the sky, or on the air, and our heaven is but a phantom-state which, determinately speaking, is just nowhere and nothing. And yet we do not think so. No Christian man or woman has any such misgiving. Again, why is it that no dogmatic solution of the cross, solid enough to hold the faith of the world, has ever yet been made, while the gospel figures of it are accepted always, rested in and regarded as the pillar of all comfort and hope?

Glancing for just a moment at one or two more strictly human illustrations, what utterance of mortal mind, in what scheme of theology or church confession, has ever proved its adamantine property as fixedly as the Apostles' Creed? And yet there is not a single word of opinion or speculated wisdom in it. It stands wholly in figure, or what is no wise different, in facts that were given to be figure. But if there is any realm of central, astronomic order, it has been this fact-form, truly Copernican confession, about which all the orbits of all the saints, have, in all ages, been revolving.

Summon again for comparison two such masters of doctrine as Turretin[9] and Bunyan,[10] one a great expounder in the school of dogma, and the other a teacher by and before the imagination. Which of these shall we say is the more solid and immovably fixed in authority? The venerable dogmatizer is already far gone by, and will

9. Francis Turretin, seventeenth-century propositional systematizer of Reformed theology.

10. John Bunyan's *Pilgrim's Progress* was widely read and quoted as a devotional handbook by New England families.

ere long be rather a milestone of history than a living part of it. His carefully squared blocks of opinion and the theologic temple he built of them for all ages to come are already time-worn, crumbling visibly away, like the stones of Tyre, and as if the burden of Tyre were upon them. But the glorious Bunyan fire still burns, because it is fire, kindles the world's imagination more and more, and claims a right to live till the sun itself dies out in the sky. His Pilgrim holds on his way still fresh and strong as ever, nay, fresher and stronger than ever, never to be put off the road till the last traveler heavenward is conducted in. And yet he saw beforehand that he was likely to be considered a very light kind of teacher, and bespoke more patience than some could think he deserved.

> "But must I needs want solidness, because
> By metaphors I speak? Were not God's laws,
> His gospel laws, in olden time, set forth,
> By Shadows, Types, and Metaphors? Yet loth
> Will any sober man be to find fault
> With them, lest he be found for to assault
> The highest Wisdom! No, he rather stoops,
> And seeks to find out, by what 'Pins,' and 'Loops,'
> By 'Calves,' and 'Sheep,' by 'Heifers,' and by 'Rams,'
> By 'Birds,' and 'Herbs,' and by the blood of 'Lambs,'
> God speaketh to him; and happy is he
> THAT FINDS THE LIGHT AND GRACE THAT IN THEM BE.''

III.

GROWTH

Since Bushnell held that Christianity is a life process, "growth" was a keynote in his rendition of Christian spirituality. Inspiration does not create a finished product; rather, it initiates a dynamic process in which the power and limits of human freedom are brought to bear on God's act of grace. Two sermons clearly sound this note of religious growth. In "The Power of an Endless Life" Bushnell designates growth as the very principle of life itself and endless growth as the principle of a human life conformed to Christ. In "Living to God in Small Things" he sets his perspective apart from those who would define Christian existence in terms of an explosive, disruptive conversion experience: life in the spirit is a process of struggling maturation in the daily, unremarkable things of existence.

Such an understanding of the religious life presupposes patience—on the part of God who calls humans to endless growth, and on the part of persons who must tolerate the defeats as well as the triumphs, the doubts as well as the assurances, entailed in human freedom. Two sermons exemplify this sub-theme of patience; they also reveal Bushnell's own patient disposition as a man and as a preacher. "The Gentleness of God" portrays the divine being as one who wins his way among humans by means of indirection rather than omnipotent exercises of will, thereby preserving and enhancing the human spirit. In "The Dissolving of Doubts," preached at the Yale College Chapel, Bushnell urges his mostly young hearers to be patient with themselves and their religious doubts. Such patience, he says, is germane to human integrity and fundamental to a life of spiritual growth.

THE POWER OF AN ENDLESS LIFE[1]

Heb. vii. 16.—Who is made, not after the law of a carnal commandment, but after the power of an endless life.

This word *after* is a word of correspondence, and implies two subjects brought in comparison. That Christ has the power of an endless life in his own person is certainly true; but to say that he is made a priest after this power subjective in himself, is awkward even to a degree that violates the natural grammar of speech. The suggestion is different; viz., that the priesthood of Christ is graduated by the wants and measures of the human soul as the priesthood of the law was not; that the endless life in which he comes, matches and measures the endless life in mankind whose fall he is to restore; providing a salvation as strong as their sin, and as long or lasting as the run of their immortality. He is able thus to save unto the uttermost. Powers of endless life though we be, falling principalities, wandering stars shooting downward in the precipitation of evil, he is able to bring us off, re-establish our dismantled eternities, and set us in the peace and confidence of an eternal righteousness.

I propose to exhibit the work of Christ in this high relation, which will lead me to consider—

I. *The power of an endless life in man, what it is, and, as being under sin, requires.*

II. *What Christ, in his eternal priesthood, does to restore it.*

I. The power of an endless life, what it is and requires.

The greatness of our immortality, as commonly handled, is one of the dullest subjects, partly because it finds apprehension asleep in us, and partly because the strained computations entered into, and the words piled up as magnifiers, in a way of impressing the sense of its eternal duration, carry no impression, start no sense of magnitude in us. Even if we raise no doubt or objection, they do little more than drum us to sleep in our own nothingness. We exist here only in the germ, and it is much as if the life power in some seed, that, for ex-

---

1. From *Sermons for the New Life* (New York: Scribner, Armstrong & Co., 1873), 304–25. Date of delivery unknown; first published in 1858.

ample, of the great cedars of the west, were to begin a magnifying of its own importance to itself in the fact that it has so long a time to live; and finally, because of the tiny figure it makes, and because the forces it contains are as yet unrealized, to settle inertly down upon the feeling that, after all, it is only a seed, a dull, insignificant speck of matter, wanting to be a little greater than it can. Instead, then, of attempting to magnify the soul by any formal computation on the score of time or duration, let us simply take up and follow the hint that is given us in this brief expression, the power of an endless life.

It is a power, a power of life, a power of endless life.

The word translated *power* in the text, is the original of our word *dynamic,* denoting a certain impetus, momentum, or causative force, which is cumulative, growing stronger and more impelling as it goes. And this is the nature of life or vital force universally,—it is a force cumulative as long as it continues. It enters into matter as a building, organizing, lifting power, and knows not how to stop till death stops it. We use the word *grow* to describe its action, and it does not even know how to subsist without growth. In which growth it lays hold continually of new material, expands in volume, and fills a larger sphere of body with its power.

Now these innumerable lives, animal and vegetable, at work upon the world, creating and new-creating, and producing their immense transformations of matter, are all immaterial forces or powers; related, in that manner, to souls, which are only a highest class of powers. The human soul can not be more efficiently described than by calling it the power of an endless life; and to it all these lower immaterialities, at work in matter, look up as mute prophets, testifying, by the magical sovereignty they wield in the processes and material transformations of growth, to the possible forces embodied in that highest, noblest form of life. And sometimes, since our spiritual nature, taken as a power of life, organizes nothing material and external by which its action is made visible, God allows the inferior lives in given examples, especially of the tree species, to have a small eternity of growth, and lift their giant forms to the clouds, that we may stand lost in amazement before the majesty of that silent power that works in life, when many centuries only are given to be the lease of its activity. The work is slow, the cumulative process silent,— viewed externally, nothing appears that we name force, and yet this living creature called a tree, throbs internally in fullness of life, circulates its juices, swells in volume, towers in majesty; till finally it gives to the very word life a historic presence and sublimity. It begins with a mere seed or germ, a tiny speck so inert and frail that we might even laugh at the bare suggestion of power in such a look of nothingness; just as at our present point of dullness and weakness, we can give no sound of meaning to any thing said of our own spiritual greatness, and yet that seed, long centuries ago, when the tremendous babyhood of Mahomet was nursing at his mother's breast, sprouted apace, gathered to itself new circles of matter, year by year and age after age, kept its pumps in play, sent up new supplies of food, piling length on length in the sky, conserving still and vitalizing all; and now it stands entire in pillared majesty, mounting upward still, and tossing back the storms that break on its green pinnacles, a bulk immense, such as being felled and hollowed would even make a modern ship of war.

And yet these cumulative powers of vegetable life are only feeble types of that higher, fearfully vaster power, that pertains to the endless life of a soul—that power that known or unknown dwells in you and in me. What Abel now is, or Enoch, as an angel of God, in the volume of his endless life and the vast energies unfolded in his growth by the river of God, they may set you trying to guess, but can by no means help you adequately to conceive. The possible majesty to which any free intelligence of God may grow, in the endless increment of ages, is after all rather hinted than imaged in their merely vegetable grandeur.

Quickened by these analogies, let us pass directly to the soul or spiritual nature itself, as a power of endless growth or increment; for it is only in this way that we begin to conceive the real magnitude and majesty of the soul, and not by any mere computations based on its eternity or immortality.

What it means, in this higher and nobler sense, to be a power of life, we are very commonly restrained from observing by two or three considerations that require to be named. First, when looking after the measures of the soul, we very naturally lay hold of what first occurs to us, and begin to busy ourselves in the contemplation of its eternal duration. Whereas the eternal duration of the soul, at any given measure, if we look no farther, is nothing but the eternal continuance of its mediocrity or comparative littleness. Its eternal growth in volume and power is in that manner quite lost sight of, and the computation misses every thing most impressive, in its future significance and history. Secondly, the growth of the soul is a merely spiritual growth, indicated by no visible and material form that is expanded by it and with it as in the growth of a tree, and therefore passes comparatively unnoticed by many, just because they can not see it with their eyes. And then again, thirdly, as the human body attains to its maturity, and, finally, in the decays of age, becomes an apparent limit to the spiritual powers and faculties, we drop into the impression that these have now passed their climacteric, and that we have actually seen the utmost volume it is in their nature ever to attain. We do not catch the significance of the fact that the soul outgrows the growth and outlives the vigor of the body, which is not true in trees; revealing its majestic properties as a force independent and qualifiedly sovereign. Observing how long the soul-force goes on to expand after the body-force has reached its maximum, and when disease and age have begun to shatter the frail house it inhabits, how long it braves these bodily decrepitudes, driving on, still on, like a strong engine in a poorly timbered vessel, through seas not too heavy for it, but only for the crazy hulk it impels,—observing this, and making due account of it, we should only be the more impressed with a sense of some inherent everlasting power of growth and progress in its endless life.

Stripping aside now all these impediments, let us pass directly into the soul's history, and catch from what transpires in its first indications the sign or promise of what it is to become. In its beginning it is a mere seed of possibility. All the infant faculties are folded up, at first, and scarcely a sign of power is visible in it. But a doom of growth is in it, and the hidden momentum of an endless power is driving it on. And a falling body will not gather momentum in its fall more naturally and certainly, than it will gather force, in the necessary struggle of its endless life now begun. We may think little of the increase; it is a matter of course, and why should we take note of it? But if no increase or development appears, if the faculties all sleep as at the first, we take sad note of that, and draw how reluctantly, the conclusion that our child is an idiot and not a proper man! And what a chasm is there between the idiot and the man; one a being unprogressive, a being who is not a power; the other a careering force started on its way to eternity, a principle of might and majesty begun to be unfolded, and to be progressively unfolded forever. Intelligence, reason, conscience, observation, choice, memory, enthusiasm, all the fires of his inborn eternity are kindling to a glow, and, looking on him as a force immortal, just beginning to reveal the symptoms of what he shall be, we call him man. Only a few years ago he lay in his cradle, a barely breathing principle of life, but in that life were gathered up, as in a germ or seed, all these godlike powers that are now so conspicuous in the volume of his personal growth. In a sense, all that is in him now was in him then, as the power of an endless life, and still the sublime progression of his power is only begun. He conquers now the sea and its storms. He climbs the heavens, and searches out the mysteries of the stars. He harnesses the lightning. He bids the rocks dissolve, and summons the secret atoms to give up their names and laws. He subdues the face of the world, and compels the forces of the waters and the fires to be his servants. He makes laws, hurls empires down upon empires in the fields of war, speaks words that can not die, sings to distant realms and peoples across vast ages of time; in a word, he executes all that is included in history, showing his tremendous energy in almost every thing that stirs the silence and changes the conditions of the world. Every thing is transformed by him even up to the stars. Not all the winds, and storms, and earthquakes, and seas, and seasons of the world, have done as much to revolutionize the world as he, the power of an endless life, has done since the day he came forth upon it, and received, as he is most truly declared to have done, dominion over it.

And yet we have, in the power thus developed, nothing more than a mere hint or initial sign of what is to be the real stature of his personality in the process of his everlasting development. We exist here only in the small, that God may have us in a state of flexibility, and bend or fashion us, at the best advantage, to the model of his own great life and character. And most of us, therefore, have scarcely a conception of the exceeding weight of glory to be comprehended in our existence. If we take, for example, the faculty of memory, how very obvious is it that as we pass eternally on, we shall have more and more to remember, and finally shall have gathered in more into this great storehouse of the soul, than is now contained in all the libraries of the world. And there is not one of our faculties that has not, in its volume, a similar power of expansion. Indeed, if it were not so, the memory would finally overflow and drown all our other faculties, and the spirits, instead of being powers, would virtually cease to be any thing more than registers of the past.

But we are not obliged to take our conclusion by inference. We can see for ourselves that the associations of the mind, which are a great part of its riches, must be increasing in number and variety forever, stimulating thought by multiplying its suggestives, and beautifying thought by weaving into it the colors of sentiment, endlessly varied.

The imagination is gathering in its images and kindling its eternal fires in the same manner. Having passed through many trains of worlds, mixing with scenes, societies, orders of intelligence and powers of beatitude—just that which made the apostle in Patmos into a poet, by the visions of a single day—it is impossible that every soul should not finally become filled with a glorious and powerful imagery, and be waked to a wonderfully creative energy.

By the supposition it is another incident of this power of endless life, that passing down the eternal galleries of fact and event, it must be forever having new cognitions and accumulating new premises. By its own contacts it will, at some future time, have touched even whole worlds and felt them through and made premises of all there is in them. It will know God by experiences correspondently enlarged, and itself by a consciousness correspondently illuminated. Having gathered in, at last, such worlds of premise, it is difficult for us now to conceive the vigor into which a soul may come, or the volume it may exhibit, the wonderful depth and scope of its judgments, its rapidity and certainty, and the vastness of its generalizations. It passes over more and more, and that necessarily, from the condition of a creature gathering up premises, into the condition of God, creating out of premises; for if it is not actually set to the creation of worlds, its very thoughts will be a discoursing in world-problems and theories equally vast in their complications.

In the same manner, the executive energy of the will, the volume of the benevolent affections, and all the active powers, will be showing, more and more impressively, what it is to be a power of endless life. They that have been swift in doing God's will and fulfilling his mightly errands, will acquire a marvelous address and energy in the use of their powers. They that have taken worlds into their love will have a love correspondently capacious, whereupon also it will be seen that their will is settled in firmness, and raised in majesty according to the vastness of impulse there is in the love behind it. They that have great thoughts, too, will be able to manage great causes, and they that are lubricated eternally in the joys that feed their activity, will never tire. What force, then, must be finally developed in what now appears to be the tenuous and fickle impulse, and the merely frictional activity of a human soul.

On this subject the scriptures indulge in no declamation, but only speak in hints and start us off by questions, well understanding that the utmost they can do is to waken in us the sense of a future scale of being unimaginable, and beyond the compass of our definite thought. Here they drive us out in the almost cold mathematical question: what shall it profit a man to gain the whole world and lose his own soul? Here they show us in John's vision, Moses and Elijah, as angels, suggesting our future classification among angels, which are sometimes called chariots of God, to indicate their excelling strength and swiftness in careering through his empire, to do his will. Here they speak of powers unimaginable as regards the volume of their personality, calling them dominions, thrones, principalities, powers, and appear to set us on a footing with these dim majesties. Here they notify us that it doth not yet appear what we shall be. Here they call us sons of God. Here they bolt upon us—But I said ye are gods; as if meaning to waken us by a shock! In these and all ways possible, they contrive to start some better conception in us of ourselves, and of the immense significance of the soul; forbidding us always to be the dull mediocrities into which, under the stupor of our unbelief, we are commonly so ready to subside. O, if we could tear aside the veil, and see for but one hour what it signifies to be a soul in the power of an endless life, what a revelation would it be!

But there is yet another side or element of meaning suggested by this expression, which requires to be noted. It looks on the soul as a falling power, a bad force, rushing downward into ruinous and final disorder. If we call it a principality in its possible volume, it is a falling principality. It was this which made the mightly priesthood of the Lord necessary. For the moment we look in upon the soul's great movement as a power, and find sin entered there, we perceive that every thing is in disorder. It is like a mighty engine in which some pivot or lever is broken, whirling and crashing and driving itself into a wreck. The disastrous effects of sin in a soul will be just according to the powers it contains, or embodies; for every force becomes a bad force, a misdirected and self-destructive force, a force which can never be restored, save by some other which is mightier and superior. What, in this view, can be more frightful than the disorders loosened in it by a state of sin.

And what shall we say of the result or end? Must the immortal nature still increase in volume without limit, and so in the volume of its miseries; or only in its miseries by the conscious depths of shame and weakness into which it is falling? On this subject I know not what to say. We do see that bad minds, in their evil life, gather force and expand in many, at least, of their capabilities, on to a certain point or limit. As far as to that point or limit, they appear to grow intense, powerful, and, as the world says, great. But they seem, at last, and apart from the mere decay of years, to begin a diminishing process: they grow jealous, imperious, cruel, and so far weak. They become little, in the girding of their own stringent selfishness. They burn to a cinder in the heat of their own devilish passion. And so, beginning as heroes and demigods, they many of them taper off into awfully intense but still little men—intense at a mere point; which appears to be the conception of a fiend. Is it so that the bitterness of hell is finally created? Is it toward this pungent, acrid, awfully intensified, and talented littleness, that all souls under sin are gravitating? However this may be, we can see for ourselves that the disorders of sin, running loose in human souls, must be driving them downward into everlasting and complete ruin, the wreck of all that is mightiest and loftiest in their immortality. One of the sublimest and most fearful pictures ever given of this you will find in the first chapter to the Romans. It reads like some battle among the gods, where all that is great and terrible and wild in the confusion, answers to the majesty of the powers engaged. And this is man, the power of an endless life, under sin. By what adequate power, in earth or in heaven, shall that sin be taken away? This brings me to consider—

II. What Christ, in his eternal priesthood, has done; or the fitness and practical necessity of it, as related to the stupendous exigency of our redemption.

The great impediment which the gospel of Christ encounters, in our world, that which most fatally hinders its reception, or embrace, is that it is too great a work. It transcends our belief, it wears a look of extravagance. We are beings too insignificant and low to engage any such interest on the part of God, or justify any such expenditure. The preparations made, and the parts acted, are not in the proportions of reason, and the very terms of the great salvation have, to our dull ears, a declamatory sound. How can we really think that the eternal God has set these more than epic machineries at work for such a creature as man?

My principal object, therefore, in the contemplations raised by this topic, has been to start some conception of ourselves, in the power of an endless life, that is more adquate. Mere immortality, or everlasting continuance, when it is the continuance only of littleness or mediocrity, does not make a platform or occasion high enough for this great mystery of the gospel. It is only when we see in human souls, taken as germs of power, a future magnitude and majesty transcending all present measures, that we come into any fit conception at all of Christ's mission to the world. Entering the gospel at this point, and regarding it as a work undertaken for the redemption of beings scarcely imagined as yet, of dominions, principalities, powers,— spiritual intelligences so transcendent that we have, as yet, no words to name them—every thing done takes a look of proportion; it appears even to be needed, and we readily admit that nothing less could suffice to restore the falling powers, or stop the tragic disorders loosened in them by their sin. How much more if, instead of drawing thus upon our imagination, we could definitely grasp the real import of our being, that which hitherto is only indicated, never displayed, and have it as a matter of positive and distinct apprehension. This power of endless life—could we lay hold of it; could we truly feel its movement in us, and follow the internal presage to its mark; or could we only grasp the bad force there is in it, and know it rushing downward, in the terrible lava-flood of its disorders, how true and rational, how magnificently divine would the great salvation of Christ appear, and in how great dread of ourselves should we hasten to it for refuge!

Then it would shock us no more that visibly it is no mere man that has arrived. Were he only a human teacher, reformer, philosopher, coming in our human plane to lecture on our self-improvement as men, in the measures of men, he would even be less credible than now. Nothing meets our want, in fact, but to see the boundaries of nature and time break way to let in a being and a power visibly not of this world. Let him be the Eternal Son of God and Word of the Father, descending out of higher worlds to be incarnate in this. As we have lost our measures, let us recover them, if possible, in the sense restored of our everlasting brotherhood with him. Let him so be made a priest for us, not after the law of a carnal commandment, but after the power of an endless life—the brightness of the Father's glory and the express image of his person—God manifest in the flesh—God in Christ, reconciling the world unto himself. All the better and more proportionate and probable is it, if he comes heralded by innumerable angels, bursting into the sky, to congratulate their fallen peers with songs of deliverance—Glory to God in the Highest, peace on earth, good will toward men. Humbled to the flesh and its external conditions, he will only the more certainly even himself with our want, if he dares to say—Before Abraham was, I am—all power is given unto me in heaven and in earth. Is he faultless, so that no man convinceth him of sin, revealing in the humble guise of humanity the absolute beauty of God; how could any thing less or inferior meet our want? If he dares to make the most astounding pretensions, all the better, if only his pretensions are borne out by his life and actions. Let him heal the sick, feed the hungry, still the sea by his word. Let his doctrine not be human, let it bear the stamp of a higher mind and be verified and sealed by the perfection of his character. Let him be transfigured, if he may, in the sight of two worlds; of angels from the upper and of men from this; that, beholding his excellent glory, no doubt may be left of his transcendent quality.

No matter if the men that follow him and love him are, just for the time, too slow to apprehend him. How could they see, with eyes holden, the divinity that is hid under such a garb of poverty and patience? How could they seize on the possibility that this man of sorrows is revealing even the depths of God's eternal love, by these more than mortal burdens? If the factitious distinctions of society pass for nothing with him, if he takes his lot among the outcast poor, how else could he show that it is not any tier of quality, but our great fallen humanity, the power of an endless life, that engages him. And when, with a degree of unconcern that is itself sublime, he says—The prince of this world cometh and hath nothing in me; how else could he convey so fitly the impression that the highest royalty and stateliest throne to him is simple man himself?

But the tragedy gathers to its last act, and fearful is to be the close. Never did the powers of eternity, or endless life in souls, reveal themselves so terribly before. But he came to break their force, and how so certainly as to let it break itself across his patience? By his miracles and reproofs, and quite as much by the unknown mystery of greatness in his character, the deepest depths of malice in immortal evil are now finally stirred; the world's wild wrath is concentered on his person, and his soul is, for the hour, under an eclipse of sorrow; exceeding sorrowful even unto death. But the agony is shortly passed; he says, I am ready; and they take him, Son of God though he be, and Word of the Father, and Lord of glory, to a cross! They nail him fast, and what a sign do they give, in that dire phrenzy, of the immortal depth of their passion! The sun refuses to look on the sight, and the frame of nature shudders! He dies! it is finished! The body that was taken for endurance and patience, has drunk up all the shafts of the world's malice, and now rests in the tomb.

No! there is more. Lo! he is not here, but is risen; he has burst the bars of death and become the first fruits of them that slept. In that sign behold his victory. Just that is done which signifies eternal redemption—the conquest and recovery of free minds, taken as powers dismantled by eternal evil. By this offering, once for all the work is finished. What can evil do, or passion, after this, when its bitterest arrows, shot into the divine patience, are by that patience so tenderly and sovereignly broken? Therefore now to make the triumph evident, he ascends, a visible conqueror, to the Father, there to stand as priest forever, sending forth his Spirit to seal, and testifying that he is able to save unto the uttermost all that come unto God by him.

This, in brief historic outline, is the great salvation. And it is not too great. It stands in glorious proportion with the work to be done. Nothing else or less would suffice. It is a work supernatural transacted in the plane of nature; and what but such a work could restore the broken order of the soul under evil? It incarnates God in the world, and what but some such opening of the senses to God or of God to the senses, could reinstate him in minds that have lost the consciousness of him, and fallen off to live apart? What but this could enter him again, as a power, into the world's life and history? We are astonished by the revelation of divine feeling; the expense of the sacrifice wears a look of extravagance. If we are only the dull mediocrities we commonly take ourselves to be, it is quite incredible. But if God, seeing through our possibilities into our real eternities, comprehends, in the view, all we are to be or become, as powers of endless life, is there not some probability that he discovers a good deal more in us than we do in ourselves; enough to justify all the concern he testifies, all the sacrifice he makes in the passion of his

Son? And as God has accurately weighed the worlds and even the atoms, accurately set him in their distance and altitudes, has he not also in this incarnate grace and passion, which offend so many by their excess, measured accurately the unknown depths and magnitudes of our eternity, the momentum of our fall, the tragic mystery of our disorder? And if we can not comprehend ourselves, if we are even a mystery to ourselves, what should his salvation be but a mystery of godliness equally transcendent? If Christ were a philosopher, a human teacher, a human example, we might doubtless reason him and set him in our present scales of proportion, but he would as certainly do nothing for us equal to our want.

Inasmuch as our understanding has not yet reached our measures, we plainly want a grace which only faith can receive; for it is the distinction of faith that it can receive a medication it can not definitely trace, and admit into the consciousness what it can not master in thought. Christ therefore comes not as a problem given to our reason, but as a salvation offered to our faith. His passion reaches a deeper point in us than we can definitely think, and his Eternal Spirit is a healing priesthood for us, in the lowest and profoundest roots of our great immortality, those which we have never seen ourselves. By our faith in him too as a mystery, he comes into our guiltiness, at a point back of all speculative comprehension, restoring that peace of innocence which is speculatively impossible; for how in mere speculation can any thing done for our sin, annihilate the fact; and without that, how take our guilt away? Still it goes! We know, as we embrace him, that it goes! He has reached a point in us by his mysterious priesthood, deep enough even to take our guiltiness away, and establish us in a peace that is even as the peace of innocence!

So, if we speak of our passions, our internal disorders, the wild, confused and even downward rush of our inthralled powers, he performs, in a mystery of love and the Spirit, what no teaching or example could. The manner we can trace by no effort of the understanding; we can only see that he is somehow able to come into the very germ principle of our life, and be a central, regulating, new-creating force in our disordered growth itself. And if we speak of righteousness, it is ours, when it is not ours; how can a being unrighteous be established in the sense of righteousness? Logically, or according to the sentence of our speculative reason, it is impossible. And yet, in Christ, we have it! We are consciously in it, as we are in him, and all we can say is, that it is the righteousness of God, by faith, unto all and upon all them that believe.

But I must draw my subject to a close. It is a common impression with persons who hear, but do not accept, the calls of Christ and his salvation, that they are required to be somewhat less in order to be Christian. They must be diminished in quantity, taken down, short-ened, made feeble and little, and then, by the time they have let go their manhood, they will possibly come into the way of salvation. They hear it declared that, in becoming little children, humble, meek, poor in spirit; in ceasing from our will and reason; and in giving up ourselves, our eagerness, revenge, and passion,—thus, and thus only, can we be accepted; but, instead of taking all these as so many figures antagonistic to our pride, our ambition, and the determined self-pleasing of our sin, they take them absolutely, as requiring a real surrender and loss of our proper manhood itself. Exactly contrary to this, the gospel requires them to be more than they are,—greater, higher, nobler, stronger,—all which they were made to be in the power of their endless life. These expressions, just referred to, have no other aim than simply to cut off weaknesses, break down infirm-ities, tear away boundaries, and let the soul out into liberty, and power, and greatness. What is weaker than pride, self-will, revenge, the puffing of conceit and rationality, the constringing littleness of all selfish passion. And, in just these things it is that human souls are so fatally shrunk in all their conceptions of themselves; so that Christ encounters, in all men, this first and most insurmountable difficulty; to make them apprised of their real value to themselves. For, no sooner do they wake to the sense of their great immortality than they are even oppressed by it. Every thing else shrinks to nothingness, and they go to him for life. And then, when they receive him, it is even a bursting forth into magnitude. A new inspiration is upon them, all their powers are exalted, a wondrous inconceivable energy is felt, and, having come into the sense of God, which is the element of all real greatness, they discover, as it were in amazement, what it is to be in the true capacity.

A similar mistake is connected with their impressions of faith. They are jealous of faith, as being only weakness. They blame the gospel, because it requires faith, as a condition of salvation. And yet, as I have here abundantly shown, it requires faith just because it is a salvation large enough to meet the measures of the soul, as a power of endless life. And, O, if you could once get away, my friends, from that sense of mediocrity and nothingness to which you are shut up, under the stupor of your self-seeking and your sin, how easy would it be for you to believe! Nay, if but some faintest suspicion could steal into you of what your soul is, and the tremendous evils working in it, nothing but the mystery of Christ's death and passion would be sufficient for you. Now you are nothing to yourselves, and therefore Christ is too great, the mystery of his cross an offense. O, thou spirit of grace, visit these darkened minds, to whom thy gospel is hid, and let the light of the knowledge of the glory of God, in the face of Jesus Christ, shine into them! Raise in them the piercing question, that tears the world away and displays the grimace of its follies,—What shall it profit a man to gain the whole world and lose his own soul?

I should do you a wrong to close this subject without conducting your minds forward to those anticipations of the future which it so naturally suggests. You have all observed the remarkable interest which beings of other worlds are shown, here and there in the scripture, to feel in the transactions of this. These, like us, are powers of endless life, intelligences that have had a history parallel to our own. Some of them, doubtless, have existed myriads of ages, and consequently now are far on in the course of their development,—far enough on to have discerned what existence is, and the amount of power and dignity there is in it. Hence their interest in us, who as yet are only candidates, in their view, for a greatness yet to be revealed. And the interest they show seems extravagant to us, just as the gospel itself is, and for the same reasons. They break into the sky, when Christ is born, chanting their All-Hail. They visit the world on heavenly errands, and perform their unseen ministries to the heirs of salvation. They watch for our repentances, and there is joy among them before God, when but one is gathered to their company, in the faith of salvation. And the reason is that they have learned so much about the proportions and measures of things, which as yet are hidden from us. These angels that excel in strength, these ancient princes and hierarchs that have grown up in God's eternity and unfolded their mighty powers in whole ages of good, recognize in us compeers that are finally to be advanced, as they are.

And here is the point where our true future dawns upon us. It doth not yet appear what we shall be. We lie here in our nest, unfledged and weak, guessing dimly at our future, and scarce believing what even now appears. But the power is in us, and that power is to be finally revealed. And what a revelation will that be! Is it possible, you will ask in amazement, that you, a creature that was sunk in such dullness, and sold to such trivialities in your bondage to the world, were, all this time, related to God and the ancient orders of his kingdom, in a being so majestic!

How great a terror to some of you may that discovery be! I can not say exactly how it will be with the bad minds, now given up finally to their disorders. Powers of endless life they still must be; but how far shrunk by that stringent selfishness, how far burned away, as magnitudes, by that fierce combustion of passion, I do not know. But, if they diminish in volume and shrink to a more intensified power of littleness and fiendishness, eaten out, as regards all highest volume, by the malice of evil and the undying worm of its regrets, it will not be so with the righteous. They will develop greater force of mind, greater volume of feeling, greater majesty of will and character, even forever. In the grand mystery of Christ and his eternal priesthood,—Christ, who ever liveth to make intercession,—they will be set in personal and experimental connection with all the great problems of grace and counsels of love, comprised in the plan by which they have been trained, and the glories to which they are exalted. Attaining thus to greater force and stature of spirit than we are able now to conceive, they have exactly that supplied to their discovery which will carry them still further on, with the greatest expedition. Their subjects and conferences will be those of principalities and powers, and the conceptions of their great society will be correspondent; for they are now coming to the stature necessary to a fit contemplation of such themes. The Lamb of redemption and the throne of law, and a government comprising both will be the field of their study, and they will find their own once petty experience related to all that is vastest and most transcendent in the works and appointments of God's empire. O, what thoughts will spring up in such minds, surrounded by such fellow intelligences, entered on such themes, and present to such discoveries! How grand their action! How majestic their communion! Their praise how august! Their joys how full and clear! Shall we ever figure, my friends, in scenes like these? O, this power of endless life!—great King of Life, and Priest of Eternity, reveal thyself to us, and us to ourselves, and quicken us to this unknown future before us.

LIVING TO GOD IN SMALL THINGS[2]

Luke xvi. 10.—''He that is faithful in that which is least, is faithful also in much; and he that is unjust in the least, is unjust also in much.''

A readiness to do some great thing is not peculiar to Naaman the Syrian. There are many Christians who can never find a place large enough to do their duty. They must needs strain after great changes, and their works must utter themselves by a loud report. Any reform in society, short of a revolution, any improvement in character, less radical than that of conversion, is too faint a work, in their view, to be much valued. Nor is it merely ambition, but often it is a truly Christian zeal, guarded by no sufficient views of the less imposing matters of life, which betrays men into such impressions. If there be any thing, in fact, wherein the views of God and the impressions of men are apt to be at total variance, it is in respect to the solemnity and importance of ordinary duties. The hurtfulness of mistake here, is of course very great. Trying always to do great things, to have extraordinary occasions every day, or to produce extraordinary changes, when small ones are quite as much needed, ends, of course, in defeat and dissipation. It produces a sort of religion in the gross, which is no religion in particular. My text leads me to speak—

Of the importance of living to God on common occasions and in small things.

He that is faithful in that which is least, says the Saviour, is faithful also in much; and he that is unjust in the least, is unjust also in much. This was a favorite sentiment with him. In his sermon on the mount, it was thus expressed—Whosoever, therefore, shall break one of these least commandments, and shall teach men so, he shall be called the least in the kingdom of heaven; but whosoever shall do and teach them, the same shall be called great in the kingdom of heaven. And when he rebuked the Pharisees, in their tything of mint, anise, and cummin, he was careful to speak very guardedly—These things ought ye to have done, and not to leave the other undone. It will instruct us in prosecuting this subject—

2. *Ibid.*, 282–303. Preached in North Church, Hartford, in 1837.

1. To notice how little we know concerning the relative importance of events and duties. We use the terms *great* and *small* in speaking of actions, occasions, plans, and duties, only in reference to the
mere outward look and first impression. Some of the most latent
agents and mean looking substances in nature, are yet the most operative; but yet, when we speak of natural objects, we call them great
or small, not according to their operativeness, but according to size,
count, report, or show. So it comes to pass, when we are classing
actions, duties, or occasions, that we call a certain class great and
another small, when really the latter are many fold more important
and influential than the former. We may suppose, for illustration, two
transactions in business, as different in their nominal amount as a
million of dollars and a single dollar. The former we call a large transaction, the latter a small one. But God might reverse these terms. He
would have no such thought as the counting of dollars. He would
look, first of all, at the principle involved in the two cases. And here
he would discover, not unlikely, that the nominally small one, owing
to the nature of the transaction, or to the humble condition of the
parties, or to their peculiar temper and disposition, took a deeper hold
of their being, and did more to settle or unsettle great and everlasting
principle, than the other. Next, perhaps, he would look at the consequences of the two transactions, as developed in the great future;
and here he would perhaps discover that the one which seems to us
the smaller, is the hinge of vastly greater consequences than the other.
If the dollars had been sands of dust, they would not have had less
weight in the divine judgment.

We are generally ignorant of the real significance of events,
which we think we understand. Almost every person can recollect
one or more instances, where the whole after-current of his life was
turned by some single word, or some incident so trivial as scarcely
to fix his notice at the time. On the other hand, many great crises of
danger, many high and stirring occasions, in which, at the time, his
total being was absorbed, have passed by, leaving no trace of effect
on his permanent interests, and are well nigh vanished from his memory. The conversation of the stage-coach is often preparing results,
which the solemn assembly and the most imposing and eloquent rites
will fail to produce. What countryman, knowing the dairyman's
daughter, could have suspected that she was living to a mightier purpose and result, than almost any person in the church of God, however

eminent? The outward of occasions and duties is, in fact, almost no index of their importance; and our judgments concerning what is great and small, are without any certain validity. These terms as we use them, are, in fact, only words of outward description, not words of definite measurement.

2. It is to be observed, that even as the world judges, small things constitute almost the whole of life. The great days of the year, for example, are few, and when they come, they seldom bring any thing great to us. And the matter of all common days is made up of little things, or ordinary and stale transactions. Scarcely once in a year does any thing really remarkable befall us. If I were to begin and give an inventory of the things you do in any single day, your muscular motions, each of which is accomplished by a separate act of will, the objects you see, the words you utter, the contrivances you frame, your thoughts, passions, gratifications, and trials, many of you would not be able to hear it recited with sobriety. But three hundred and sixty-five such days make up a year, and a year is a twentieth, fiftieth, or seventieth part of your life. And thus, with the exception of some few striking passages, or great and critical occasions, perhaps not more than five or six in all, your life is made up of common, and as men are wont to judge, unimportant things. But yet, at the end, you have done up an amazing work, and fixed an amazing result. You stand at the bar of God, and look back on a life made up of small things—but yet a life, how momentous, for good or evil!

3. It very much exalts, as well as sanctions, the view I am advancing, that God is so observant of small things. He upholds the sparrow's wing, clothes the lily with his own beautifying hand, and numbers the hairs of his children. He holds the balancings of the clouds. He maketh small the drops of rain. It astonishes all thought to observe the minuteness of God's government, and of the natural and common processes which he carries on from day to day. His dominions are spread out, system beyond system, system above system, filling all height and latitude, but he is never lost in the vast or magnificent. He descends to an infinite detail, and builds a little universe in the smallest things. He carries on a process of growth in every tree, and flower, and living thing; accomplishes in each an internal organization and works the functions of an internal laboratory, too delicate all for eye or instrument to trace. He articulates the members and impels the instincts of every living mote that shines in the sunbeam.

As when we ascend toward the distant and the vast, so when we descend toward the minute, we see his attention acuminated, and his skill concentrated on his object; and the last discernible particle dies out of our sight with the same divine glory on it, as on the last orb that glimmers in the skirt of the universe. God is as careful to finish the mote as the planet, both because it consists only with his perfection to finish every thing, and because the perfection of his greatest structures is the result of perfection in their smallest parts or particles. On this patience of detail rests all the glory and order of the created universe, spiritual and material. God could thunder the year round; he could shake the ribs of the world with perpetual earthquakes; he could blaze on the air, and brush the affrighted mountains, each day with his comets. But if he could not feed the grass with his dew, and breathe into the little lungs of his insect family; if he could not expend his care on small things, and descend to an interest in their perfection, his works would be only crude and disjointed machines, compounded of mistakes and malformations, without beauty and order, and fitted to no perfect end.

The works of Christ are, if possible, a still brighter illustration of the same truth. Notwithstanding the vast stretch and compass of the work of redemption, it is a work of the most humble detail in its style of execution. The Saviour could have preachd a sermon on the mount every morning. Each night he could have stilled the sea, before his astonished disciples, and shown the conscious waves lulling into peace under his feet. He could have transfigured himself before Pilate and the astonished multitudes of the temple. He could have made visible ascensions in the noon of every day, and revealed his form standing in the sun, like the angel of the apocalypse. But this was not his mind. The incidents of which his work is principally made up, are, humanly speaking, very humble and unpretending. The most faithful pastor in the world was never able, in any degree, to approach the Saviour, in the lowliness of his manner and his attention to humble things. His teachings were in retired places, and his illustrations drawn from ordinary affairs. If the finger of faith touched him in the crowd, he knew the touch and distinguished also the faith. He reproved the ambitious housewifery of an humble woman. After he had healed a poor being, blind from his birth—a work transcending all but divine power—he returned and sought him out, as the most humble Sabbath-school teacher might have done; and when he had found him, cast out and persecuted by men, he taught him privately the highest secrets of his Messiahship. When the world around hung darkened in sympathy with his cross, and the earth was shaking with inward amazement, he himself was remembering his mother, and discharging the filial cares of a good son. And when he burst the bars of death, its first and final conquerer, he folded the linen clothes and the napkin, and laid them in order apart, showing that in the greatest things, he had a set purpose also concerning the smallest. And thus, when perfectly scanned, the work of Christ's redemption, like the created universe, is seen to be a vast orb of glory, wrought up out of finished particles. Now a life of great and prodigious exploits would have been comparatively an easy thing for him, but to cover himself with beauty and glory in small things, to fill and adorn every little human occasion, so as to make it divine,—this was a work of skill, which no mind or hand was equal to, but that which shaped the atoms of the world. Such everywhere is God. He nowhere overlooks or despises small things.

4. It is a fact of history and of observation, that all efficient men, while they have been men of comprehension, have also been men of detail. I wish it were possible to produce as high an example of this two-fold character among the servants of God and benevolence in these times, as we have in that fiery prodigy of war and conquest, who, in the beginning of the present century, desolated Europe. Napoleon was the most effective man in modern times—some will say of all times. The secret of his character was, that while his plans were more vast, more various, and, of course, more difficult than those of other men, he had the talent, at the same time, to fill them up with perfect promptness and precision, in every particular of execution. His vast and daring plans would have been visionary in any other man; but with him every vision flew out of his brain, a chariot of iron; because it was filled up, in all the particulars of execution, to be a solid and compact framework in every part. His armies were together only one great engine of desolation, of which he was the head or brain. Numbers, spaces, times, were all distinct in his eye. The wheeling of every legion, however remote, was mentally present to him. The tramp of every foot sounded in his ear. The numbers were always supplied, the spaces passed over, the times met, and so the work was done. The nearest moral approximation I know of, was Paul the apostle. Paul had great principles, great plans, and a great enthusiasm. He

had the art, at the same time, to bring his great principles into a powerful application to his own conduct, and to all the common affairs of all the disciples in his churches. He detected every want, understood every character; set his guards against those whom he distrusted; kept all his work turning in a motion of discipline; prompted to every duty. You will find his epistles distinguished by great principles; and, at the same time, by a various and circumstantial attention to all the common affairs of life; and, in that, you have the secret of his efficiency. There must be detail in every great work. It is an element of effectiveness, which no reach of plan, no enthusiasm of purpose, can dispense with. Thus, if a man conceives the idea of becoming eminent in learning, but cannot toil through the million of little drudgeries necessary to carry him on, his learning will be soon told. Or, if a man undertakes to become rich, but despises the small and gradual advances by which wealth is ordinarily accumulated, his expectations will, of course, be the sum of his riches. Accurate and careful detail, the minding of common occasions and small things, combined with general scope and vigor, is the secret of all the efficiency and success in the world. God has so ordered things, that great and sudden leaps are seldom observable. Every advance in the general must be made by advances in particular. The trees and the corn do not leap out suddenly into maturity, but they climb upward, by little and little, and after the minutest possible increment. The orbs of heaven, too, accomplish their circles not by one or two extraordinary starts or springs, but by traveling on through paces and roods of the sky. It is thus, and only thus, that any disciple will become efficient in the service of his Master. He can not do up his works of usefulness by the prodigious stir and commotion of a few extraordinary occasions. Laying down great plans, he must accomplish them by great industry, by minute attentions, by saving small advances, by working out his way as God shall assist him.

5. It is to be observed, that there is more of real piety in adorning one small than one great occasion. This may seem paradoxical, but what I intend will be seen by one or two illustrations. I have spoken of the minuteness of God's works. When I regard the eternal God as engaged in polishing an atom, or elaborating the functions of a mote invisible to the eye, what evidence do I there receive of his desire to perfect his works! No gross and mighty world, however plausibly shaped, would yield a hundredth part the intensity of evidence. An

illustration from human things will present a closer parallel. It is perfectly well understood, or if not, it should be, that almost any husband would leap into the sea, or rush into a burning edifice to rescue a perishing wife. But to anticipate the convenience or happiness of a wife in some small matter the neglect of which would be unobserved, is a more eloquent proof of tenderness. This shows a mindful fondness, which wants occasions in which to express itself. And the smaller the occasion seized upon, the more intensely affectionate is the attention paid. Piety toward God may be well tested or measured, in the same way. Peter found no difficulty in drawing his sword and fighting for his Master, even at the hazard of his life, though but an hour or less afterward he forsook him and denied him. His valor on that great and exciting occasion was no proof of his piety. But when the gentle Mary came, with her box of ointment, and poured it on the Saviour's head—an act which satisfied no want, met no exigency, and was of no use, except as a gratuitous and studied proof of her attachment to Jesus, he marks it as an eminent example of piety; saying—Verily I say unto you wheresoever this gospel shall be preached in the world, there also shall this, that this woman hath done, be told for a memorial of her.

My brethren, this piety which is faithful in that which is least, is really a more difficult piety than that which triumphs and glares on high occasions. Our judgments are apt to be dazzled by a vain admiration of the more public attempts and the more imposing manifestations of occasional zeal. It requires less piety, I verily believe, to be a martyr for Christ, than it does to love a powerless enemy; or to look upon the success of a rival without envy; or even to maintain a perfect and guileless integrity in the common transactions of life. Precisely this, in fact, is the lesson which history teaches. How many, alas! of those who have died in the manner of martyrdom, manifestly sought that distinction, and brought it on themselves by instigation of a mere fanatical ambition! Such facts seem designed to show us that the common spheres of life and business, the small matters of the street, the shop, the hearth, and the table, are more genial to true piety, than any artificial extraordinary scenes of a more imposing description. Excitement, amibition, a thousand questionable causes, may elevate us occasionally to great attempts; but they will never lead us into the more humble duties of constancy and godly industry; or teach us to adorn the unpretending spheres of life with a heavenly spirit.

We love to do great things; our natural pride would be greatly pleased, if God had made the sky taller, the world larger, and given us a more royal style of life and duty. But he understands us well. His purpose is to heal our infirmity; and with this very intent, I am persuaded, he has ordained these humble spheres of action, so that no ostentation, no great and striking explosions of godliness shall tempt our heart. And in the same way, his word declares, that bestowing all one's goods to feed the poor, or giving his body to be burned, and of consequence, that great speeches and donations, that a mighty zeal for reform, that a prodigious jealousy for sound doctrine, without something better—without charity, profiteth nothing. And the picture of charity is humble enough;—It suffereth long and is kind, envieth not, vaunteth not itself; is not puffed up, doth not behave itself unseemly; seeketh not her own, is not easily provoked, thinketh no evil, beareth all things, believeth all things, hopeth all things, endureth all things.

6. The importance of living to God, in ordinary and small things, is seen, in the fact that character, which is the end of religion, is in its very nature a growth. Conversion is a great change; old things are passed away; behold all things are become new. This however is the language of a hope or confidence, somewhat prophetic, exulting, at the beginning, in the realization of future victory. The young disciple, certainly, is far enough from a consciousness of complete deliverance from sin. In that respect, his work is but just begun. He is now in the blade; we shall see him next in the ear; and after that, he will ripen to the full corn in the ear. His character, as a man and a Christian, is to accomplish its stature by growing. And all the offices of life, domestic, social, civil, useful, are contrived of God to be the soil, as Christ is the sun, of such a growth. All the cares, wants, labors, dangers, accidents, intercourses of life, are adjusted for the very purpose of exercising and ripening character. They are precisely adapted for this end, by God's all-perfect wisdom. This, in fact, is the grand philosophy of the structure of all things. And, accordingly, there never has been a great and beautiful character, which has not become so by filling well the ordinary and smaller offices appointed of God.

The wonderful fortunes of Joseph seem, at first, to have fallen suddenly upon him, and altogether by a miracle. But a closer attention to his history will show you that he rose only by a gradual progress, and by the natural power of his virtues. The astonishing art he had of winning the confidence of others had, after all, no magic in it save the magic of goodness; and God assisted him, only as he assists other good men. The growth of his fortunes was the shadow only of his growth in character. By his assiduity, he made every thing prosper; and by his good faith, he won the confidence, first of Potiphar, then of the keeper of the prison, then of Pharaoh himself. And so he grew up gently and silently till the helm of the Egyptian kingdom was found in his hand.

Peter, too, after he had flourished so vauntingly with his sword, entered on a growing and faithful life. From an ignorant fisherman, he became a skillful writer, a finished Christian, and a teacher of faithful living, in the common offices of life. He occupied his great apostleship in exhorting subjects to obey the ordinances of governors for the Lord's sake; servants to be subject to their masters; wives to study such a carriage as would win their unbelieving husbands; and husbands to give honor to the wife, as being heirs together of the grace of life. But in a manner to comprehend every thing good, he said:— Giving all diligence (this is the true notion of Christian excellence)— giving all diligence, add to your faith virtue, to virtue knowledge, to knowledge temperance, to temperance patience, to patience godliness, to godliness brotherly kindness, and to brotherly kindness charity. The impression is unavoidable, that he now regarded religion, not as a sword fight, but as a growth of holy character, kept up by all diligence in the walks of life.

Every good example in the word of God, is an illustration of the same truth. To finish a character on a sudden, or by any but ordinary duties, carefully and piously done, by a mere religion of Sundays and birth-days, and revivals and contributions, and orthodoxies, and public reforms, is nowhere undertaken. They watered the plant in secret, trained it up at family altars, strengthened it in the exposures of business, till it became a beautiful and heavenly growth, and ready, with all its blooming fruit, to adorn the paradise of God.

It ought also to be noticed, under this head, that all the mischiefs which befall Christian character and destroy its growth, are such as lie in the ordinary humble duties of life. Christians do not fall back into declension or disgraceful apostacy on a sudden, or by the overcoming power of great and strange temptations. They are stolen away rather by little and little, and almost insensibly to themselves. They commonly fall into some lightness of carriage; some irritation of temper in their family or business; some neglect of duty to children, apprentices, or friends; some artfulness; some fault of integrity in business. These are the beginnings of evil. At length they grow a little more remiss. They begin to slight their secret duties. The world and its fashions become more powerful, and they yield a little farther; till at length they are utterly fallen from the spirit and standing of Christians. And thus, you perceive that all the dangers which beset our piety, lie in the humble and ordinary matters of life. Here then is the place where religion must make her conquests. Here she must build her barriers and take her stand. And if it be a matter of consequence that the people of God should live constant and godly lives; that they should grow in the strength of their principles, and the beauty of their example; that the church should clear herself of all reproach, and stand invested with honor in the sight of all mankind,—if this be important, so important is it that we live well in small things, and adorn the common incidents of life with a heavenly temper and practice. Religion must forever be unstable, the people of Christ must fall into declension and disgrace, if it be not understood that here is the true field of the Christian life.

These illustrations of the importance of living to God in ordinary and common things might be carried to almost any extent; but I will arrest the subject here, and proceed to suggest some applications which may be useful.

1. Private Christians are here instructed in the true method of Christian progress and usefulness. It is a first truth with you all, I doubt not, brethren, that divine aid and intercourse are your only strength and reliance. You know, too well, the infirmity of your best purposes and endeavors, to hope for any thing but defeat, without the Spirit of God dwelling in you and superintending your warfare. In what manner you may secure this divine indwelling permanently is here made plain. It is not by attempts above your capacity, or by the invention of great and extraordinary occasions; but it is by living unto God daily. If you feel the necessity of making spiritual attainments, of growing in holiness; if you think as little of mere starts and explosions in religous zeal as they deserve, and as much of growths, habits, and purified affections as God does, you will have a delightful work to prosecute in the midst of all your ordinary cares and employments, and you will have the inward witness of divine communion ever vouchsafed you. The sins, by which God's Spirit is ordinarily

grieved, are the sins of small things—laxities in keeping the temper, slight neglects of duty, lightness, sharpness of dealing. If it is your habit to walk with God in the humblest occupations of your days, it is very nearly certain that you will be filled with the Spirit always.

If it be a question with you, how to overcome bad and pernicious habits, the mode is here before you. The reason why those who are converted to Christ, often make so poor a work of rectifying their old habits, is that they lay down their work in the very places where it needs to be prosecuted most carefully, that is, in their common employments. They do not live to God in that which is least. They reserve their piety for those exercises, public and private, which are immediately religious, and so a wide door is left open in all the common duties of life for their old habits to break in and take them captive. As if it were enough, in shutting out a flood, to dike the higher points of the ground and leave the lower!

If the question be, in what manner you may grow in knowledge and intellectual strength, the answer is readily given. You can do it by no means save that of pertinacious, untiring application. No one becomes a Christian who can not by the cultivation of thought, and by acquiring a well-discriminated knowledge of the scriptures, make himself a gift of four fold, and perhaps even an hundred fold value to the church. This he can do by industry, by improving small opportunities, and, not least, by endeavoring to realize the principles and the beauty of Christ in all his daily conduct. In this point of view, religion is cultivation itself, and that of the noblest kind. And never does it truly justify its nature, except when it is seen elevating the mind, the manners, the whole moral dignity of the subject.

Why is it that a certain class of men, who never thrust themselves on public observation, by any very signal acts, do yet attain to a very commanding influence, and leave a deep and lasting impression on the world? They are the men who thrive by constancy and by means of small advances, just as others do who thrive in wealth. They live to God in the common doings of their daily life, as well as in the more extraordinary transactions, in which they mingle. In this way, they show themselves to be actuated by good principle, not from respect to the occasions where it may be manifested, but from respect to principle itself. And their carefulness to honor God in humble things, is stronger proof to men of their uprightness, than the most distinguished acts or sacrifices. Such persons operate principally by the weight of confidence and moral respect they acquire, which is the most legitimate and powerful action in the world. At first, it is not felt, because it is noiseless, and is not thoroughly appreciated. It is action without pretense, without attack, and therefore, perhaps, without notice for a time. But by degrees the personal motives begin to be understood, and the beauty and moral dignity of the life are felt. No proclamation of an aim or purpose has, in the mean time, gone before the disciple to awaken suspicion or start opposition. The simple power of his goodness and uprightness flows out as an emanation on all around him. He shines like the sun, not because he purposes to shine, but because he is full of light. The bad man is rebuked, the good man strengthened by his example; every thing evil and ungraceful is ashamed before him, every thing right and lovely is made stronger and lovelier. And now, if he has the talent to undertake some great enterprise of reform or of benevolence, in the name of his Master, he has something already prepared in the good opinions of mankind, to soften or neutralize the pretense of such attempts, and give him favor in them. Or, if a Christian of this stamp has not the talents or standing necessary to lead in the more active forms of enterprise, he will yet accomplish a high and noble purpose in his life. The silent savor of his name may, perhaps, do more good after he is laid in his grave, than abler men do by the most active efforts.

I often hear mentioned, by the Christians of our city, the name of a certain godly man, who has been dead many years; and he is always spoken of with so much respectfulness and affection, that I, a stranger of another generation, feel his power, and the sound of his name refreshes me. That man was one who lived to God in small things. I know this, not by any description which has thus set forth his character, but from the very respect and homage with which he is named. Virtually, he still lives among us, and the face of his goodness shines upon all our Christian labors. And is it not a delightful aspect of the Christian faith, that it opens so sure a prospect of doing good, on all who are in humble condition, or whose talents are too feeble to act in the more public spheres of enterprise and duty? Such are called to act by their simple goodness more than others are; and who has not felt the possibility that such, when faithful, do actually discharge a calling, the more exalted, because of its unmixed nature? If there were none of these unpretending but beautiful examples, blooming in depression, sweetening affliction by their Christian patience, adorning poverty by their high integrity, and dying in the Christian heroism of faith,—if, I say, there were no such examples making their latent impressions in the public mind, of the dignity and truth of the gospel, who shall prove that our great men, who are supposed to accomplish so much by their eloquence, their notable sacrifices and far-reaching plans, would not utterly fail in them? However this may be, we have reason enough, all of us, for living to God in every sphere of life. Blessed are they that keep judgment, and he that doeth righteousness at all times.

2. Our subject enables us to offer some useful suggestions, concerning the manner in which churches may be made to prosper.

First of all, brethren, you will have a care to maintain your purity and your honor, by the exercise of a sound discipline. And here you will be faithful in that which is least. You will not wait until a crisis comes, or a flagrant case arises, where the hand of extermination is needed. That is often a very cruel discipline, rather than one of brotherly love. Nothing, of course, should be done in a meddlesome spirit; for this would be more mischievous than neglect. But small things will yet be watched, the first gentle declinings noted and faithfully but kindly reproved. Your church should be like a family, not waiting till the ruin of a member is complete and irremediable, but acting preventively. This would be a healthy discipline, and it is the only sort, I am persuaded, on which God will ever smile.

The same spirit of watchfulness and attention is necessary to all the solid interests of your church. It is not enough that you attempt to bless it occasionally by some act of generosity or some fit of exertion. Your brethren, suffering from injustice or evil report, must have your faithful sympathy; such as are struggling with adversity must have your aid; when it is possible, the more humble and private exercises of your church must be attended.

The impression can not be too deeply fixed, that a church must grow chiefly by its industry and the personal growth of its members. Some churches seem to feel that, if any thing is to be done, some great operation must be started. They can not even repent without concert and a general ado. Have you not the preaching of God's word, fifty-two sabbaths in the year? Have you not also families, friendships, interchanges of business, meetings for prayer, brotherly vows, opportunities of private and public charity? Do not despise these common occasions—God has not planned the world badly. Christ did not want higher occasions than the Father gave him. The grand maxim of his mission was, that the humblest spheres give the greatest weight and dignity to principles—He was the good carpenter, saving the world! Rightly viewed, my brethren, there are no small occasions in this world, as in our haste we too often think. Great principles, principles sacred even to God, are at stake in every moment of life. What we want, therefore, is not invention, but industry; not the advantages of new and extraordinary times, but the realizing of our principles by adorning the doctrine of God our Saviour in all times.

One of the best securities for the growth and prosperity of a church, is to be sought in a faithful exhibition of religion in families. Here is a law of increase, which God has incorporated in his church, and by which he designs to give it strength and encouragement. But why is it—I ask the question with grief and pain—why is it that so many children, so many apprentices and servants are seen to grow up, or to live many years in Christian families, without any regard, or even respect for religion? It is because their parents, guardians, or masters have that sort of piety which can flourish only like Peter's sword, on great occasions. Then, perhaps, they are exceedingly full of piety, and put forth many awkward efforts to do good in their families; enough, it may be, to give them a permanent disgust for religious things. But when the great occasion is past, their work is done up. A spirit of worldliness now rolls in again, a want of conscience begins to appear, a light and carnal conversation to show itself. The preaching of the gospel is very critically, and somewhat wittily canvassed on the Sabbath. The day itself, in the mean time, fares scarcely better than the preacher. It is shortened by degrees at both ends, and again by a newspaper or some trifling conversation, in the middle. There is no instructive remark at the family prayers, and perhaps no family instruction anywhere. There is no effort to point the rising family toward a better world, and apparently no living for such a world. Bad tempers are manifested in government and in business. Arts are practiced below dignity and wide of integrity. How is it possible that the children and youth of a family should not learn to despise such a religion? How different would be the result, if there were a simple unostentatious piety kept up with constancy, and the fear of God were seen to be a controlling principle, in all the daily conduct and plans of life! I have heard of many striking cases of conversion, which were produced, under God, by simply seeing the godly life of a Christian in his family without a word of direct address, and in a time of general inattention to religious things. In such a family every child and inmate will certainly respect religion. And the church, in fact, may count on receiving a constant and certain flow of increase from the bosom of such families.

I will not pursue this head farther. But feel assured of this, brethren, that an every-day religion; one that loves the duties of our common walk; one that makes an honest man; one that accomplishes an intellectual and moral growth in the subject; one that works in all weather, and improves all opportunities, will best, and most healthily promote the growth of a church, and the power of the gospel. God prescribes our duty; and it were wrong not to believe that if we undertake God's real work, he will furnish us to it, and give us pleasure in it. He will transfuse into us some portion of his own versatility; he will attract us into a nicer observation of his wisdom in our humble duties and concerns. We shall more admire the healthiness of that which grows up in God's natural springtimes, and ripens in the air of his common days. The ordinary will thus grow dignified and sacred in our sight; and without discarding all invention in respect to means and opportunities, we shall yet especially love the daily bread of a common grace, in our common works and cares. And all the more that it was the taste of our blessed Master, to make the ordinary glow with mercy and goodness. Him we are to follow. We are to work after no set fashion of high endeavor, but to walk with him, performing as it were, a ministry on foot, that we may stop at the humblest matters and prove our fidelity there.

THE GENTLENESS OF GOD.[3]

"Thy gentleness hath made me great."—Ps. xviii. 35.

Gentleness in a deity—what other religion ever took up such a thought? When the coarse mind of sin makes up gods and a religion

---

3. From *Christ and His Salvation, In Sermons Variously Related Thereto* (New York: Charles Scribner, 1864), 28–50. Date of delivery unknown; first published in 1864.

by its own natural light, the gods, it will be seen, reveal both the coarseness and the sin together, as they properly should. They are made great as being great in force, and terrible in their resentments. They are mounted on tigers, hung about with snakes, cleave the sea with tridents, pound the sky with thunders, blow tempests out of their cheeks, send murrain upon the cattle, and pestilence on the cities and kingdoms of other gods—always raging in some lust or jealousy, or scaring the world by some vengeful portent.

Just opposite to all these, the great God and creator of the world, the God of revelation, the God and Father of our Lord Jesus Christ, contrives to be a gentle being; even hiding his power, and withholding the stress of his will, that he may put confidence and courage in the feeling of his children. Let us not shrink then from this epithet of scripture, as if it must imply some derogation from God's real greatness and majesty; for we are much more likely to reach the impression, before we have done, that precisely here do his greatness and majesty culminate.

What then, first of all, do we mean by gentleness? To call it sweetness of temper, kindness, patience, flexibility, indecisiveness, does not really distinguish it. We shall best come at the true idea, if we ask what it means when applied to a course of treatment? When you speak, for example, of dealing gently with an enemy, you mean that, instead of trying to force a point straight through with him, you will give him time, and ply him indirectly with such measures and modes of forbearance as will put him on different thoughts, and finally turn him to a better mind. Here then is the true conception of God's gentleness. It lies in his consenting to the use of indirection, as a way of gaining his adversaries. It means that he does not set himself, as a ruler, to drive his purpose straight through, but that, consciously wise and right, abiding in his purposes with majestic confidence, and expecting to reign with a finally established supremacy, he is only too great to fly at his adversary, and force him to the wall, if he does not instantly surrender; that, instead of coming down upon him thus, in a manner of direct onset, to carry his immediate submission by storm, he lays gentle seige to him, waiting for his willing assent and choice. He allows dissent for the present, defers to prejudice, watches for the cooling of passion, gives room and space for the weaknesses of our unreasonable and perverse habit to play themselves out, and so by leading us round, through long courses of kind but faithful exercise, he counts on bringing us out into the ways of obedience and duty freely chosen. Force and crude absolutism are thus put by; the irritations of a jealous littleness have no place; and the great God and Father, intent on making his children great, follows them and plies them with the gracious indirections of a faithful and patient love.

It is scarcely necessary to add that there are many kinds of indirection, which are wide, as possible, of any character of gentleness. All policy, in the bad sense of the term, is indirection. A simply wise expedient has often this character. But the indirections of God are those of a ruler, perfectly secure and sovereign, and their object is, not to turn a point of interest for himself, but simply to advance and make great the unworthy and disobedient subjects of his goodness.

This character of gentleness in God's treatment, you will thus perceive, is one of the greatest spiritual beauty and majesty, and one that ought to affect us most tenderly in all our sentiments and choices. And that we may have it in its true estimation, observe, first of all, how far off it is from the practice and even capacity generally of mankind. We can do almost any thing more easily than consent to use any sort of indirection, when we are resisted in the exercise of authority, or encounter another at some point of violated right.

There is a more frequent approach to gentleness, in the parental relation, than any where else among men. And yet even here, how common is the weak display of a violent, autocratic, manner, in the name of authority and government. Seeing the child daring to resist his will, the parent is, how often, foolishly exasperated. With a flush of anger and a stern, hard voice, he raises the issue of peremptory obedience; and when, either by force or without, he has carried his way, he probably congratulates himself that he has been faithful enough to break his child's will. Whereas, raising an issue between his own passions and his child's mere fears, he is quite as likely to have broken down his conscience as his will, unnerving all the forces of character and capacities of great manhood in him for life. Alas how many parents, misnamed fathers and mothers, fancy, in this manner, that when self-respect is completely demolished in their poor defenseless child, the family government is established. They fall into this barbarity, just because they have too little firmness to hold their ground in any way of indirection or gentleness. They are violent because they are weak, and then the conscious wrong of their violence weakens them still farther, turning them, after the occasion is past, to such a misgiving, half apologizing manner, as just completes their weakness.

It will also be observed, almost universally, among men, that where one comes to an issue of any kind with another, matters are pressed to a direct point-blank Yes or No. If it is a case of personal wrong, or a quarrel of any kind, the parties face each other, pride against pride, passion against passion, and the hot endeavor is to storm a way through to victory. There is no indirection used to soften the adversary, no waiting for time, nothing meets the feeling of the moment but to bring him down upon the issue, and floor him by a direct assault. To redress the injury by gentleness, to humble an adversary by his own reflections, and tame his will by the circuitous approach of forbearance and a siege of true suggestion—that is not the manner of men, but only of God.

True gentleness, we thus perceive, is a character too great for any but the greatest and most divinely tempered souls. And yet how ready are many to infer that, since God is omnipotent, he must needs have it as a way of majesty, to carry all his points through to their issue by force, just as they would do themselves. What, in their view, is it for God to be omnipotent, but to drive his chariot where he will. Even Christian theologians, knowing that he has force enough to carry his points at will, make out pictures of his sovereignty, not seldom, that stamp it as a remorseless absolutism. They do not remember that it is man, he that has no force, who wants to carry every thing by force, and that God is a being too great for this kind of infirmity; that, having all power, he glories in the hiding of his power; that holding the worlds in the hollow of his hand, and causing heaven's pillars to shake at his reproof, He still counts it the only true gentleness for Him to bend, and wait, and reason with his adversary, and turn him round by His strong Providence, till he is gained to repentance and a volunteer obedience.

But God maintains a government of law, it will be remembered, and enforces his law by just penalties, and what room is there for gentleness in a government of law? All room, I answer; for how shall he gain us to his law as good and right, if he does not give us time to make the discovery of what it is? To receive law because we are crammed with it, is not to receive it as law, but only to receive it as force, and God would spurn that kind of obedience, even from the meanest of his subjects. He wants our intelligent, free choice, of duty—that we should have it in love, nay have it even in liberty. Doubtless it is true that he will finally punish the incorrigible; but He need not therefore, like some weak, mortal despot, hurry up his force, and drive straight in upon his mark. If he were consciously a little faint-hearted he would, but he is great enough in his firmness to be gentle and wait.

But some evidence will be demanded that God pursues any such method of indirection, or of rectoral gentleness with us. See then, first of all, how openly he takes this attitude in the scriptures.

When our first father breaks through law, by his act of sin, he does not strike him down by his thunders, but he holds them back, comes to him even with a word of promise, and sends him forth into the rough trials of a world unparadised by guilt, to work, and suffer, and learn, and, when he will, to turn and live. The ten brothers of Joseph are managed in the same way. When they could not speak peaceably to him, or even endure his presence in the family, God lets them sell him to the Egyptians, then sends them down to Egypt, by the instigations of famine, and passes them back and forth with supplies to their father, allowing them to feed even the life of their bodies out of Joseph's bounty, till finally, when he is revealed as their brother and their father's son, they are seen doing exactly what they had sworn in their wrath should never be done—bowing their sheaf to the sheaf of Joseph. Here too is the solution of that very strange chapter of history, the forty years' march in the wilderness. The people were a slave-born people, having all the vices, superstitions, and unmanly weaknesses, that belong to slavery. God will not settle his land with such, and no thunders or earthquakes of discipline can drive the inbred weakness suddenly out of them. So he takes the indirect method, puts them on a milling of time and trial, marches them round and round to ventilate their low passions, lets some die and others be born, till finally they become quite another people, and are fitted to inaugurate a new history.

But I need not multiply these minor examples, when it is the very genius of Christianity itself to prevail with man, or bring him back to obedience and life by a course of loving indirection. What we call the gospel is only a translation, so to speak, of the gentleness of God—a matter in the world of fact, answering to a higher matter, antecedent, in the magnanimity of God. I do not say that this gospel is a mere effusion of divine sentiment apart from all counsel and government. It comes by counsel older than the world's foundations. The salvation it brings is a governmental salvation. It is, at once, the crown of God's purposes and of his governmental order. And the gentleness of God must institute this second chapter of gracious indirection, because no scheme of rule could issue more directly in good without it. For it was impossible in the nature of things that mere law—precept driven home by the forces of penalty—should ever establish a really principled obedience in us. How shall we gladly obey and serve in love, which is the only obedience having any true character, till we have had time to make some experiments, try some deviations, sting ourselves in some bitter pains of trials, and so come round into the law freely chosen, because we have found how good it is; and, what is more than all, have seen how good God thinks it himself to be, from what is revealed in that wondrous indirection of grace, the incarnate life and cross of Jesus. Here the very plan is to carry the precept of law by motives higher than force; by feeling, and character, and sacrifice. We could not be driven out of sin by the direct thrust of omnipotence; for to be thus driven out is to be in it still. But we could be overcome by the argument of the cross, and by voices that derive a quality from suffering and sorrow. And thus it is that we forsake our sins, at the call of Jesus and his cross, freely, embracing thus in trust, what in willfulness and ignorance we rejected.

Nor does it vary at all our account of this gospel, that the Holy Spirit works concurrently in it, with Christ and his cross. For it is not true, as some Christian teachers imagine, that the Holy Spirit works conversion by a direct, soul-renewing fiat or silent thunderstroke of omnipotence. He too works by indirection, not by any short method of absolute will. Working efficiently and, in a certain sense, immediately in the man, or subject, he still circles round the will, doing it respect by laying no force upon it, and only raising appeals to it from what he puts in the mind, the conscience, the memory, the sense of want, the fears excited, the aspirations kindled. He moves upon it thus by a siege, and not by a fiat, carries it finally by a process of circumvallation, commonly much longer even than the ministry of Jesus. He begins with the child, opening his little nature to gleams of religious truth and feeling—at the family prayers, in his solitary hours and dreams, in the songs of praise that warble on the strings of his soul, and among the heavenly affinities of his religious nature. And thenceforward he goes with him, in all the future changes and unfoldings of his life, turning his thoughts, raising tender questions in him, working private bosom scenes in his feeling, forcing nothing, but pleading and insinuating every thing good; a better presence keeping him company, and preparing, by all modes of skill and holy inducement, to make him great. So that, if we could follow a soul onward in its life-history, we should see a Spirit-history running parallel with it. And when it is really born of God, it will be the result of what the Spirit has wrought, by a long, and various, and subtle, and beautiful process, too delicate for human thought to trace.

Holding this view of God's gentleness in the treatment of souls, and finding even the Christian gospel in it, we ought also to find that his whole management of us and the world corresponds. Is it so—is there such a correspondence?

See, some will say, what terrible forces we have ravening and pouring inevitably on about us day and night—roaring seas, wild hurricanes, thunder-shocks that split the heavens, earthquakes splitting the very world's body itself, heat and cold, drought and deluge, pestilences and deaths in all forms. What is there to be seen but a terrible, inexorable going on, still on, everywhere. The fixed laws everywhere refuse to bend, hearing no prayers, the great worlds fly through heaven as if slung by the Almighty like the smooth stone of David, and the atoms rush together in their indivertible affinities, like the simples of gunpowder touched by fire, refusing to consider any body. Where then is the gentleness of such a God as we have signaled to us, in these unpitying, inexorable, fated, powers of the world? Is it such a God that moves by indirection? Yes, and that all the more properly, just because these signs of earth and heaven, these undiverted, undivertible, all-demolishing and terrible forces permit him to do it. He now can hide his omnipotence, for a time, just at the point where it touches us; he can set his will behind his love for to-day and possibly tomorrow; simply because he has these majestic inexorabilities for the rear-guard of his mercies. For we can not despise him now, when he bends to us in favor, because it is the bending, we may see, of firmness. Able to use force, he can now use character, and time, and kindness. Real gentleness in Him, as in every other being, supposes counsel, order, end, and a determinate will. A weak man can be weak and that is all. Not even a weak woman can be properly called gentle. No woman will so much impress others by her gentleness, when she is gentle, as one that has great firmness and decision. And so it is the firm, great God, he that goes on so inflexibly in the laws, and the inexorable forces and causes of the creation—He it is that can, with so much better dignity, gentle himself to a child or a sinner.

See then how it goes with us in God's management of our experience. Doing every thing to work on our feeling, temperament, thought, will, and so on our eternal character, He still does nothing by direct impulsion. It is with us here, in every thing, as it was with Jonah when the Lord sent him to Nineveh. It was a good long journey inland, but Jonah steers for Joppa, straight the other way, and there puts to sea, sailing off upon it, and then under it, and through the belly of hell, and comes to land nobody knows where. After much perambulation, he gets to Nineveh and gives his message doggedly, finally to be tamed by a turn of hot weather and the wilting of a gourd. Just so goes the course of a soul whom God is training for obedience and life. It may be the case of a young man, setting off willfully, with his face turned away from God. Whereupon God lets him please himself a little in his folly, and finally pitch himself into vice, there to learn, by the bitter woes of his thraldom, how much better God is to him than he is to himself, how much worthier of trust than he ever can be to himself. Or he takes, it may be, a longer course with him— gives him a turn of sickness, then of bankruptcy, then of desertion by friends, then of slander by enemies, taming thus his pride, sobering his feeling, making the world change color, but not yet gaining him to the better life. Then he fetches him out of his disasters by unexpected vindications and gifts of mercy, such as soften unwontedly the pitch of his sensibilities. A faithful Christian wife, gilding his lot of adversity before, by her gentle cares, and quite as much, his recovery now, by the beautiful spirit she has formed in his and her children, by her faithful training—making them an honor to him as to herself— wins upon his willful habit, melts into his feeling, and operates a change in his temperament itself. Meantime his years will have been setting him on, by a silent drift, where his will would never carry him,

and changing, in fact, the current of his inclination itself. Till at
length, dissatisfied with himself, as he is more softened to God, and
more softened to God, as he is more diverted from the satisfaction he
once had in himself, he turns, with deliberate consent, to the call of
Jesus, and finds what seemed to be a yoke, to be easy as liberty itself.

The change is great, nay almost total in his life, and yet it has
been carried by a process of indirection so delicate, that he is scarcely
sensible by what steps and curiously turned methods of skill it has
been brought to pass. And so God is managing every man, by a process and history of his own; for he handles him as he does no other,
adapting every turn to his want and to the points already gained, till
finally he is caught by the gentle guile of God's mercies and drawn
to the rock of salvation; even as some heavy and strong fish, that has
been played by the skillful angler, is drawn, at last, to land, by a
delicate line, that would not even hold his weight.

In a similar way God manages, not seldom, to gain back infidels
and doubters. First he commonly makes them doubt their doubts.
Their conceit he moderates, meantime, by the sobering effect of years
and sorrow. By and by he sharpens their spiritual hunger, by the consciously felt emptiness of their life, and the large blank spaces of their
creed. Then he opens some new vista into the bright field of truth,
down which they never looked before, and the mole eyes of their
skepticism are even dazed by the new discovered glory of God's light.

Disciples who are lapsed into sin, and even into looseness of
life, are recovered in the same way of indirection. God does not pelt
them with storms, nor jerk them back into their place by any violent
seizure. He only leads them round by his strong-handed yet gentle
tractions, till he has got them by, or out of, their fascinations, and
winnowed the nonsense out of their fancy or feeling, by which they
have been captivated. And so at length he gets their feet upon the rock
again never to be moved.

Indeed I may go farther. Even if you desire it, God will not thrust
you on to higher attainments in religion, by any forcible and direct
method. He will only bring you out into the rest you seek, just as soon
as you are sufficiently untwisted, and cleared, and rectified, under
his indirect methods, to be there. Commonly your light will spring
up in quarters where you look not for it, and even the very hidings
and obscurations you suffer, will give you out some spark of light,
as they leave you. The obstacles you conquer will turn out to be, in

some sense, aids, the discouragements that tried you will open, when they part, as windows of hope.

Having traced the manner and fact of God's condescension to these gentle methods, let us now pass on to another point where the subject properly culminates; viz., to the end he has in view; which is, to make us great. He may have a different opinion of greatness from that which is commonly held by men—he certainly has. And what is more, he has it because he has a much higher respect for the capabilities of our human nature, and much higher designs concerning it, than we have ourselves. We fall into a mistake here also, under what we suppose to be the Christian gospel itself; as if it were a plan to bring down, not the loftiness of our pride, and the willfulness of our rebellion, but the stature and majesty of our nature itself. Thus we speak of submitting, or losing our will, being made weak and poor, becoming little children, ceasing to have any mind of our own, falling into nothingness and self-contempt before God. All which are well enough as Christian modes of expression; but we take them too literally. They are good as relating to our wrong will and wrong feeling, not as relating to our capacity of will and feeling itself. On the contrary, while God is ever engaged to bring down our loftiness in evil and perversity, he is just as constantly engaged to make us loftier and stronger in every thing desirable—in capacity, and power, and all personal majesty. We do not understand him, in fact, till we conceive it as a truth profoundly real and glorious, that he wants to make us great—great in will, great in the breadth and honest freedom of our intellect, great in courage, enthusiasm, self-respect, firmness, superiority to things and matters of condition; great in sacrifice and beneficence; great in sonship with Himself; great in being raised to such common counsel, and such intimate unity with him in his ends, that we do, in fact, reign with him.

Take, for example, the first point named, the will; for this, it will be agreed, is the spinal column even of our personality. Here it is that we assert ourselves with such frightful audacity in our sin. Here is the tap-root of our obstinacy. Hence come all the woes and disorders of our fallen state. Is it then His point to crush our will, or reduce it in quantity? If that were all, he could do it by a thought. No, that is not his way. His object is, on the contrary, to gain our will— gain it, that is, in such a manner as to save it, and make it finally a thousand fold stouter in good and sacrifice, than it has been, or could be, in wrong and evil. He will make it the chariot, as it were, of a great and mighty personality, inflexible, unsubduable, tremendous in good forever.

So of the intellect. Blinded by sin, wedded to all misbelief and false seeing, he never requires us to put violence upon it, never to force an opinion or a faith, lest we break its integrity; he only bids us set it for seeing, by a wholly right intent and a willingness even to die for the truth; assured that, in this manner, Time, and Providence, and Cross, and Spirit, will bring it into the light, clearing, as in a glorious sun-rising, all the clouds that obscure it, and opening a full, broad heaven of day on its vision. Recovered thus without being forced or violated, it feels itself to be a complete integer in power, as never before; and having conquered such obstacles under God, by the simple honesty of its search, it has a mighty appetite sharpened for the truth, and a glorious confidence raised, that time and a patient beholding will pierce all other clouds, and open a way for the light.

And so it is that God manages to save all the attributes of force and magnanimity in us, while reducing us to love and obedience. Take such an example as Paul. Do we speak of will? why he has the will-force of an empire in him. Of intelligence? let it be enough that he goes down into Arabia, and that in three years' time his mind has gone over all the course of Christian truth and doctrine, helped by no mortal, but only by God's converse with him, and his own free thought. Of courage, firmness, self-respect? what perils has he met, what stripes endured, and what offscouring of the world has he been taken for, unhumbled still, and erect in the consciousness of his glorious manhood in Christ—sorrowful yet always rejoicing, poor yet making many rich, having nothing yet possessing all things; confounding Athens and Ephesus and the mob at Jerusalem, out-pleading Tertullus the lawyer, convincing Felix and Agrippa, commanding in the shipwreck, winning disciples to the faith in the household of Caesar, and planting, in fact, all over Caesar's world-wide empire, the seeds of a loftier and stronger empire by which it is finally to be mastered.

Such now are God's mighty ones—humble it may be and poor, or if not such by social position, most effectually humbled, some will think, by their faith, yet how gloriously exalted. God renounces all the point-blank methods of dealing, that he may give scope and verge to our liberty, and win us to some good and great feeling, in glorious affinity with his own. He wants us to be great enough in the stature of our opinions, principles, courage and character, that he may enjoy us and be Himself enjoyable by us. Hence also it is that, when we are born of God, and the divine affinities of our great nature come into play unbroken, unimpaired, and even wondrously raised in volume, we, for the first time, make discovery of ourselves. Our heads touch heaven, as it were, in the sense of our regenerated dignity, and joys like the ocean roll through our nature, that before could only catch some rill or trickling drop of good. And with it comes what strength, a mighty will, a sense of equilibrium recovered, an all appropriating faith, superiority to things, immovable repose.

And now at the crowning of this great subject, what shall more impress us than the sublime and captivating figure God maintains for Himself and his government in it. Easy enough were it for him to lay his force upon us, and dash our obstinacy to the ground. He might not thrust us into love, he could not into courage and confidence, but he might instantly crush out all willfulness in us forever. But he could not willingly reduce us, in this manner, to a weak and cringing submission. He wants no slaves about his throne. If he could not raise us into liberty and make us great in duty, he would less respect both duty and Himself. He refuses therefore to subdue us unless by some such method that we may seem, in a certain other sense, to subdue ourselves. Most true it is that he carries a strong hand with us. He covers up no principle, tempers the exactness of no law. There is no connivance in his methods, no concealment of truths disagreeable and piercing, no proposition of compromise or halving, in a way of settlement. His Providence moves strong. His terrors flame out on the background of a wrathful sky. He thunders marvelously with his voice. And so his very gentleness stands glorious and strong and sovereignly majestic round us. Were he only soft or kind, bending like a willow to our wicked state, there were little to move and affect us even in his goodness itself. But when we look on Him as the Almighty Rock, the immovable Governor and Keeper of the worlds, girding himself in all terrible majesty, when he must, to let us know that impunity in wrong is impossible, then it is that we behold Him in the true meaning of his gentleness—how good! how firm! how adorably great! Come nigh O thou sinning, weary prodigal, and acknowledge and receive, in blissful welcome, the true greatness of thy God! Be not jealous any more that religion is going to depress your manly parts, or weaken the strength of your high aspirations. In your lowest humiliations and deepest repentances, you will be consciously raised and exalted. Every throb of heaven's life in your bosom will be only a throb of greatness. Every good affection, every holy action, into which your God may lead you, all your bosom struggles, your hungers and tears and prostrations, will be the travailing only of a princely birth, and a glorious sonship with God.

Holding such a view too of God's ends and the careful indirections by which he pursues them, we can not fail to note the softened aspect given to what are often called the unaccountable severities of human experience. The woes of broken health and grim depression; the pains, the unspeakable agonies by which human bodies are wrenched for whole years; the wrongs of orphanage; pestilence, fire, flood, tempest and famine—how can a good God launch his bolts on men, we ask, in severities like these? And the sufferers themselves sometimes wonder, even in their faith, how it is that if God is a Father, he can let fall on his children such hail-storms of inevitable, unmitigated disaster. No, suffering mortal! a truce to all such complainings. These are only God's merciful indirections, fomentations of trouble and sorrow that he is applying, to soften the rugged and hard will in you. These pains are only switches to turn you off from the track of his coming retributions. If your great, proud nature could be won to the real greatness of character, by a tenderer treatment, do you not see, from all God's gentle methods of dealing with mankind, that he would gladly soften your troubles? And if diamonds are not polished by soap, or oil, or even by any other stone, but only by their own fine dust, why should you complain that God is tempering you to your good, only by such throes and lacerations and wastings of life, as are necessary?

Again, to vary the strain of our thought, how strangely weak and low, is the perversity of many, when they require it of God to convert them by force, or drive them heavenward by storm. You demand, it may be, that God shall raise the dead before you, or that He shall speak to you in an audible voice from the sky, or that he shall regenerate your life by some stroke of omnipotence in your sleep—something you demand that shall astound your senses, or supersede your freedom. You require it of God, in fact, that He shall manage you as he did Sennacherib, that He shall put his hook into your nose, and his bridle into your lips, and lead you back, in that manner, out of sins you will not consentingly forsake. How preposterous and base to ask it thus of your Father, that He will storm you with his power and thrust you into goodness by his thunder-bolts! Instead of being jealous, with a much finer class of souls, that God and religion are going to reduce your level, you even require to be made little by Him, nay, to be unmade, and even thrust out of your personal manhood. How much better to give a ready welcome to what God is doing for you and in you, without force, doing in a way to save and even to complete your personal manhood.

Last of all let us not omit, in such a subject as this, the due adjustment of our conceptions to that which is the true pitch and scale of our magnanimity and worth as Christian men. It is easy, at this point, to flaunt our notions of dignity, and go off, as it were, in a gas of naturalism, prating of manliness, or manly character. And yet there is such a thing to be thought of, revelation being judge, as being even great—great in some true scale of Christian greatness. A little, mean-minded, shuffling, cringing, timorous, selfish soul—would that many of our time could see how base the figure it makes under any Christian name. I will not undertake to say how little a man may be and be a Christian; for there are some natures that are constitutionally mean, and it may be too much to expect that grace will ennoble them all through in a day. Judging them in all charity, it must none the less be our conception for ourselves, that God is calling us even to be great, great in courage and candor, steadfast in honor and truth, immovable in our promises, heroic in our sacrifices, right, and bold, and holy—men whom He is training, by His own great spirit, for a world of great sentiment, and will, and might, and majesty. For when we conceive the meeting in that world, and being there compeers with such majestic souls as Moses, and Paul, and Luther, and Cromwell, nay with thrones and dominions otherwise nameless, we do not seem, I confess, to be so much raised in the sense of our possible stature in good, as when we simply meditate God's gentle methods with us here, to raise our fallen manhood to its place; his careful respect for our liberty, the hidings of His power, the detentions of his violated feeling, the sending of his Son, and his Son's great cross, the silent intercessions of his Spirit—all the changes through which he is leading us, all the careful trainings of care and culture by which he is bringing us back at last, stage by stage, to the final erectness and glory of a perfect life. Even as when the mother eagle lifts her young upon the edge of her nest, holding them back that they may not topple off, and puts them fluttering there and waving their pinions that they may get strength to lift their bodies, and finally to scale the empyreal heights. And when we shall be able, ascending thus our state of glory, to look back and trace all this, in a clear and orderly review, what a wonderful and thrilling retrospect will it be.

Conscious there of powers not broken down or crushed into servility, but of wills invigorated rather by submission, with what sense of inborn dignity and strength shall we sing—Thy gentleness hath made us great. All the littleness of our sin is now quite gone. We are now complete men, such as God meant us to be;—great in the stature of our opinions, great in our feelings, principles, energies of will and joy; greatest of all in our conscious affinity with God and the Lamb. Be it ours to live, then, with a sense of our high calling upon us, abiding in all the holy magnanimities of love, honor, sacrifice and truth; sincere, exact, faithful, bountiful and free; showing thus to others and knowing always in ourselves, that we do steadily aspire to just that height of good, into which our God himself has undertaken to exalt us.

THE DISSOLVING OF DOUBTS.[4]

"And I have heard of thee, that thou canst make interpretations and dissolve doubts."—Dan. 5: 16.

Doubts and questions are not peculiar to Nebuchadnezzar, but they are the common lot and heritage of humanity. They vary in their subjects and times, but we have them always on hand. We live just now in a specially doubting age, where almost every matter of feeling is openly doubted, or, it may be, openly denied. Science puts every thing in question, and literature distils the questions, making an atmosphere of them. We doubt both creation and Creator; whether there be second causes or only primal causes running *ab æterno in æter-*

---

4. From *Sermons on Living Subjects* (New York: Scribner, Armstrong & Co., 1872), 166–84. Preached at the Yale College Chapel in 1871.

num; whether God is any thing more than the sum of such causes; whether he works by will back of such causes; whether he is spirit working supernaturally through them; whether we have any personal relation to him, or he to us. And then, when we come to the matter of revelation, we question the fact of miracles and of the incarnation. We doubt free agency and responsibility, immortality and salvation, the utility of prayer and worship, and even of repentance for sin. And these sweeping, desolating doubts run through all grades of mind, all modes and spheres of life, as it were telegraphically, present as powers of the air to unchristen the new born thoughts of religion as fast as they arrive. The cultivated and mature have the doubts ingrown they know not how, and the younger minds encounter their subtle visitations when they do not seek them. And the more active minded they are, and the more thoughts they have on the subject of religion, the more likely they are, (unless anchored by true faith in God,) to be drifted away from all the most solid and serious convictions, even before they are aware of it. Their mind is ingenuous, it may be, and their habit is not over speculative, certainly not perversely speculative; they only have a great many thoughts raising a great many questions that fly, as it were, loosely across their mental landscape, and leave no trace of their passage—that is, none which they themselves perceive,—and yet they wake up by and by, startled by the discovery that they believe nothing. They can not any where put down their foot and say, "here is truth." And it is the greatest mystery to them that they consciously have not meant to escape from the truth, but have, in a certain sense, been feeling after it. They have not been ingenious in their questions and arguments. They have despised all tricks of sophistry, they have only been thinking and questioning as it seemed to be quite right they should. And yet, somehow, it is now become as if all truth were gone out, and night and nowhere had the world. The vacuity is painful, and they are turned to a wrestling with their doubts, which is only the more painful that they wrestle, as it were, in mid-air, unable to so much as touch ground any where.

The point I am sketching here is certainly in the extreme, and yet it is an extreme often reached quite early, and one toward which all young minds gravitate, as certainly as they consent to live without God and carry on their experience, steadied by no help from the practical trust of religion. Probably some of you, my friends here before me, are at one point of doubt or unbelieving, and some at another; I sincerely hope that none of you have reached the dark extreme just described. But whatever point you have reached, I propose for my object this morning to bring in what I can of countervailing help. I shall speak of the dissolving of your doubts, showing how you may have them dissolved in all their degrees and combinations. If they do not press you, or at all trouble you; if you like to have them, and amuse yourself in what you count the brilliancy of their play, if you love to be inventive and propagate as many and plausible as you may, I have nothing for you. But if you want to know the truth—all truth—and be in it, and have all the fogs of the mind cleared away, I think I can tell you in what manner it may, without a peradventure, be done. Shall I go on? Give me then your attention, nothing more. I shall not ask you to surrender up your will or suppress your intelligence, would not even consent to have you force your convictions or opinions. All that I ask is a real desire to find the truth and be in it.

Before proceeding, however, in the principal matter of the subject, it may be well to just note the three principal sources and causes whence our doubts arise, and from which they get force to make their assault. They never come of truth or high discovery, but always of the want of it.

In the first place, all the truths of religion are inherently dubitable. They are only what are called probable, never necessary truths like the truths of geometry or of numbers. In these we have the premises in our very minds themselves. In all other matters we have the premise to find. And there is almost no premise out of us that we do not some time or other doubt. We even doubt our senses, nay, it takes a very dull, loose-minded soul, never to have, or to have had a doubt of the senses. Now this field of probable truth is the whole field of religion, and of course it is competent for doubt to cover it in every part and item.

In the second place, we begin life as unknowing creatures that have every thing to learn. We grope, and groping is doubt; we handle, we question, we guess, we experiment, beginning in darkness and stumbling on towards intelligence. We are in a doom of activity, and can not stop thinking—thinking every thing, knocking against the walls on every side; trying thus to master the problems, and about as often getting mastered by them. Yeast works in bread scarcely more blindly. When I draw out this whole conception of our life as it is, the principal wonder, I confess, is that we doubt so little and accept so much.

And, again, thirdly, it is a fact, disguise it as we can, or deny it as we may, that our faculty is itself in disorder. A broken or bent telescope will not see any thing rightly. A filthy window will not bring in even the day as it is. So a mind wrenched from its true lines of action or straight perception, discolored and smirched by evil, will not see truly, but will put a blurred, misshapen look on every thing. Truths will only be as good as errors, and doubts as natural as they.

Now it will be seen that as long as these three sources or originating causes of doubt continue, doubts will continue, and will, in one form or another, be multiplied. Therefore, I did not propose to show how they may be stopped, for that is impossible, but only how they may be dissolved, or cleared away. I may add, however, that the method by which they are to be dissolved, will work as well preventively as remedially; for though it will not stop their coming, it will stop their coming with damage and trouble to the mind, and keep it clear for all steadiest repose and highest faith in religion.

And the first thing here to be said, and it may be most important, is negative; viz., that the doubters never can dissolve or extirpate their doubts by inquiry, search, investigation, or any kind of speculative endeavor. They must never go after the truth to merely find it, but to practice it and live by it. It is not enough to rally their inventiveness, doing nothing to polarize their aim. To be simply curious, thinking of this and thinking of that, is only a way to multiply doubts; for in doing it they are, in fact, postponing all the practical rights of truth. They imagine, it may be, that they are going first, to settle their questions, and then, at their leisure, to act. As if they were going to get the perfect system and complete knowledge of truth before they move an inch in doing what they know! The result is that the chamber of their brain is filled with an immense clatter of opinions, questions, arguments, that even confound their reason itself. And they come out wondering at the discovery, that the more they investigate the less they believe! Their very endeavor mocks them,—just as it really ought. For truth is something to be lived, else it might as well not be. And how shall a mind get on finding more truth, save as it takes direction from what it gets; how make farther advances when it tramples what it has by neglect? You come upon the hither side of a vast intricate forest region, and your problem is to find your way through it. Will you stand there inquiring and speculating forty years, expecting first to make out the way? or, seeing a few rods into it, will you go on as far as you see, and so get ability to see a few rods farther? proceeding in that manner to find out the unknown, by advancing practically in the known.

No, there is no fit search after truth which does not, first of all, begin to live the truth it knows. Alas! to honor a little truth is not in the doubters, or they do not think of it, and so they dishonor beforehand all the truth they seek, and swamp it, by inevitable consequence, in doubts without end.

Dropping now this negative matter, we come to the positive. There is a way for dissolving any and all doubts,—a way that opens at a very small gate, but widens wonderfully after you pass. Every human soul, at a certain first point of its religious outfit, has a key given it which is to be the *open sesame* of all right discovery. Using this key as it may be used, any lock is opened, any doubt dissolved. Thus every man acknowledges the distinction of right and wrong, feels the reality of that distinction, knows it by immediate consciousness even as he knows himself. He would not be a man without that distinction. It is even this which distinguishes him from the mere animals. Having it taken away, he would, at the same instant, drop into an animal. I do not say, observe, that every man is clear as to what particular things may be fitly called right and what wrong. There is a great disagreement here in men's notions; what is right to some, or in some ages and some parts of the world, being wrong to others, in other times and countries. I only say that the distinction of *idea* or *general principle* is the same in all ages and peoples, without a shade of difference. Their ideas of space and time are not more perfectly identical. So far they are all in the same great law; constituted, in that fact, men, moral beings, subjects of religion. Their whole nature quivers responsively to this law. To be in the right, and of it, to mean the right, and swear allegiance to it forever, regardless of cost, even though it be the cost of life itself,—they can as well disown their existence as disown this law. There may be now and then a man who contrives to raise a doubt of it, and yet, driven out with rods, it will come back, a hundred times a day, and force its recognition; especially if any one does him a wrong.

Here, then, is the key that opens every thing. And the only reason why we fall into so many doubts, and get unsettled by our inquiries, instead of being settled by them as we undertake to be, is that we do not begin at the beginning. Of what use can it be for a man to push on his inquiries after truth, when he throws away, or does not practically honor, the most fundamental and most determinating of all truths? He goes after truth as if it were coming in to be with him in wrong! even as a thief might be going after honest company in stolen garments. How can a soul, unpolarized by wrong, as a needle by heat, settle itself in the poles of truth? or who will expect a needle, hung in a box of iron, turning every way and doubting at every point of compass, to find the true North? But a right mind has a right polarity, and discovers right things by feeling after them. Not all right things in a moment, though, potentially, all in a moment; for its very oscillations are true, feeling after only that which is, to know it as it is.

The true way, therefore, of dissolving doubts, as I just now said, is to begin at the beginning, and do the first thing first. Say nothing of investigation, till you have made sure of being grounded everlastingly, and with a completely whole intent, in the principle of right doing as a principle. And here it is, let me say, that all unreligious men are at fault, and often without knowing, or even suspecting it. They do right things enough in the out-door, market sense of the term, and count that being right. But let them ask the question, "Have I ever consented to be, and am I really now, in the right, as in principle and supreme law; to live for it, to make any sacrifice it will cost me, to believe every thing it will bring me to see, to be a confessor of Christ as soon as it appears to be enjoined upon me, to go on a mission to the world's end, if due conviction sends me, to change my occupation for good conscience' sake, to repair whatever wrong I have done to another, to be humbled, if I should before my worst enemy, to do complete justice to God, and, if I could, to all worlds?—in a word, to be in wholly right intent, and have no mind but this forever?" Ah, how soon do they discover possibly, in this manner, that they are right only so far as they can be, and not be at all right as in principle— right as doing some right things, nothing more. Of course, they are not going to be martyrs in this way, and they have not had a thought of it.

After this there is not much use in looking farther, for if we can not settle ourselves practically in this grand first law which we do know, how can we hope to be settled in what of truth we do not? Are we ready, then, to undertake a matter so heavy? for the struggle it requires will be great, as the change itself must be well nigh total; a revolution so nearly complete, that we shall want every help we can get. And let us not be surprised by the suggestion that God, perchance, may come to our help unseen, when we do not so much as know how to believe in him, only let it occur to us how great a comfort it should be, to have a God so profoundly given to the right; for that subtle gleam of sympathy may be itself a kind of prayer,—prayer that he will answer before the call is heard. And then, as certainly as the new right mind begins, it will be as if the whole heaven were bursting out in day. For this is what Christ calls the single eye, and the whole body is inevitably full of light. How surely and how fast fly away the doubts, even as fogs are burned away by the sun.

Now to make this matter plain, I will suppose a case in which the dissolving of doubt in this manner is illustrated. Suppose that one of us, clear all the vices, having a naturally active-minded, inquiring habit, occupied largely with thoughts of religion,—never meaning to get away from the truth, but, as he thinks, to find it, only resolved to have a free mind, and not allow himself to be carried by force or fear or any thing but real conviction,—suppose that such a one going on thus, year by year, reading, questioning, hearing all the while the gospel in which he has been educated, sometimes impressed by it, but relapsing shortly into greater doubt than before, finds his religious beliefs wearing out, and vanishing, he knows not how, till finally he seems to really believe nothing. He has not meant to be an atheist, but he is astonished to find that he has nearly lost the conviction of God, and can not, if he would, say with any emphasis of conviction that God exists. The world looks blank, and he feels that existence is getting blank also to itself. This heavy charge of his possibly immortal being oppresses him, and he asks again and again, "What shall I do with it?" His hunger is complete, and his soul turns every way for bread. His friends do not satisfy him. His walks drag heavily. His suns do not rise, but only climb. A kind of leaden aspect overhangs the world. Till finally, pacing his chamber some day, there comes up suddenly the question,—"Is there, then, no truth that I do believe?— Yes, there is this one, now that I think of it, there is a distinction of right and wrong, that I never doubted, and I see not how I can; I am even quite sure of it." Then, forthwith, starts up the question, "Have I, then, ever taken the principle of right for my law? I have done right

things as men speak, have I ever thrown my life out on the principle
to become all it requires of me? No, I have not, consciously I have
not. Ah! then here is something for me to do! No matter what becomes
of my questions,—nothing ought to become of them, if I can not take
a first principle so inevitably true and live in it.'' The very suggestion
seems to be a kind of revelation; it is even a relief to feel the conviction
it brings. "Here, then," he says, "will I begin. If there is a God, as
I rather hope there is, and very dimly believe, he is a right God. If I
have lost him in wrong, perhaps I shall find him in right. Will he not
help me, or, perchance, even be discovered to me?" Now the decisive
moment is come. He drops on his knees, and there he prays to the
dim God dimly felt, confessing the dimness for honesty's sake, and
asking for help, that he may begin a right life. He bows himself on it
as he prays, choosing it to be henceforth his unalterable, eternal endeavor.

It is an awfully dark prayer, in the look of it, but the truest and
best he can make,—the better and more true that he puts no orthodox
colors on it; and the prayer and the vow are so profoundly meant that
his soul is borne up into God's help, as it were by some unseen chariot,
and permitted to see the opening of heaven even sooner than he opens
his eyes. He rises and it is as if he had gotten wings. The whole sky
is luminous about him,—it is the morning, as it were, of a new eternity. After this, all troublesome doubt of God's reality is gone, for
he has found Him! A being so profoundly felt, must inevitably be.

Now this conversion, calling it by that name, as we properly
should, may seem, in the apprehension of some, to be a conversion
for the gospel and not *in* it or *by* it; a conversion by the want of truth,
more than by the power of truth. But that will be a judgment more
superficial than the facts permit. No, it is exactly this: it is seeking
first the kingdom of God, and his righteousness,—exactly that and
nothing less. And the dimly groping cry for help—what is that but a
feeling after God, if haply it may find him, and actually finding him
not far off. And what is the help obtained, but exactly the true Christ-
help? And the result—what also is that, but the Kingdom of God
within; righteousness, and peace, and joy, in the Holy Ghost?

Now the result will be that a soul thus won to its integrity of
thought and meaning, will rapidly clear all tormenting questions and
difficulties. They are not all gone, but they are going. Revelation, it
may be, opens some troublesome chapters. Preaching sometimes

stumbles the neophyte, when he might better be comforted by it. The great truths of God often put him in a maze. The creation story, the miracles, the incarnation, the trinity, the relations of justice and mercy,—in all these he may only see, for a time, men walking that have the look of trees. But the ship is launched, he is gone to sea, and has the needle on board. He is going now to sell every thing for the truth,—not the truth to keep as a knowledge, but the truth to live by. He is going henceforth to be concentered in the right, nay, the right-eousness itself of God; and his prayers he will be hanging, O how tenderly, on God, for the inward guidance of his Spirit. He will un-dertake shortly some point that is not cleared at once by the daylight of his new experience, and will, by and by, master it. That will give him courage to undertake shortly another, and he will go to it with new appetite. And so he will go on, not afraid to have questions even to the end of his life, and will be nowise disturbed by them. He will be in the gospel as an honest man, and will have it as a world of wonderfully grand, perpetually fresh discovery. He comes now to the lock with the key that opens it in his hand, fumbling no more in doubt, unresolved, because he has no key.

The menstruum, then, by which all doubts may be dissolved, appears to be sufficiently shown or provided. It only remains to add a few more promiscuous points of advice that relate to the general conduct of the mind in its new conditions.

1. Be never afraid of doubt. Perhaps a perfectly upright angelic mind well enough might, though I am not sure even of that. We, at least, are in the fog eternal of wrong, and there is no way for us to get clear but to prove all things and hold fast. Make free use of all the intelligence God has given you, only taking care to use it in a con-sciously supreme allegiance to right and to God. Your questions then will only be your helpers, and the faster they come, the better will be your progress in the truth.

2. Be afraid of all sophistries, and tricks, and strifes of disin-genuous argument. Doting about questions, and doubting about them are very different things. Any kind of cunning art or dodge of strat-agem in your words and arguments will do you incalculable mischief. They will damage the sense of truth, which is the worst possible kind of damage. False arguments make the soul itself false, and then a false, uncandid soul can see nothing as it is. No man can fitly seek

after truth who does not hold truth in the deepest reverence. Truth must be sacred even as God, else it is nothing.

3. Have it as a fixed principle also, that getting into any scornful way is fatal. Scorn is dark, and has no eyes; for the eyes it thinks it has are only sockets in the place of eyes. Doubt is reason, scorn is disease. One simply questions, searching after evidence; the other has got above evidence, and turns to mockery the modest way that seeks it. Even if truth were found, it could not stay in any scorning man's bosom. The tearing voice, the scowling brow, the leer, the sneer, the jeer, would make the place a robber's cave to it, and drive the delicate and tender guest to make his escape at the first opportunity. There was never a scorner that gave good welcome to truth. Knaves can as well harbor honesty, and harlots' chastity, as scorners' truth.

4. Never settle upon any thing as true, because it is safer to hold it than not. I will not say that any one is to have it as a point of duty to be damned, or willing to be, for the truth. I only say that truth brings often great liabilities of cost, and we must choose it, cost what it will. To accept the Bible even because it is safest, as some persons do, and some ministers very lightly preach, is to do the greatest dishonor both to it and to the soul. Such faith is cowardly, and is even a lie besides. It is basing a religion, not in truth, but in the doctrine of chances, and reducing the salvation of God to a bill of insurance. If the Bible is true, believe it, but do not mock it by assuming for a creed the mere chance that it may be. For the same reason, take religion, not because it will be good for your family, or good for the state, but because it is the homage due inherently from man to God, and the kingdom of God. What more flashy conceit can there be, than a religion accepted as a domestic or political nostrum?

5. Have it as a law never to put force on the mind, or try to make it believe; because it spoils the mind's integrity, and when that is gone, what power of advance in the truth is left? I know very well that the mind's integrity is far enough gone already, and that all our doubts and perpetual self-defeats come upon us for just that reason. All the more necessary is it that we come into what integrity we can, and stay there. Let the soul be immovable as rock, by any threat of danger, any feeling of risk; any mere scruple, any call to believe by sheer, self-compelling will. The soul that is anchored in right will do no such thing. There must, of course, be no obstinacy, no stiff holding

out after conviction has come. There must be tenderness, docility, and, with these, a most firmly kept equilibrium. There must be no gustiness of pride or self-will to fog the mind and keep right conviction away.

6. Never be in a hurry to believe, never try to conquer doubts against time. Time is one of the grand elements in thought as truly as in motion. If you can not open a doubt to-day, keep it till to-morrow; do not be afraid to keep it for whole years. One of the greatest talents in religious discovery, is the finding how to hang up questions and let them hang without being at all anxious about them. Turn a free glance on them now and then as they hang, move freely about them, and see them, first on one side, and then on another, and by and by when you turn some corner of thought, you will be delighted and astonished to see how quietly and easily they open their secret and let you in! What seemed perfectly insoluble will clear itself in a wondrous revelation. It will not hurt you, nor hurt the truth, if you should have some few questions left to be carried on with you when you go hence, for in that more luminous state, most likely, they will soon be cleared,—only a thousand others will be springing up even there, and you will go on dissolving still your new sets of questions, and growing mightier and more deep-seeing for eternal ages.

Now, my friends, it would not be strange if I had in the audience before me all sorts of doubts, and varieties of questions, all grades of incipient unbelief, or, it may be, of unbelief not incipient, but ripe and in full seed. But I have one and the same word for you all, that is, look after the day, and the night itself will join you in it. Or, better still, set your clock by the sun; then it will be right all day, and even all night besides, and be ready when he rises, pointing its finger to the exact minute where he stands, in the circle of his swift motion. Be right, that is, first of all, in what you know, and your soul will be faithfully chiming with all you ought to know. All evidences are with you then, and you with them. Even if they seem to be hid, they will shortly appear, and bring you their light. But this being right implies a great deal, observe, and especially these two things:—First, that you pray for all the help you can get; for without this you can not believe, or feel, that you truly want to be right. Secondly, that you consent, in advance, to be a christian, and begin a religious life, fulfilling all the sacrifices of such a life, provided you may find it necessary to do so, in order to carry out and justify yourself in acting up to the principle you have accepted. Undertaking to be right, only resolving not to be a christian, is but a mockery of right. You must go where it carries you. You must even be a Mahometan, a Jew, a Pagan,—any thing to have a clear conscience. There is no likelihood, it is true, that you will have to be either of these, but there is an almost certainty that you must be a christian. Be that as it may, you must consent to go where right conviction carries you. And there is even some proper doubt whether you can get out of this place of worship without being carried to Christ, if you undertake to go out as a thoroughly right man. For Christ is but the Sun of Righteousness, and you will assuredly find that, in being joined to the RIGHT, you are joined eternally to him, and walking with him in the blessed daylight of his truth.

IV.

DARKNESS AND LIGHT

In his sermon on *"The Gentleness of God"* Bushnell says that God's indirect method of winning human hearts does not preclude the thunder of his voice, does not conceal *"truths disagreeable and piercing,"* does not eliminate the *"terrible forces we have ravening and pouring inevitably on about us day and night."* In fact, the sin, evil, suffering, and horror of existence are part and parcel of God's indirection.

For all of its emphasis on freedom, growth, and patient optimism, Bushnell's vision of life has its dark side. That is nowhere more apparent than in his essay *"Of the Animal Infestations."* Nothing so powerfully betokens the nightmarish quality of human existence for Bushnell than venomous creatures, especially stinging insects. Such dark creatures, however, have their uses in the process of religious spirituality: they can build rugged character in beings possessed of freedom; and they can symbolize the consequences of a human will bent on evil for evil's sake.

The paradoxical nature of human sin is depicted in Bushnell's sermon *"Dignity of Human Nature Shown From its Ruins,"* in which he develops the complementary motifs of darkness and light. The radical fall of man is proof of the high state and calling from which he has lapsed; the darkness of the doom which he has freely chosen implies the realm of light to which he belongs. In a sermon based on a passage from the Book of Job, *"Light on the Cloud,"* Bushnell expands on the implications of a life lived within the dialectical tension between darkness and light. And in *"The Immediate Knowledge of God,"* another sermon preached at Yale, Bushnell delineates what, despite the realities of darkness, illumination available to faith can mean in daily existence: an intuitive sense of God's presence as unmediated, direct and personal as self-awareness.

OF THE ANIMAL INFESTATIONS.[1]

It is a difficulty encountered by the Paleyizing,[2] or Bridgewater school of theologians,[3] that what they gain by their argument from design, they sometimes appear to lose by the discredit they bring on the ends for which designs are made. Thus, if we take it for a fact that the whole creation is a framework of design—every object, and creature, and member, being nicely adapted to its uses—then it follows of necessity, that all beaks and talons, all claws and cuspidal teeth, all fangs and stings and bags of venom, are adapted to their particular uses as accurately and studiously as any thing else is seen to be; and then again it follows that as some creative builder is shown to exist by so many tokens of design, the apparent badness of the design indicates a malign power in him, working just as evidently for ends not good. Various devices are planned, it is true, for turning the argument, but, as far as I have seen, with very little show of success. If then, it be as great a matter to discover the goodness of God as to discover God; if indeed we make no discovery of God at all when we trace him in designs that are related to ends either bad or doubtfully good, there ought certainly to be some explication of the difficulties referred to that is more satisfactory.

Thus it is put forward by Kirby,[4] that "all organized beings have a natural tendency to increase and multiply," and that Providence "sets necessary bounds to their increase, by letting them loose upon each other." "In our first view of nature," he says, "we are struck by a scene which seems to be one of universal conflict—man constantly engaged in a struggle with his fellowman, laying waste the

---

1. Essay XIII in *Moral Uses of Dark Things* (New York: Charles Scribner & Co., 1868), 274–95.

2. Reference to the theories of William Paley, an eighteenth-century English thinker who, in his popular *Natural Theology*, argued that an intricately designed universe with its material parts serving given ends implies a divine designer, just as a watch implies a watchmaker.

3. A series of eight treatises published in the years 1833–36; their authors summarized scientific information that allegedly attested to "the Power, Wisdom, and Goodness of God as Manifest in Creation."

4. William Kirby, whose 1835 Bridgewater Treatise was entitled *The Power, Wisdom, and Goodness of God as Manifested in the Creation of Animals and in their History, Habits, and Instincts.*

earth, and slaughtering its inhabitants; his subjects of the animal kingdom following the example of their master, and pitilessly destroying each other.'' And the solution which he thinks sufficient is that, ''unless the tendency to multiply had been met by some such check, animated beings would be perpetually encroaching upon each other, and would finally perish for want of sufficient food.'' And why not as well let them perish in that way, as by devouring each other? What comfort is it to the lamb that a lion has eaten him up, and prevented the over-multiplication of sheep by the larger multiplication of lions? Is it not also the precise point of objection here, that such kind of arguments look for the increase of just those creatures that are worthless and destructive, and a limitation of increase in the harmless and useful? Besides, how easy was it for the Creator to keep down the over-population of the animal races, by making them less fruitful, or shortening the time of their life!

In another connection, when speaking of animals ''particularly injurious to man,'' Kirby suggests that they have their object in ''his punishment.'' And this, he thinks, may be true, more particularly of ''those personal pests, that not only attempt to derive their nutriment from him by occasionally sucking his blood, as the flea, the horse-fly, and others, but of those which make a settlement within him, infesting him with a double torment.'' But almost every kind of animal, as truly as man, suffers by injury from some other, and has in fact its pests without and pests within, after the same manner. Are we then to say that every such animal is undergoing punishment? A far more general fact may indeed be true, viz., that the whole creation, animals and men together, is groaning in the common liabilities and corporate reactions of evil; which, if we call it punishment, is not a private dealing in terms of personal justice, but only a shock of general disorder in the world itself.

At still another point, Mr. Kirby contrives to get a semblance of comfort in the supposition, that the tormenting insects are blood-letters which prevent the cattle from overfeeding by their annoyance, and so promote their health; also that man is compensated here, as regards the torment he experiences, ''by the care of the wise Physician, who prescribes the painful operation, and furnishes his chirurgical operators with the necessary knives and lancets.'' But unhappily the amount of blood taken by such infestations is too small to support the argument, and the amount of poison or pain dispensed too large to allow us any thought or care, whether some drops of blood are gone or not. If we could be let off with the blood-letting, taken without the poison, we should scarcely want any such chirurgical analogy for our comfort.

In still another place, Mr. Kirby launches a different suggestion, in which he appears to have a more theologic satisfaction; observing, with regard to "this constant scene of destruction, this never-intermitted war of one part of the creation upon another, that the sacrifice of a part maintains the health and life of the whole, and the great doctrine of *vicarious suffering* forms an article of physical science. Thus does the animal kingdom, in some sort, preach the gospel of Christ." The capitals in which this last clause is put do not appear to be wanted; for the meaning it conveys is sufficiently horrible, I think, without additional emphasis. That there is a really answering relation, between a bullock eaten by a grizzly and the death of the cross, is simply revolting. As little will a sparrow killed by a hawk be conceived to have died for the hawk, or a child for a viper that bit him, or a man for the gorilla that clubbed him in the wood. Such attempts at Christian argument are doubtless well meant, but they are, to say the least, very unfortunate.

Dr. Paley himself handles the argument here with better effect. Admitting distinctly, at the outset, that "venomous animals and animals preying upon one another" are constructed with organs that must be referred to design, and obliged also to allow that "we cannot avoid the difficulty, by saying that the effect was not intended," he only imagines that our trouble is created by our ignorance, and that, having so many and preponderant cases of beneficent design discovered to us, we are required to have it as "a reasonable presumption," that the goodness of his purpose would sufficiently appear, if we understood his purpose more deeply. And exactly this we shall by and by see to be true, only we shall find the truth outside of all mere physical ends and reasons. Not satisfied, however, with this merely excusing way of vindication, he goes on to specify something which may "extenuate the difficulty;" (1) that the venomous creatures, for example, have their venom faculty only as a good to themselves, because it is the power by which they subdue their prey, and so are able to feed their bodies—which is far as possible from being true of whole tribes of venomous insects, like the gnat, or mosquito, taking the sleeper off his defense, humming first their poisonous note in his ear, to vex the quiet of his rest, and then having sucked their fill with his blood, leaving the poisonous toll of their blessing in the wound for compensation; the very complaint against them being, not that they kill, not that they get their living, but that they bestow their venom gratis, and with no conceivable reason; (2) that such kinds of venomous creatures and beasts of prey do not, after all, kill as many people as we think, and much oftener kill other animals and not men—a very small comfort, if we can not know that their venom does no killing at all but for good; (3) that the venomous species, vipers and rattlesnakes for example, stand guard, so to speak, for "whole tribes" that have a similar look and no venom—a very farfetched argument, to say the least, which does not even show that the protected tribes are not themselves more terribly harassed by the venom of their protectors, than by the other enemies these are supposed to intimidate, or affect with shyness; (4) that it is our fault, in which we are to blame ourselves, that we crowd after and annoy the venomous creatures, and do not let them have the dens and dry places where they belong, unmolested—a much better argument, if they did not crowd after us, into our cities, and houses, and chambers.

Having exhausted this line of argument with little apparent success, he finally subsides into the same field, where Mr. Kirby is but a follower, showing how it was necessary, in order to keep the world full, that all creatures should be over-fecund in their increase, and then when the spaces are stocked to have such thinning off provided for, that all populations will be graduated by their supplies, and the contracted or expanded limits of their field. Thus he imagines, "that immense forests in North America would be lost to sensitive existence, if it were not for gnats, and that vast plains in Siberia would be lifeless without mice." But the great difficulty is to see what interest eternal benevolence has, whether in the population of gnats or of mice—how there should be any complaint of a lack of "sensitive existence," because there is a lack of gnats in the forests, if only there is enough of them in the populated regions; or why we should be much concerned for the plains of Siberia, because of the want of mice, as long as the cities and towns are so far from being "lifeless" on that account. However this may be, it is really a considerable impeachment of Providence, to say that God can no other way limit the superfecundity of his creatures, than by giving them venom to poison, and claws to tear each other. God is conditioned only by what is absolute or unconditional; but venom-bags and claws do not belong to the absolute.

There is plainly no solution for this difficulty which stops short in the mere physical economy, considering only ends and uses that pertain to mechanical and bodily conditions. Nobody ever saw far enough into God's designs to justify him, who did not see far enough to distinguish what ends his designs are for; viz., the moral ends and uses of existence. This frame of things was never understood, and never will be, without going back of things; it is mere jargon otherwise, confusion, absurdity, poison, torment—any thing and every thing but rationality and goodness. Here, then, is our question—viz., whether any sufficient account of venom and destructiveness in the animal infestations is to be discovered in the moral wants and uses of existence? And here we are met by the discovery—

1. That a great part of the evils of life are on us purposely, and not by accident, or by any kind of fatality, or pantheistic necessity. Many of us would like to imagine that our pests, and poisons, and various kinds of torments are at least not designed; that however they may come, they are only mysterious; or that if they must be allowed to be, in some sense, from God, the Universal Creator, it must in reverence be held, that he did not mean to have them as annoying and deadly as we find them to be. Then let any one dissect a talon, or a claw, or a carnivorous jaw, and decide whether there is any contrivance here for tearing and devouring flesh; and whether any preparation for scenting is deliberately contrived, in the outspread nervous texture of the nostril. Whence came that terrible vise in the mouth of a shark, and whose invention is it? That viper fang, both sharp and hollow, laid down flat upon the jaw when there is no occasion for it, but hung with pulleys of muscle to throw it up when attack is to be made, allowing it now, in the bite, to be pressed directly down upon a bag of liquid venom deposited just under its roots—whose invention is this? Is it not plainly a deliberate contrivance, as truly, visibly deliberate as any injecting or ejecting engine in the world? And how many venomous creatures are there—spiders, ants, ticks, scorpions, serpents, flies, mosquitoes, centipedes, that have their bags of poison made ready, as the fearful artillery of their otherwise contemptible life! Let no one imagine that such kind of artillery is not meant; there is no other that is gotten up with a machinery more skillful, or with better ammunition. All that may be done with such tools is plainly

meant to be done. Whatever else may be true, God has created venom, and we must not scruple to say it. If we have any conception of goodness that forbids this kind of possibility in God, then our God plainly enough does not exist, or the God that does exist is not he. The really existent God, as we can see with our eyes, is such a being as can use contrivance in adjusting the due apparatus, both of prey and of poison. And we need not scruple to confess a degree of satisfaction in this kind of discovery, showing that goodness is no such innocent, mawkishly insipid character, no such mollusc softness swimming in God's bosom as many affect to suppose; that it has resolve, purpose, thunder in it, able to contrive hard things, when hard are wanted. No other impression is at all equal to the moral training for which we are sent hither. If we could not see distinctly that God is able to plan for suffering, and prepare the machinery to produce it, what we call his goodness would only be a weak, emasculated virtue, which, if we should praise it, would not long keep our respect. One of the very first and most necessary conditions of a right moral government in souls is vigor; a will that is visibly asserting itself everywhere in acts of sovereignty that do not ask our consent. It is better for us even to be shocked sometimes, than never to be impressed. Mere safe-keeping is not rugged enough to answer the moral uses of our life. Elemental forces, grinding hard about us and upon us, are necessary to the due unfolding of our moral and religious ideas, and it is in just these severities of discipline that we afterward discover the deepest counsels of beneficence, and the highest culminations of eternal goodness itself.

2. We here perceive that not only dangerous and fierce animals are wanted as the necessary furniture of our discipline, but a large supply of annoyances, irritants, and disgusting infestations. We laugh at these creatures many times, and try to amuse ourselves at their expense, and it might not be desirable to take them more seriously, but it is a very serious matter, nevertheless, that we have them to laugh at. Indeed it is even a fair subject of doubt whether we get as much real discipline, after all, from all the beasts of prey together, as we do from any single one of a half dozen tribes of pests that infest the world—ants, mosquitoes, wood-flies, jiggers, and the like. A part of their value is that they annoy us enough to keep us awake, and if they sometimes keep us awake when we are really demanding sleep, it is

not altogether ill. Unmolested sleep might settle us at length into lethargy. We want irritants to stir us up and nettle us into vivacity, as truly as we do the lull of music and breeze to quiet us. Besides, we are always trying to get the world into a law of happiness, as if that were the main errand here, or as if God made it and must needs take it to be the law of his will. How often do we say this, and sometimes we even set our speculation upon it, to show that so it must be. It was very important, therefore, to keep us off this ground, and worry and sting us away from it. And to this end doubtless it is that God lets in upon us, on our face, and hands, and whole bodily skin, such numberless troops of hostile infestation. They come with bite, and creeping feet, and slimy touch, and sting, and stinging voice. They break no bones, they stir in general no fear, they seem to have no errand that could not as well be dispensed with. And yet, they do bring irritations, annoyances, disgusts upon us, that have a considerable significance, and ought to have, must have, a considerable use. Not all the elephants, and tigers, and hyenas, and crocodiles of the world, have a thousandth part of the power exerted by these on our feeling and temperament. And it is a great thing they do, when they only keep us off the folly of conceiving that God is principally concerned with us here to make us happy. Therefore he shows us that he is not, by instrumentations most unremorseful, most deliberately contrived; leaving us nothing less or different to believe, than that he is shaping us to good, moral good, let the happiness and all the fine computations of pleasures fare as they may. But these are things by the way; the grand determining reason for the existence of these creatures and the divine contrivance in them is to be found, I have no doubt—

3. In the fact that, in order to our highest moral benefit, there is a fixed necessity that we have a world so prepared in its furniture, as to be a representation of man to himself. It would be impossible to carry on our moral training, if we could not be insphered in conditions that reflect, express, and continually raise in us the idea of what we are. It is not enough that what may be known of God should be clearly seen in things that are made; other great purposes of existence can be secured only as we have images and a language to mirror the nature, and state, and moral quality of our action. The world must be a dictionary where objects are supplied, that may serve as bases of words inherently significant of what is in us to be signified. And it is

here that Swedenborg[5] comes in with his doctrine—whence derived I really do not know—of correspondences. Nothing is more certain, however he came by his doctrine, than that all moral terms of language suppose pre-existing terms of correspondence in the world's objects, that fitly represent or express the moral ideas and facts of our personality. It is also remarkable that all most expressive words and images, in this department of speech, are derived from animals; which, again, he says, were not created as we know them, but "exist from man." By which I suppose him to mean, that while they exist, in a sense, from God's appointment, they take their evil type, whatever it be, from the evil in man. A similar thought appears to be laboring in the story of the curse reported in Genesis; viz., that in some sense there is a general unmaking of the world by transgression, in which it changes type and falls with the fall of the occupant. So far, accordingly, it will be *from man*, bearing the expressional stamp of man; and it makes no difference whether it is changed after such a fall and by it, or adapted to it by anticipation. Be this matter as it may, all the animal types especially; the bats, and owls, and unclean birds of night; the tigers, wolves, foxes, alligators; all the serpents, and venomous creatures, and base vermin, with all the disgusting or annoying infestations of insect life, are appointed to serve grand purposes of benefit in the moral training of souls. Their destructive, poisonous, and loathsome nature, carrying all nicest, most deliberative marks of design, is good because it is evil; that is, because it expresses so faithfully what most needs to be expressed, in these four particulars: (1) the ferocity of our sin; (2) the venom principle there is in it; (3) the immense disturbing power it obtains, even under the limitations of our human insignificance; and (4) the interior efficacy it has in its working. These four factors let us consider more deliberatively, and each by itself.

First, then, nothing is more certain than that evil, as a law of selfishness, begets rapacity, violence, and even a certain ferocity in wrong, which wants reminders set on every side, and a world packed full of images to show the picture of it; and then that these same im-

---

5. Emanuel Swedenborg (1688–1772), Swedish scientist, philosopher and theologian whose spiritualist ideas—especially those concerning the correspondence of divine and material realities—influenced a number of American Romantic thinkers.

ages should pack the languages with words, to be the coins of inter-change, description, observation, accusation, reflective thought, concerning it. The moral uses of life would fail if the outward state were not made answerable and largely analogous to the state within. Hell in the bosom could not see or know itself in a paradise. If prey is the element within, it must be duly objectivized in the element without. To say that animals are organized for prey, and made crea-tures of prey, just to keep down over-multiplication, is to fool our-selves in a very slim pretext of physical adaptation, and miss altogether the grand symbolism in the stupendous engineering of God for our moral and immortal benefit. Indeed, the only good point there is in that physical solution is, that the tribes thinned away are the least harmful and most useful, and the tribes of extermination that remain precisely those which are most utterly worthless and piratical; for there seems to be some use in that, when taken as a revelation of the terrible devastations of wrong, extirpating innocence always, and emptying the world of righteousness. Still there is not much in this; for it will be seen that, in the long run, the more harmless and useful animals, having a domestic value, will obtain defenders, and will over-live and over-multiply their destroyers, and will even stock the world after these are extinct. However this may be, the general pur-pose of God in these creatures of prey is plain as it well can be. They are given to be our kinsmen, the cousins-german of our sin. They are the moral furniture of a world in selfishness and evil. There is a kind of bad litany in them, howling congenially with all wrong feeling and doing. They not only kill and devour savagely, by sting, and fang, and beak, and claw, but some of the least of them march out man-nishly in columns and fight pitched battles, lasting for whole days; and they even take on airs of high civility, by reducing fellow tribes to a condition of regular slavery; where, as they were heroes in fight, they become lords in mastership and exaction. Sometimes they work by satire, as in the case of the ants here referred to; sometimes by terror, by spitefulness, by cunning stealthiness and tricks of decoy, by immense deglutitions, by any and all sorts of animal habits that connect with prey, ferocities, voracities and disgusts that make it symbolic of evil. In this way they give us profitable company, and keep us at home in surroundings morally adapted to the omnivorous habit of our sin—no very honorable calling for them, but an excel-lently useful and even morally indispensable one for us.

I proposed also to speak, secondly, of the venom principle incorporated in a great many animals, and especially of the moral analogy it fills in relationship with evil. The number of animals that have the gift of poison, and have bags of poison carefully prepared, in connection with a hollow sting, or bill, or fang, or claw, for the injection of it, is larger than many appear to know. Sometimes the object is to repel, or disable an attack, and is only defensive. Sometimes it is to incapacitate and prostrate the animal that is to be taken as prey, where it classes with all other contrivances for the capture of supplies. But there are cases where the venom appears to be dispensed gratis, just because it belongs to a venomous nature to put forth that kind of power. What can the venomous spider, or the venomous ant, Solpuga, mean, but simply mischief, when, creeping over a man by night, he vaccinates him with a mortal poison? The mosquito comes, we know, to get his supply of blood, and so we may not object; for if he is to exist, he must live. But the strange thing is that he pays for the blood he gets with the poison he leaves. His victim was asleep, we may suppose, and there was no resistance. All that he wanted he took, but he must needs distil a poison before he goes; without any pretext of self-defense, or of doing it to capture supplies, but sometimes even waking his victim by it, after he has gotten his fill. It is as if the very bill of the animal exuded poison by the simple instigation of pleasure itself. Other infestations of the forest and the chamber impart their venom in a similar way, when, apparently, they have nothing to gain by it. What, then, does it mean, that infusions of venom have so large a place in the very contrivance of so many animal natures? The natural theologians give us no plausible, or even tolerable answer. Their whole scheme of argument from design is at fault in this matter, and must be, till they ascend above the mere physical ends of contrivance, and behold those moral ends which are the sovereign, all-controlling reasons of God, in what he creates or designs.

The fearful truth, never to be hid or lost sight of, though indignantly repelled by many, is that the state of wrong or sin in mankind goes beyond selfishness and the rapacious instincts of prey, and does sometimes become a venomous principle, doing evil because it is evil, perpetrating mischief because it is mischief, and havoc because it has that kind of power. More commonly, the crimes committed—arson, robbery, rape, murder—are such as gain or some hope of advantage instigates. Indeed, we seldom encounter examples where wrong is done for the mere sake of wrong; though now and then we do meet even such. Our poor freedmen of the South, for example, hunted, whipped, hung upon trees, burned up in their huts by night— what have they done, what are they going to attempt, that such barbarous severities are put upon them? The simple answer is, that men who are fiends will fulfill the definition, doing deeds of havoc, or of torment, for the enjoyment of it! Fearful is the truth that such beings can exist, appalling is the fact that they do. Even so madly inspired by evil is it possible for man to be. These hapless creatures, lately slaves, are free by no offense of their own. The hares of the wood are scarcely less capable of harm than they. No, their crime is that they have been injured; for as Tacitus, with true insight, declares, ''Whom a man hath injured him he hates.'' Dear sport is it, therefore, to set them flying into the bush; music itself to hear them howl and beg under a limb! This element of mischief for the sake of mischief, not often displayed in as flagrant examples, still enters largely into human conduct. We have not made up the full inventory of evil, when we have simply shown what selfishness will do for selfish ends. Evil has a demonizing power, not working always by calculation, but sometimes by a spell, and becoming thus, by its own bad inspiration, an end to itself. So far there is nothing in nature to represent it, or be its analogy. The revenge of elephants, the cunning stealth of foxes, the prey of wolves and tigers, the blood-hunger of leeches—not all the powers of damage and destruction wielded by all the animals can at all represent this kind of evil-doing. Only venom can sufficiently do it; and without the venom-bags, and bills, and fangs, and stings, and claws, the moral furniture of the world would not be complete. Evil for evil's sake, disinterested evil, is the fearful possibility and fact that must have signs and a language provided. In this office all the venomous animals do service, and more especially such as do not use their functions for self-defense, or the conquest of supplies, but distill their poison *gratis* or without reason.

Again, thirdly, it was necessary to a true understanding of our responsibility in evil-doing, that the plea of insignificance be taken away from us,—which appears to be done most effectively by the fact that we are made to suffer so great torment or damage, often, by creatures of prey, or venom, that are exceedingly small. We are perfectly defenseless against them in a great many cases, because they are small. A single mosquito will defy and torture a man all night,

when if it were a horse or an elephant, he would very shortly have
him in control. A single jigger, scarcely visible to the eye, will hide
himself under the skin and have a populous city there, before there
is even a thought of such occupancy. The land-leeches of the woods
of Ceylon will scent a man before he arrives, and, hurrying toward
him, will dart their thread-like bodies through his clothing, pinning
it to his skin, so that when he comes out, fifty heads will be pumping
at his blood. Sometimes the diminutive creatures come in armies, and
there is no conquering host of men whose march is half as destructive,
or half as difficult to resist. The weevil, the fly, the caterpillar, the
army-worm, the locust, the military hornet, that "drove out the
Amorites before Israel"—who can withstand? When the latter loom
up as a cloud on the plains of Syria, they fill the company of travelers
with greater consternation than a water-spout, and set them flying
madly every way, if only the torture permits,—otherwise they lie
down with their animals and die. It is even reported that Papor, king
of Persia, was compelled by a cloud of gnats to raise the siege of
Nisibij; where the very point of contest lay between the gnats on one
side, and his elephants on the other, and the latter were put to rout,
with his whole army, just because the insect creatures had too great
advantage over creatures in such mark for bulkiness and indefensible
majesty. In all which examples we discover, that the most fearful,
most perfectly irresistible enemies we encounter are the smallest, the
mere living specks of the creation. They come in greatest power, be
it as one or as many, and we are most appalled by them, because we
are least capable of defense against them. In this manner they invert
all our notions of size, and make diminutiveness a terror. So that when
we shrink away from all terrors of responsibility, because we are practically dwarfed and sunk out of sight before the oppressive weight
and magnitude of God, we have a mental correction already prepared,
in the fact that size has come to signify so little as regards real power
and consequence. There is no size, either in agents or actions, that
has consequence. If we die for the bite of an ant, it signifies as much
as that we die for the bite of a tiger. Doubtless God is a very great
being, and it may seem that we can do little against his immensity,
but all the more does it signify that we can sting the immense sensibility of his goodness. It is the moral significance of actions that creates their true guiltiness, not their size, or report, or show, or linear
sphere of dimensional effect. The ingratitude, the falsity, the venom,

the poison, the monstrous filthiness and corruption—these are the offense, and the measure is quality of meaning, not any bulk of movement or physical effect. We are not too small, however diminutive, to do great injuries to God, and move revulsions in his pure feeling that are only the more prodigious offense, because they wound sensibilities essentially infinite and infinitely tender.

I proposed also, fourthly, to speak of these destructive and venomous animals considered as types of the interior working of evil. We might easily get occupied with wrong as a merely exterior affair— the annoyance, misrule, destructiveness, oppressiveness, and the numberless inconveniences and desolations of it. Almost everybody is so far against wrong, and many are stirred up by the dreadful miseries of it, to become reformers against it. The danger was that we might always be looking outwardly to find it, and not realizing at all the deep, all-penetrating, thoroughgoing infection of it—humanity pricked through with evil infestations and disorders might, perchance, not be at all conceived. What then does it signify, that we are not only beset with so many external infestations and infections, but are so commonly attacked within, by hideous creatures that undertake to be co-inhabitants with us! It is no pleasant subject, but the naturalists are obliged in mere science to make out at least twenty species of these pestiferous creatures, that inwardly inhabit and are peculiar to man; even as the cattle to the pastures, or the fishes to the sea. They fix on any organ of the body, too, according to their kind, from the brain downward, and many of them have such power that life is finally sure to be discomfited by them. A symbol so impressive can not but impress, and will even more deeply impress, when the revelations of science are more familiarly known. We do, in fact, have this impression largely verified in us, before such revelations arrive; we believe that powers of death are lurking everywhere in us, as that we are wrong in fact all through. The infection, we say, is deep, and mortality has the touch of every thing that lives—which touch is internal. That which is within defileth. The immense value of all such impressions, recognizing evil as infesting life at the core, is greater than we often imagine. We sometimes call it corruption, imagining in the very word a kind of venomous action; all which is figure of course, representing the tremendous body-and-soul-dissolving infestations of evil working inwardly. Life has been so contrived, that we can not well miss the idea, however much or little we

know of the verminous infestations referred to, as therapeutically discovered and scientifically taught.

On the whole, I think it will be seen that the destructive and
venomous animals of the world have a good reason for their existence.
If there is any thing dark in their existence, it is not solved in the very
shallow philosophy that supposes their introduction for mere physical
ends. There is no solution massive enough, and grand enough, to meet
the real scope of the problem, save that they are all the outfit and
furniture of a moral system, and the uses such a system is ordained
to serve. They belong to the revelation and fit discipline of evil, being
symbols, physical analogies, such as draw their type from man, and
not from the beauty and goodness of God. What he is they become
for his sake; for in him, as a creature going into wrong, they all received their law and came forth, in their time, to work with him in
the sad but really wild and terribly sublime history of his life.

DIGNITY OF HUMAN NATURE SHOWN FROM ITS RUINS[6]

Romans iii., 13–18.—"Their throat is an open sepulchre;
with their tongues they have used deceit; the poison of asps
is under their lips. Whose mouth is full of cursing and bitterness. Their feet are swift to shed blood. Destruction and
misery are in their ways. And the way of peace they have
not known. There is no fear of God before their eyes.

A most dark and dismal picture of humanity, it must be admitted;
and yet it has two sides or aspects. In one view, it is the picture of
weakness, wretchedness, shame and disgust; all which they discover
in it who most sturdily resent the impeachment of it. In the other, it
presents a being higher than even they can boast; a fearfully great
being; great in his evil will, his demoniacal passions, his contempt
of fear, the splendor of his degradation, and the magnificence of his
woe.

It is this latter view of the picture to which, at the present time,
I propose to call your attention, exhibiting,—

---

6. From *Sermons for the New Life* (New York: Scribner, Armstrong & Co.,
1873), 50–70. Date of delivery unknown; first published in 1858.

The dignity of man, as revealed by the ruin he makes in his fall and apostacy from God.

It has been the way of many, in our time, to magnify humanity, or the dignity of human nature, by tracing its capabilities and the tokens it reveals of a natural affinity with God and truth. They distinguish lovely instincts, powers and properties allied to God, aspirations reaching after God; many virtues, according to the common use of that term; many beautiful and graceful charities; and, by such kind of evidences, or proofs, they repel, sometimes with scorn, what they call the libelous, or even the insulting doctrine of total depravity. And this they do, as I will add, not without some show of reason, when the fact of our depravity is asserted in a manner that excludes the admission of any such high aspirations and amiable properties, or virtues, as we certainly discover in human conduct, apart from any gifts and graces of religion. And it must be admitted that some teachers have given occasion for this kind of offense; not observing the compatibility of great aspirations and majestic affinities with a state of deep spiritual thraldom; assuming, also, with as little right, the want of all appropriate sensibilities and receptivities for the truth, as a necessary inference from the complete destitution of holiness. They make out, in this manner, a doctrine of human depravity, in which there is no proper humanity left.

I am not required by my subject to settle the litigation between these two extremes; one of which makes the gospel unnecessary, because there is no depravation to restore; and the other of which makes it impossible, because there is nothing left to which any holy appeal can be made; but I undertake, in partial disregard of both, to show the essential greatness and dignity of man from the ruin itself which he becomes; confident of this, that in no other point of view, will he prove the spiritual sublimity of his nature so convincingly.

Nor is it any thing new, or a turn more ingenious than just, that we undertake to raise our conceptions of human nature in this manner; for it is in just this way that we are accustomed to get our measures and form our conceptions of many things;—of the power, for example, of ancient dynasties and the magnificence of ancient works and cities. Falling thus, it may be, on patches of paved road here and there, on lines leading out divergently from ancient Rome, uncovering and deciphering the mile-stones by their sides, marked with postal distances, here for Britain, here for Germany, here for Ephesus and Babylon, here for Brundusium, the port of the Appian Way, and so for Egypt, Numidia and the provinces of the sun; imagining the couriers flying back and forth, bearing the mandates of the central authority to so many distant nations, followed by the military legions trailing on to execute them; we receive an impression of the empire, from these scattered vestiges, which almost no words of historic description could give us. So, if we desire to form some opinion of the dynasty of the Pharaohs, of whom history gives us but the faintest remembrances and obscurest traditions, we have only to look on the monumental mountains, piled up to molder on the silent plain of Egypt, and these dumb historians in stone will show us more of that vast and populous empire, measuring by the amount of realized impression, more of the imperial haughtiness of the monarchs, more of the servitude of their people and of the captive myriads of the tributary nations, than even Heroditus and Strabo, history and geography, together.

The same is true, even more strikingly, of ancient cities. Though described by historians, in terms of definite measurement, with their great structures and defenses and the royal splendor of their courts, we form no sufficient conception of their grandeur, till we look upon their ruins. Even the eloquence of Homer describing the glory and magnificence of Thebes, the vast circuit of its walls, its hundred gates, and the chariots of war pouring out of all, to vanquish and hold in subjection the peoples of as many nations, yields only a faint, unimpressive conception of the city; but, to pass through the ruins of Karnac and Luxor, a vast desolation of temples and pillared avenues that dwarf all the present structures of the world, solemn, silent and hoary, covered with historic sculptures that relate the conquest of kingdoms—a journey to pass through, a maze in which even comprehension is lost—this reveals a fit conception of the grandest city of the world as no words could describe it. Beheld and judged by the majesty of its ruins, there is a poetry in the stones surpassing all majesty of song. So, when the prophet Jonah, endeavoring, as he best can, to raise some adequate opinion of the greatness of Nineveh, declares that it is an exceeding great city, of three days' journey; and, when Nahum follows, magnifying its splendor in terms of high description that correspond; still, so ambiguous and faint is the impression made, that many were doubting whether, after all, "the exceeding great city" was any thing more than a vast inclosure of gardens and pasture grounds for sheep, where a moderate population subsisted under the protection of a wall. No one had any proper conception of the city till just now, when a traveler and antiquary digs into the tomb where it lies, opens to view, at points many miles asunder, its temples and palaces, drags out the heavy sculptures, shows the inscriptions, collects the tokens of art and splendor, and says, "this is Nineveh, the 'exceeding great city;' " and then, judging of its extent from the vast and glorious ruin, we begin to have some fit impression of its magnitude and splendor. And so it is with Babylon, Ephesus, Tadmor of the desert, Baalbec and the nameless cities and pyramids of the extinct American race. All great ruins are but a name for greatness in ruins, and we see the magnitude of the structure in that of the ruin made by it, in its fall.

So it is with man. Our most veritable, though saddest, impressions of his greatness, as a creature, we shall derive from the magnificent ruin he displays. In that ruin we shall distinguish fallen powers, that lie as broken pillars on the ground; temples of beauty, whose scarred and shattered walls still indicate their ancient, original glory; summits covered with broken stones, infested by asps, where the palaces of high thought and great aspiration stood, and righteous courage went up to maintain the citadel of the mind,—all a ruin now, "archangel ruined."

And exactly this, I conceive, is the legitimate impression of the scripture representations of man, as apostate from duty and God. Thoughtfully regarded, all exaggerations and contending theories apart, it is as if they were showing us the original dignity of man, from the magnificence of the ruin in which he lies. How sublime a creature must that be, call him either man or demon, who is able to confront the Almighty and tear himself away from his throne. And, as if to forbid our taking his deep misery and shame as tokens of contempt, imagining that a creature so humiliated is inherently weak and low, the first men are shown us living out a thousand years of lustful energy, and braving the Almighty in strong defiance to the last. "The earth is corrupt before God, and the earth is filled with violence." We look, as it were, upon a race of Titans, broken loose from order and making war upon God and each other; beholding, in their outward force, a type of that original majesty which pertains to the moral nature of a being, endowed with a self-determining liberty, capable of choices against God, and thus of a character in evil that shall be his own. They fill the earth, even up to the sky, with wrath and the demoniacal tumult of their wrongs, till God can suffer them no longer, sending forth his flood to sweep them from the earth. So of the remarkable picture given by Paul, in the first chapter of the epistle to the Romans. In one view we are disgusted, in another shocked, doubting whether it presents a creature most foolish and vile or most sublimely impious and wicked: and coming out, finally, where the chapter ends—''who knowing the judgment of God that they which commit such things are worthy of death, not only do the same but have pleasure in them that do them''—there to confess the certain greatness of a being whose audacity is so nearly infinite, whose adherence to the league with evil is maintained with a pertinacity so damnably desperate and relentless. And the picture of the text corresponds, yielding no impression of a merely feeble and vile creature, but of a creature rather most terrible and swift; destructive, fierce and fearless; miserable in his greatness; great as in evil. Their throat is an open sepulchre; with their tongues they have used deceit; the poison of asps is under their lips; whose mouth is full of cursing and bitterness; their feet are swift to shed blood. Destruction and misery are in their way; and the way of peace have they not known; there is no fear of God before their eyes.

But we come to the ruin as it is, and we look upon it with our own eyes, to receive the true, original impression for ourselves.

We look, first of all, upon the false religions of the world; pompous and costly rites transacted before crocodiles and onions; magnificent temples built over all monkeyish and monstrous creatures, carved by men's hands; children offered up, by their mothers, in fire, or in water; kings offered on the altars, by their people, to propitiate a wooden image; gorgeous palaces and trappings of barbaric majesty, studded all over with beetles in gold, or precious stones, to serve as a protection against pestilences, poisons and accidents. I can not fill out a picture that so nearly fills the world. Doubtless it is a picture of ruin—yet of a ruin how visibly magnificent. For, how high a nature must that be, how intensely allied to what is divine, that it must prepare such pomps, incur such sacrifices, and can elevate such trifles of imposture to a place of reverence. If we say that, in all this, it is feeling after God if haply it may find him, which in one view is the truth, then how inextinguishable and grand are those religious instincts by which it is allied to the holy, the infinite, the eternal, but invisible one.

The wars of the world yield a similar impression. What opinion should we have of the energy, ferocity and fearful passion of a race of animals, could any such be found, who marshal themselves by the hundred thousand, marching across kingdoms and deserts to fight, and strewing leagues of ground with a covering of dead, before they yield the victory. One race there is that figure in these heroics of war, in a small way, viz., the tiny race of ants; whom God has made a spectacle to mock the glory and magnificence of human wars; lest, carried away by so many brave shows and by the applauses of the drunken ages of the world, we pass, undiscovered, the meanness and littleness of that selfish ambition, or pride, by which human wars are instigated. These are men such as history, in all past ages, shows them to be; swift to shed blood, swifter than the tiger race, and more terrible. Cities and empires are swept by their terrible marches, and become a desolation in their path. Destruction and misery are in their ways—O what destruction, misery, how deep and long! And what shall we think of any creature of God displayed in signs like these. Plainly enough he is a creature in ruins, but how magnificent a creature! Mean as the ant in his passions, but erecting, on the desolations he makes, thrones of honor and renown, and raising himself into the attitude of a god, before the obsequious ages of mankind; for who of us can live content, as we are tempered, without some hero to admire and worship?

Consider again the persecutions of the good; fires for the saints of all ages, dungeons for the friends of liberty and benefactors of their times, poison for Socrates, a cross for Jesus Christ. What does it mean? What face shall we put on this outstanding demonstration of the world? No other but this, that cursing and bitterness, the poison even of asps, and more, is entered into the heart of man. He hates with a diabolical hatred. Feeling "how awful goodness is," the sight of it rouses him to madness, and he will not stop till he has tasted blood. And what a being is this that can be stung with so great madness, by the spectacle of a good and holy life. The fiercest of animals are capable of no such devilish instigation; because they are too low to be capable of goodness, or even of the thought. But here is a creature who can not bear the reminder, even of good, or of any thing above the ruin where his desolated glory lies. O how great is the nature which is capable of this dire phrenzy.

The great characters of the world furnish another striking proof of the transcendent quality of human nature, by the dignity they are able to connect even with their littleness and meanness. On a small island of the southern Atlantic, is shut up a remarkable prisoner,[7] wearing himself out there in a feeble mixture of peevishness and jealousy, solaced by no great thoughts and no heroic spirit; a kind of dotard before the time, killing and consuming himself by the intense littleness into which he has shrunk. And this is the great conqueror of the modern world, the man whose name is the greatest of modern names, or, some will say, of all names the human world has pronounced; a man, nevertheless, who carried his greatest victories and told his meanest lies in close proximity, a character as destitute of private magnanimity, as he was remarkable for the stupendous powers of his understanding and the more stupendous and imperial leadership of his will. How great a being must it be, that makes a point of so great dignity before the world, despite of so much that is really little and contemptible.

But he is not alone. The immortal Kepler, piloting science into the skies, and comprehending the vastness of heaven, for the first time, in the fixed embrace of definite thought, only proves the magnificence of man as a ruin, when you discover the strange ferment of irritability and "superstition wild," in which his great thoughts are brewed and his mighty life dissolved.

So also Bacon proves the amazing wealth and grandeur of the human soul only the more sublimely that, living in an element of cunning, servility and ingratitude, and dying under the shame of a convict, he is yet able to dignify disgrace by the stupendous majesty of his genius, and commands the reverence even of the world, as to one of its sublimest benefactors. And the poet's stinging line—

"The greatest, wisest, meanest of mankind,"

pictures, only with a small excess of satire, the magnificence of ruin comprehended in the man.

---

7. Napoleon.

Probably no one of mankind has raised himself to a higher pitch of renown by the superlative attributes of genius displayed in his writings, than the great English dramatist;[8] flowering out, nevertheless, into such eminence of glory, on a compost of fustian, buffoonery and other vile stuff, which he so magnificently covers with splendor and irradiates with beauty, that disgust itself is lost in the vehemence of praise. And so we shall find, almost universally, that the greatness of the world's great men, is proved by the inborn qualities that tower above the ruins of weakness and shame, in which they appear, and out of which, as solitary pillars and dismantled temples they rise.

But we must look more directly into the contents of human nature, and the internal ruin by which they are displayed. And here you may notice, first of all, the sublime vehemence of the passions. What a creature must that be, who, out of mere hatred, or revenge, will deliberately take the life of a fellow man, and then dispatch his own to avoid the ignominy of a public execution. Suppose there might be found some tiger that, for the mere bitterness of his grudge against some other whelp of his mother, springs upon him in his sleep and rends him in pieces, and then deliberately tears open his own throat to escape the vengeance of the family. No tiger of the desert is ever instigated by any so intense and terrible passion, that, for the sweetness of revenge, is willing afterward to rush on death itself. This kind of phrenzy plainly belongs to none but a creature immortal, an archangel ruined, in whose breast a fire of hell may burn high enough and deep enough to scorch down even reason and the innate love of life. Or take the passion of covetousness, generally regarded as one essentially mean and degraded. After all, how great a creature must that be, who is goaded by a zeal of acquisition so restless, so self-sacrificing, so insatiable. The poor, gaunt miser, starving for want, that he may keep the count of his gold—whom do we more naturally pity and despise. And yet he were even the greatest of heroes, if he could deny himself with so great patience, in a good and holy cause. How grand a gift that immortality, how deep those gulfs of want in the soul, that instigate a madness so desolating to character, a self-immolation so relentless, a niggard suffering so sublime. The same is true even of the licentious and gluttonous lusts and their loathsome

8. Shakespeare.

results. No race of animals can show the parallel of such vices; because they are none of them instigated by a nature so insatiable, so essentially great, in the magnificence of wants that find no good to satisfy their cravings. The ruin we say is beastly, but the beasts are clear of the comparison; it requires a mold vaster than theirs, to burst the limits of nature in excesses so disgusting.

Consider again the wild mixtures of thought, displayed both in the waking life and the dreams of mankind. How grand! how mean! how sudden the leap from one to the other! how inscrutable the succession! how defiant of orderly control! It is as if the soul were a thinking ruin; which it verily is. The angel and the demon life appear to be contending in it. The imagination revels in beauty exceeding all the beauty of things, wails in images dire and monstrous, wallows in murderous and base suggestions that shame our inward dignity; so that a great part of the study and a principal art of life, is to keep our decency, by a wise selection from what we think and a careful suppression of the remainder. A diseased and crazy mixture, such as represents a ruin, is the form of our inward experience. And yet, a ruin how magnificent, one which a buried Nineveh, or a desolated Thebes can parallel only in the faintest degree; comprehending all that is purest, brightest, most divine, even that which is above the firmament itself; all that is worst, most sordid, meanest, most deformed.

Notice, also, the significance of remorse. How great a creature must that be that, looking down upon itself from some high summit in itself, some throne of truth and judgment which no devastation of order can reach, withers in relentless condemnation of itself, gnaws and chastises itself in the sense of what it is! Call it a ruin, as it plainly is, there rises out of the desolated wreck of its former splendor, that which indicates and measures the sublimity of the original temple. The conscience stands erect, resisting all the ravages of violence and decay, and by this, we distinguish the temple of God that was; a soul divinely gifted, made to be the abode of his spirit, the vehicle of his power, the mirror of his glory. A creature of remorse is a divine creature of necessity, only it is the wreck of a divinity that was.

So again, you may conceive the greatness of man, by the ruin he makes, if you advert to the dissonance and obstinacy of his evil will. It is dissonant as being out of harmony with God and the world, and all beside in the soul itself; viz., the reason, the conscience, the wants, the hopes, and even the remembrances of the soul. How great a creature is it that, knowing God, can set itself off from God and resist him, can make itself a unit, separate from all beings beside, and maintain a persistent rebellion even against its own convictions, fears and aspirations. Like a Pharaoh it sits on its Egyptian throne, quailing in darkness, under the successive fears and judgments of life, relenting for the moment, then gathering itself up again to re-assert the obstinacy of its pride, and die, it may be, in its evil. What a power is this, capable of a dominion how sublime, a work and sphere how transcendent! If sin is weak, if it is mean, little, selfish and deformed, and we are ready to set humanity down as a low and paltry thing of nothing worth, how terrible and tragic in its evil grandeur does it appear, when we turn to look upon its defiance of God, and the desperate obstinacy of its warfare. Who, knowing the judgment of God, that they which commit such things are worthy of death, not only do the same, but have pleasure in them that do them. Or as we have it in the text,—There is no fear of God before their eyes. In one view there is fear enough, the soul is all its life long haunted by this fear, but there is a desperation of will that tramples fear and makes it as though it were not.

Consider once more the religious aspirations and capacities of religious attraction that are garnered up, and still live in the ruins of humanity. How plain it is, in all the most forward demonstrations of the race, that man is a creature for religion; a creature secretly allied to God himself, as the needle is to the pole, attracted toward God, aspiring consciously, or unconsciously, to the friendship and love of God. Neither is it true that, in his fallen state, he has no capacity left of religious affection, or attraction, till it is first new created in him. All his capacities of love and truth are in him still, only buried and stifled by the smoldering ruin in which he lies. There is a capacity in him still to be moved and drawn, to be charmed and melted by the divine love and beauty. The old affinity lives though smothered in selfishness and lust, and even proves itself in sorrowful evidence, when he bows himself down to a reptile or an idol. He will do his most expensive works for religion. There is a deep panting still in his bosom, however suppressed, that cries inaudibly and sobs with secret longing after God. Hence the sublime unhappiness of the race. There is a vast, immortal want stirring on the world and forbidding it to rest. In the cursing and bitterness, in the deceit of tongues, in the poison

of asps, in the swiftness to blood, in all the destruction and misery of
the world's ruin, there is yet a vast insatiate hunger for the good, the
true, the holy, the divine, and a great part of the misery of the ruin is
that it is so great a ruin; a desolation of that which can not utterly
perish, and still lives, asserting its defrauded rights and reclaiming
its lost glories. And therefore it is that life becomes an experience to
the race so tragic in its character, so dark and wild, so bitter, so incapable of peace. The way of peace we can not know, till we find our
peace, where our immortal aspirations place it, in the fullness and the
friendly eternity of God.

Regarding man then, as immersed in evil, a being in disorder,
a spiritual intelligence in a state of ruin, we derogate nothing from
his dignity. Small conception has any one of the dignity of human
nature, who conceives it only on the side of praise, or as set off by
the figments of a merely natural virtue. As little could he apprehend
the tragic sublimity of Hamlet, considered only as an amiable son
ingenuously hurt by the insult done his father's name and honor. The
character is great, not here, but in its wildness and its tragic mystery;
delicate and fierce, vindictive and cool, shrewd and terrible, a reasonable and a reasoning madness, more than we can solve, all that
we can feel. And so it is that we discover the true majesty of human
nature itself, in the tragic grandeur of its disorders, nowhere else.
Nothing do we know of its measures, regarded in the smooth plau-
sibilities and the respectable airs of good breeding, and worldly virtue. It is only as a lost being that man appears to be truly great. Judge
him by the ruin he makes, wander among the shattered pillars and
fallen towers of his majesty, behold the immortal and eternal vestiges,
study his passions, thoughts, aspirations, woes; behold the destruction and misery that are in his ways,—destruction how sublime, misery how deep, clung to with how great pertinacity, and then say,—
this is man, this is the dignity of human nature. It will kindle no pride
in you, stimulate no pompous conceit, but it will reveal a terror, discover a shame, speak a true conviction, and, it may be, draw forth a
tear.

Having reached this natural limit of our subject, let us pause a
moment, and look about us on some of the practical issues to which
it is related.

It is getting to be a great hope of our time, that society is going to slide into something better, by a course of natural progress; by the advance of education, by great public reforms, by courses of self-culture and philanthropic practice. We have a kind of new gospel that corresponds; a gospel which preaches not so much a faith in God's salvation as a faith in human nature; an attenuated moralizing gospel that proposes development, not regeneration; showing men how to grow better, how to cultivate their amiable instincts, how to be rational in their own light and govern themselves by their own power. Sometimes it is given as the true problem, how to reform the shape and re-construct the style of their heads, and even this it is expected they will certainly be able to do! Alas that we are taken, or can be, with so great folly. How plain it is that no such gospel meets our want. What can it do for us but turn us away, more and more fatally, from that gospel of the Son of God, which is our only hope. Man as a ruin, going after development, and progress, and philanthropy, and social culture, and, by this fire-fly glimmer, to make a day of glory! And this is the doctrine that proposes shortly to restore society, to settle the passion, regenerate the affection, re-glorify the thought, fill the aspiration of a desiring and disjointed world! As if any being but God had power to grapple with these human disorders; as if man, or society, crazed and maddened by the demoniacal frenzy of sin, were going to rebuild the state of order, and re-construct the shattered harmony of nature, by such kind of desultory counsel and unsteady application as it can manage to enforce in its own cause; going to do this miracle by its science, its compacts, and self-executed reforms! As soon will the desolations of Karnac gather up their fragments and re-construct the proportions out of which they have fallen. No, it is not progress, not reforms that are wanted as any principal thing. Nothing meets our case, but to come unto God and be medicated in him; to be born of God, and so, by his regenerative power, to be set in heaven's own order. He alone can re-build the ruin, he alone set up the glorious temple of the mind; and those divine affinities in us that raven with immortal hunger—he alone can satisfy them in the bestowment of himself.

And this brings me to speak of another point, where the subject unfolded carries an important application. The great difficulty with christianity in our time is, that, as a fact, or salvation, it is too great for belief. After all our supposed discoveries of dignity in human nature, we have commonly none but the meanest opinion of man. How can we imagine or believe that any such history as that of Jesus Christ is a fact, or that the infinite God has transacted any such wonder for man? a being so far below his rational concern, or the range of his practical sympathy. God manifest in the flesh! God in Christ reconciling the world unto himself! the birth of the manger! the life of miracle! the incarnate dying! and the world darkening in funeral grief around the mighty sufferer's cross!—it is extravagant, out of proportion, who can believe it? Any one, I answer, who has not lost the magnitude of man. No work of God holds a juster proportion than this great mystery of godliness, and if we did but understand the great mystery of ungodliness we should think so. No man will ever have any difficulty in believing the work of Christ who has not lost the measures of humanity. But for this, no man will ever think it reason to deny his divinity, explain away his incarnation, or reject the mystery of his cross. To restore this tragic fall required a tragic salvation. Nor did ever any sinner who had come to himself, felt the bondage of his sin, trembled in the sense of his terrible disorders, groaned over the deep gulfs of want opened by his sin, struggled with himself to compose the bitter struggles of his nature, heaved in throes of anguish to emancipate himself,—no such person, however deep in philosophy, or scepticism, ever thought, for one moment, that Christ was too great a Saviour. O, it was a divine Saviour, an almighty Saviour, coming out from God's eternity, that he wanted! none but such was sufficient! Him he could believe in, just because he was great,—equal to the measures of his want, able to burst the bondage of his sin. "For God so loved the world that he gave his only begotten son, that whosoever believeth in him should not perish, but should have everlasting life."—O, it is the word of reason to his soul. He believes, and on this rock, as a rock of adequate salvation, he rests.

Once more, it is another and important use of the subject we have here presented, that the magnitude and real importance of the soul are discovered in it, as nowhere else. For it is not by any computations of reason, but in your wild disorders, your suppressed affinities for God, the distempers and storms of your passions, and the magnificent chaos of your immortality, that you will get the truest opinion of your consequence to yourselves. Just that which makes you most oblivious and blindest to your own significance, ought to make you most aware of it and press you most earnestly to God. I know not how it is but the soul appears under sin, all selfish as it is, to shrink and grow small in its own sight. Perhaps it is due, in part, to the consciousness we have, in sin, of moral littleness and meanness. We commonly speak of it in figures of this kind, we call it low and weak and degraded, and fall into the impression that these words are real measures of our natural magnitude. Whereas, in another sense, the sin we speak of is mighty, terrible, God-defying and triumphant. Let this thought come to you, my friends, as well as the other, and if sin is morally little, let it be, in power, mighty as it really is. The shadow by which most convincingly your true height is measured, is that which is cast athwart the abyss of your shame and spiritual ignominy. Just here it is that you will get your most veritable impressions of your immortality; even as you get your best impression of armies, not by the count of numbers, but by the thunder-shock of battle, and the carnage of the field when it is over. We try all other methods, but in vain, to rouse in men's bosoms some barely initial sense of their consequence to themselves, and get some hold, in that manner, of the stupendous immortality Christ recognizes in them and throws off his glory to redeem. We take the gauge of your power as a mind, showing what this power of mind has been able, in the explorations of matter and light and air, of sea and land, and the distant fields of heaven, to do. We display its inventions, recount its victories over nature. We represent, as vividly as we can, and by computations as vast and far-reaching as we are master of, in our finite arithmetic, the meaning of the word, eternity. All in vain. What are you still but the insect of some present hour, in which you live and flutter and die? But here we take another method, we call you to the battle field of sin. We show you the vestiges. This we say is man, the fallen principality. In these tragic desolations of intelligence and genius, of passion, pride and sorrow, behold the import of his eternity. Be no mere spectator, turn the glass we give you round upon yourself, look into the ruin of your own conscious spirit, and see how much it signifies, both that you are a sinner and a man. Here, within the soul's gloomy chamber, the loosened passions rage and chafe, impatient of their law; here huddle on the wild and desultory thoughts; here the imagination crowds in shapes of glory and disgust, tokens both and mockeries of its own creative power, no longer in the keeping of reason; here sits remorse scowling and biting her chain; here creep out the fears, a meagre and pale multitude; here drives on the will in his chariot of war; here lie trampled the great aspirations, groaning in immortal thirst; here the blasted affections weeping out their life in silent injury; all that you see without, in the wars, revenges and the crazed religions of the world, is faithfully represented in the appalling disorders of your own spirit. And yet, despite all this, a fact which overtops and crowns all other evidence, you are trying and contriving still to be happy—a happy ruin! The eternal destiny is in you, and you can not break loose from it. With your farthing bribes you try to hush your stupendous wants, with your single drops, (drops of gall and not of water,) to fill the ocean of your immortal aspirations. You call on destruction to help you, and misery to give you comfort, and complain that destruction and misery are still in all your ways. O, this great and mighty soul, were it something less, you might find what to do with it; charm it with the jingle of a golden toy, house it in a safe with ledgers and stocks, take it about on journeys to see and be seen! Any thing would please it and bring it content. But it is the godlike soul, capable of rest in nothing but God; able to be filled and satisfied with nothing but his fullness and the confidence of his friendship. What man that lives in sin can know it, or conceive it; who believe what it is!

O, thou Prince of Life! come in thy great salvation to these blinded and lost men, and lay thy piercing question to their ear,— What shall it profit a man to gain the whole world and lose his own soul? Breathe, O breathe on these majestic ruins, and rouse to life again, though it be but for one hour, the forgotten sense of their eternity, their lost eternity.

Even so, your lost eternity. The great salvation coming, then, is not too great; nought else, or less could suffice. For if there be any truth that can fitly appall you, rive you with conviction, drive you home to God, dissolve you in tears of repentance, it is here, when you discover yourself and your terrible misdoings, in the ruins of your desolated majesty. In these awful and scarred vestiges, too, what type is given you of that other and final ruin, of which Christ so kindly and faithfully warned you, when, describing the house you are building on these treacherous sands, he showed the fatal storm beating vehemently against it, with only this one issue possible—And immediately it fell, and the ruin of that house was great.

LIGHT ON THE CLOUD.[9]

Job xxxvii. 21.—"And now men see not the bright light which is in the clouds: but the wind passeth, and cleanseth them."

The argument is, let man be silent when God is dealing with him; for he can not fathom God's inscrutable wisdom. Behold, God is great, and we know him not. God thundereth marvelously with his voice: great things doeth he which we can not comprehend. Dost thou know the wondrous works of him that is perfect in knowledge? Teach us what we shall say unto him; for we can not order our speech by reason of darkness. If a man speak, surely he shall be swallowed up.

Then follows the text, representing man's life under the figure of a cloudy day. The sun is in the heavens, and there is always a bright light on the other side of the clouds; but only a dull, pale beam pierces through. Still, as the wind comes at length to the natural day of clouds, clearing them all away, and pouring in, from the whole firmament, a glorious and joyful light, so will a grand clearing come to the cloudy and dark day of life, and a full effulgence of light, from the throne of God, will irradiate all the objects of knowledge and experience.

Our reading of the text, you will observe, substitutes for *cleansing, clearing away*, which is more intelligible. Perhaps, also, it is better to read "on the clouds," and not "in." Still, the meaning is virtually the same. The words, thus explained, offer three points which invite our attention.

I. *We live under a cloud, and see God's way only by a dim light.*

II. *God shines, at all times, with a bright light, above the cloud, and on the other side of it.*

III. *This cloud of obscuration is finally to be cleared away.*

1. We live under a cloud, and see God's way only by a dim light.

As beings of intelligence, we find ourselves hedged in by mystery on every side. All our seeming knowledge is skirted, close at

9. From *Sermons for the New Life*, 143–64. Date of delivery unknown; first published in 1858.

hand, by dark confines of ignorance. However drunk with conceit we may be, however ready to judge every thing, we still comprehend almost nothing.

What then does it mean? Is God jealous of intelligence in us? Has he purposely drawn a cloud over his ways to baffle the search of our understanding? Exactly contrary to this; he is a being who dwelleth in light, and calls us to walk in the light with him. He has set his works about us, to be a revelation to us always of his power and glory. His word he gives us, to be the expression of his will and character, and bring us into acquaintance with himself. His Spirit he gives us, to be a teacher and illuminator within. By all his providential works, he is training intelligence in us and making us capable of knowledge.

No view of the subject, therefore, can be true that accuses him. The true account appears to be that the cloud, under which we are shut down, is not heavier than it must be. How can a being infinite be understood, or comprehended, by a being finite? And, when this being infinite has plans that include infinite quantities, times and relations, in which every present event is the last link of a train of causes reaching downward from a past eternity, and is to be connected also with every future event of a future eternity, how can a mortal, placed between these two eternities, without knowing either, understand the present fact, whatever it be, whose reasons are in both?

Besides, we have only just begun to be; and a begun existence is, by the supposition, one that has just begun to know, and has every thing to learn. How then can we expect, in a few short years, to master the knowledge of God and his universal kingdom? What can he be to such but a mystery? If we could think him out, without any experience, as we do the truths of arithmetic and geometry, we might get on faster and more easily. But God is not a mere thought of our own brain, as these truths are, but a being in the world of substance, fact and event, and all such knowledge has to be gotten slowly, through the rub of experience. We open, after a few days, our infantile eyes and begin to look about, perceive, handle, suffer, act and be acted on, and, proceeding in this manner, we gather in, by degrees, our data and material of knowledge; and so, by trial, comparison, distinction, the study of effects and wants, of rights and wrongs, of uses and abuses, we frame judgments of things, and begin to pass our verdict on the matters we know. But how long will it take us to penetrate, in this manner, the real significance of God's dealings with us and the world, and pass a really illuminated judgment on them? And yet, if we but love the right, as the first father did before his sin, God will be revealed in us internally, as the object of our love and trust, even from the first hour. He will not appear to be distant, or difficult. We shall know him as a friendly presence in our heart's love, and we shall have such a blessed confidence in him that if, in the outer world of fact and event, clouds and darkness appear to be round about him, we shall have the certainty within that justice and judgment are the habitation of his throne. Meanwhile, he will be teaching us graciously, and drawing us insensibly, through our holy sympathies, into the sense of his ways, and widening, as fast as possible, the circle of our human limitation, that we may expatiate in discoveries more free. And thus it comes to pass that, as the eyelids of the infant are shut down, at first, over his unpracticed eyes, which are finally strengthened for the open day, by the little, faint light that shines through them, so our finite, childish mind, saved from being dazzled, or struck blind, by God's powerful effulgence, and quickened by the gentle light that streams through his cloud, is prepared to gaze on the fullness of his glory, and receive his piercing brightness undimmed.

But there is another fact less welcome that must not be forgot, when we speak of the darkness that obscures our knowledge of God. There is not only a necessary, but a guilty limitation upon us. And therefore we are not only obliged to learn, but, as being under sin, are also in a temper that forbids learning, having our mind disordered and clouded by evil. Hence, come our perplexities; for, as the sun can not show distinctly what it is in the bottom of a muddy pool, so God can never be distinctly revealed in the depths of a foul and earthly mind. To understand a philosopher requires, they tell us, a philosopher; to understand patriotism, requires a patriot; to understand purity, one that is pure; so, to understand God, requires a godlike spirit. Having this, God will as certainly be revealed in the soul, as light through a transparent window. He that loveth knoweth God, for God is love. What darkness then must be upon a mind that is not congenially tempered, a mind unlike to God, opposite to God, selfish, lustful, remorseful, and malignant! Even as an apostle says—Having the understanding darkened, being alienated from the life of God, through the ignorance that is in them, because of the blindness of their heart.

The very activity of reason, which ought to beget knowledge, begets only darkness now, artificial darkness. We begin a quarrel with limitation itself, and so with God. He is not only hid behind thick walls of mystery, but he is dreaded as a power unfriendly, suspected, doubted, repugnantly conceived. Whatever can not be comprehended, and how very little can be, is construed as one construes an enemy, or as an ill-natured child construes the authority of a faithful father. An evil judgment taken up yesterday prepares another to-day, and this another tomorrow, and so a vast complicated web of false judgments, in the name of reason, is spread over all the subjects of knowledge. We fall into a state thus of general confusion, in which even the distinctions of knowledge are lost. Presenting our little mirror to the clear light of God, we might have received true images of things, and gotten by degrees a glorious wealth of knowledge, but we break the mirror, in the perversity of our sin, and offer only the shivered fragments to the light; when, of course, we see distinctly nothing. Then, probably enough, we begin to sympathize with ourselves and justify the ignorance we are in, wondering, if there be a God, that he should be so dark to us, or that he should fall behind these walls of silence, and suffer himself to be only doubtfully guessed, through fogs of ignorance and obscurity. Reminded that he is and must be a mystery, we take it as a great hardship, or, it may be, an absurdity, that we are required to believe what we can not comprehend. We are perplexed by the mode of his existence and action—how can he fill all things, and yet have no dimensions? How is it that he knows all things, before the things known exist? Foreknowing what we will do, how can we be blamed for what we were thus certain beforehand to do? How is it that he creates, governs, redeems, and yet never forms a new purpose, or originates a new act, which is not from eternity? How is he infinitely happy, when a great many things ought to be, and are declared to be, repugnant or abhorrent to his feeling? How does he produce worlds out of nothing, or out of himself, when nothing else exists? How did he invent forms and colors, never having seen them?

Entering the field of supposed revelation, the difficulties are increased in number, and the mysteries are piled higher than before. God is here declared to be incarnate, in the person of Jesus Christ, and the whole history of this wonderful person is made up of things logically incompatible. He is the eternal son of God, and the son of Mary; he is Lord of all, and is born in a manger; stills the sea by his word, and traveling on foot is weary; asks, who convinceth me of sin? and prays like one wading through all the deepest evils of sin; dies like a man and rises like a god, bursting the bars of death by his power. Even God himself is no more simply God, but a threefold mystery that mocks all understanding,—Father, Son, and Holy Ghost. Is it revelation, then, that only burdens faith with mysteries more nearly impossible? Exactly so; nothing is more clear to any really thoughtful person than that, until some high point is passed, God ought to be enveloped in greater mystery, and will be, the closer he is brought to the mind. Knowing nothing of him, he is no mystery at all; knowing a little, he is mystery begun; knowing more, he is a great and manifold deep, not to be fathomed. We are, and ought to be, overwhelmed by his magnitudes, till we are able to mount higher summits of intelligence than now. Or, if it be answered that, in some of these things, we have contradictions, and not mere difficulties, it is enough to reply that the highest truths are wont to be expressed in forms of thought and language that, as forms, are repugnant. Nor is it any fault of these mere instrumental contradictions that we can not reconcile them, if only they roll upon us senses of God's deep majesty and love, otherwise impossible. Our amazement itself is but the vehicle of his truth.

Turning next to the creative works of God, we find the cloud also upon these. The Lord by wisdom hath founded the earth, by understanding hath he established the heavens, there is no searching of his understanding; why he created the worlds when he did, and not before; what he could have been doing, or what enjoyment having, previous to their creation; and, if all things are governed by inherent laws, what more, as the universal governor, he can find any place to do since:—these are questions, again, before which speculative reason reels in amazement. If the baffled inquirer then drops out of the search after God, as many do, and says,—I will go down to nature, and it shall, at least, be my comfort that nature is intelligible, and even a subject of definite science, he shortly discovers that science only changes the place of mystery and leaves it unresolved. Hearing, with a kind of scientific pity, Job's question about the thunder,—who can understand the noise of his tabernacle? he at first thinks it something of consequence to say that thunder is the noise of electricity, and not of God's tabernacle at all. But he shortly finds himself asking, who can understand electricity? and then, at last, he is with Job again.

So, when he hears Job ask, Knowest thou the ordinances of heaven,—
he recollects the great Newtonian discovery of gravity, and how, by
aid of that principle, even the weights of the stars have been exactly
measured, and their times predicted, and imagines that, now the secrets of astronomy are out, the ordinances of heaven are understood.
But here, again, it finally occurs to him to ask, what is gravity? and
forthwith he is lost in a depth of mystery as profound as that of Job
himself. And so, asking what is matter,—what is life, animal and
vegetable,—what is heat, light, attraction, affinity,—he discovers
that, as yet, we really comprehend nothing, and that nature is a realm
as truly mysterious even as God. Not a living thing grows out of the
earth, or walks upon it, or flies above it; not an inanimate object exists, in heaven, earth, or sea, which is not filled and circled about
with mystery as truly as in the days of Adam or Job, and which is not
really as much above the understanding of science, as the deepest
things of God's eternity or of his secret life.

But there is, at least, one subject that he must understand and
know even to its center; viz., himself. Is he not a self-conscious being,
and how can there be a cloud over that which is comprehended even
by consciousness itself? Precisely contrary to this, there are more
mysteries and dark questions grouped in his own person, than he has
ever met in the whole universe beside. He can not even trace, with
any exactness, the process by which he has been trained to be what
he is, or the subtle forces by which his character has been shaped.
Only the smallest fraction of his past history can he distinctly remember, all the rest is gone. Even the sins for which he must answer before
God are gone out of his reach, and can no more be reckoned up in
order, till the forgotten past gives up its dead things, to be again remembered. As little can he discover the manner of his own spirit,
how he remembers, perceives objects, compares them, and, above
all, how he wills and what it is that drives him to a sentence against
himself when he wills the wrong. He knows too that, in wrong, he is
after self-advantage; and every wrong, he also knew at the time, must
be to his disadvantage; why then did he do it? He can not tell. The
sin of his sin will be, when he is judged before God, that he can not
tell. Even the familiar fact of his connection with a body is altogether
inexplicable; and why any act of his will should produce a motion of
his body, he can no more discover than why it should produce a mo-

tion among the stars. The beating of his heart and the heaving of his lungs are equally mysterious. In his whole nature and experience, he is, in fact, a deep and inscrutable mystery to himself. God breathes unseen in his heart, and yet he wonders that God is so far off. Death comes in stealthily, and distills the fatal poison that will end his life, unseen and unsuspected. He goes down to his grave, not knowing, by any judgment of his own, apart from God's promise, (which he does not believe,) that he shall live again. What shall be the manner of his resurrection and with what body he shall come, he can as little comprehend, as he can the mystery of the incarnation.

Finding, therefore, God, nature, himself, overhung with this same cloud, it is not wonderful that he suffers bitter afflictions and galls himself against every corner of God's purposes. Why is society a weight so oppressive on the weak and the poor? If sin is such an evil, as it certainly is, why did the Creator, being Almighty, suffer it? Indeed, there is almost nothing that meets us, between our first breathing and our graves, that does not, to an evil mind, connect, in one way or another, some perplexity, some accusing or questioning thought, some inference that is painful, or perhaps atheistical. Can it be? Why should it be? How can a good God let it be? If he means to have it otherwise, is he not defeated? if defeated, is he God? If he has no plan, how can I trust him? if his plan will suffer such things, how then can I trust him?—these are the questions that are continually crowding upon us. The cloud is all the while over us. He hath made darkness his pavilion and thick clouds of the skies. This man's prosperity is dark; that man's adversity is dark. The persecutions of the good, the afflictions of the righteous, the desolations of conquest, the fall of nations and their liberties, the extinction of churches, the sufferings of innocence, the pains of animals, the removal by death of genius and character just ripened to bless the world—there is no end to our dark questions. There are times, too, when our own personal experience becomes enveloped in darkness. We not only can not guess what it means, or what God will do with us in it, but it wears a look contrary to what appear to be our just expectations. We are grieved, perplexed, confounded. Other men are blessed in things much worse. We ourselves have been successful in things far more questionable, and when our deserts were less. What does it mean that God is covering his way, under these thick clouds of mystery and seeming caprice? In short, we may sum it up, as a general truth, that nothing in the world is really luminous, to a mind unilluminated by religion; and, if we say that the Christian walks in the light, it is not so much that he can always understand God as it is that he has confidence in him, and has him always near.

Thus we live. Practically, much is known about God and his ways, all that we need to know; but, speculatively, or by the mere understanding, almost nothing, save that we can not know. The believing mind dwells in continual light; for, when God is revealed within, curious and perplexing questions are silent. But the mind that judges God, or demands a right to comprehend him before it believes, stumbles, complains, wrangles, and finds no issue to its labor. Still there is light, and we pass on now to show,—

II. That there is abundance of light on the other side of the cloud, and above it.

This we might readily infer, from the fact that so much of light shines through. When the clouds overhead are utterly black, too black to be visible, we understand that it is night, or that the sun is absent; but, when there is a practical and sufficient light for our works, we know that the sun is behind them, and we call it day. So it is when God spreadeth a cloud upon his throne. We could not see even the mystery, if there were no light behind it, just as we could not see the clouds if no light shone through.

The experience of every soul that turns to God is a convincing proof that there is light somewhere, and that which is bright and clear. Was it a man struggling with great afflictions, an injured man crushed by heavy wrongs, was it a man desolated and broken down by domestic sorrows; was it a rich man stripped by sore losses and calamities, was it a proud man blasted by slander; was it an atheist groping after curious knowledge and starving on the chaff of questions unresolved—be it one or another of these, for all alike were tormented in the same perplexities of the darkened understanding, every thing was dark and dry and empty; but when they come to Christ and believe in him, it is their common surprise to find how suddenly every thing becomes luminous. Speculatively, they understand nothing which before was hidden, and yet there is a wondrous glory shining on their path. God is revealed within, and God is light. The flaming circle of

skirts the horizon of the mind. Their dark questions are
left behind. They are even become insignificant. Their dignity is gone, and the soul, basking in the blessed sunshine of God's
love, thinks it nothing, any more, if it could understand all mysteries.
In all which it is made plain that, if we are under the cloud, there is
yet a bright light above.

It will also be found, as another indication, that things which,
at some time, appeared to be dark,—afflictions, losses, trials,
wrongs, defeated prayers, and deeds of suffering patience yielding
no fruit,—are very apt, afterward, to change color and become visitations of mercy. And so where God was specially dark, he commonly brings out, in the end, some good, or blessing in which the
subject discovers that his Heavenly Father only understood his wants
better than he did himself. God was dark in his way, only because
his goodness was too deep in counsel, for him to follow it to its mark.
It is with him as with Joseph, sold into slavery, and so into the rule
of a kingdom; or as it was with Job, whose latter end, after he had
been stripped of every thing, was more blessed than his beginning;
or as with Nehemiah, whose sorrowing and disconsolate look itself
brought him the opportunity to restore the desolations over which he
sorrowed. Even the salvation of the world is accomplished through
treachery, false witness, and a cross. All our experience in life goes
to show that the better understanding we have of God's dealings, the
more satisfactory they appear. Things which seemed dark or inexplicable, or even impossible for God to suffer without wrong in himself, are really bright with goodness in the end. What then shall we
conclude, but that, on the other side of the cloud, there is always a
bright and glorious light, however dark it is underneath.

Hence it is that the scriptures make so much of God's character
as a light-giving power, and turn the figure about into so many forms.
In God, they say, is light and no darkness at all. According to John's
vision of the Lord—His countenance was as the sun that shineth in
his strength. The image of him given by another apostle is even more
sublime,—Who only hath immortality dwelling in light that no man
can approach unto,—language, possibly, in which he had some reference to his own conversion, when a light, above the brightness of
the sun, bursting upon him and shining round about him, seared his
eye-balls, so that afterward there fell off from them, as it had been,

scales of cinder. God, therefore, he conceives to be light-inapproach-able, as figured in that experience. And probably enough he would say that, as the astronomers in looking at the sun arm their sight with a smoky or colored medium, so the very clouds we complain of are mercifully interposed, in part, and rather assist than hinder our vision.

It is little therefore to say, and should never be a act incredible, that however dark our lot may be, there is light enough on the other side of the cloud, in that pure empyrean where God dwells, to irradiate every darkness of the world; light enough to clear every difficult ques-tion, remove every ground of obscurity, conquer every atheistic sus-picion, silence every hard judgment; light enough to satisfy, nay to ravish the mind forever. Even the darkest things God has explanations for, and it is only necessary to be let into his views and designs, as when we are made capable of being we certainly shall, to see a tran-scendent wisdom and beauty in them all. At present, we have no ca-pacity broad enough to comprehend such a revelation. We see through a glass darkly, but we see what we can. When we can see more, there is more to be seen. On the other side of the cloud there is abundance of light. This brings me to say,—

III. That the cloud we are under will finally break way and be cleared.

On this point we have many distinct indications. Thus it coin-cides with the general analogy of God's works, to look for obscurity first, and light afterward. According to the scripture account of the creation, there was, first, a period of complete darkness; then a period of mist and cloud, where the day light is visible, but not the sun; then the sun beams out in a clear open sky, which is called, in a way of external description, the creation of the sun. How many of the animals begin their life at birth with their eyes closed, which are afterward opened to behold the world into which they have come. How many myriads of insects begin their existence underground, emerging af-terward from their dark abode, to take wings and glitter in the golden light of day. If we observe the manner too of our own intellectual discoveries, we shall generally see the inquirer groping long and pain-fully under a cloud, trying and experimenting in a thousand guesses to no purpose, till finally a thought takes him and behold the difficulty is solved! At a single flash, so to speak, the light breaks in, and what before was dark is clear and simple as the day. Darkness first and light afterward, this is the law of science universally. By so many and various analogies, we are led to expect that the cloud, under which we live in things spiritual, will finally be lifted, and the splendor of eternal glory poured around us.

Our desire of knowledge, and the manner in which God manages to inflame that desire, indicate the same thing. This desire he has planted naturally in us, as hunger is natural in our bodies, or the want of light in our eyes. And the eye is not a more certain indication that light is to be given, than our desire to know divine things is that we shall be permitted to know them. And the evidence is yet further increased, in the fact that the good have a stronger desire of this knowledge than mere nature kindles. And if we say, with the scripture, that the fear of the Lord is the beginning of knowledge, doubtless the body of it is to come after. It is the glory of God, indeed, to conceal a thing, but not absolutely, or for the sake of concealment. He does it only till a mind and appetite for the truth is prepared, to make his revelation to. He gives us a dire light and sets us prying at the walls of mystery, that he may create an appetite and relish in us for true knowledge. Then it shall be a joyful and glorious gift—drink to the thirsty, food to the hungry, light to the prisoner's cell. And he will pour it in from the whole firmament of his glory. He will open his secret things, open the boundaries of universal order, open his own glorious mind and his eternal purposes.

The scriptures also notify us of a grand assize, or judgment, when the merit of all his doings with us, as of our doings toward him, will be revised, and it appears to be a demand of natural reason that some grand exposition of the kind should be made, that we may be let into the manner of his government far enough to do it honor. This will require him to take away the cloud, in regard to all that is darkest in our earthly state. Every perplexity must now be cleared, and the whole moral administration of God, as related to the soul, must be sufficiently explained. Sin, the fall, the pains and penalties and disabilities consequent, redemption, grace, the discipline of the righteous, the abandonment of the incorrigibly wicked—all these must now be understood. God has light enough to shed on all these things, and he will not conceal it. He will shine forth in glorious and transcendent brightness, unmasked by cloud, and all created minds, but

the incorrigible outcasts and enemies of his government, will respond;—Alleluia, salvation, and glory, and honor, and power be unto
the Lord our God; for just and true are his judgments.

Precisely what is to be the manner and measure of our knowledge, in this fuller and more glorious revelation of the future, is not
clear to us now, for that is one of the dark things, or mysteries, of
our present state. But the language of scripture is remarkable. It even
declares that we shall see God as he is; and the intensity of the expression is augmented, if possible, by the effects attributed to the sight—
we shall be like him, for we shall see him as he is. We shall be so
irradiated and penetrated, in other words, by his glory, as to be transformed into a spiritual resemblance; partaking his purity, reflecting
his beauty, ennobled by his divinity. It is even declared that our
knowledge of him shall be complete. Now we know in part, then shall
we know even as also we are known. To say that we shall know God
as he knows us, is certainly the strongest declaration possible, and it
is probably hyperbolical; for it would seem to be incredible that a
finite mind should at once, or even at any time in its eternity, comprehend the infinite, as it is comprehended by the infinite. It is also
more agreeable to suppose that there will be an everlasting growth in
knowledge, and that the blessed minds will be forever penetrating
new depths of discovery, clearing up wider fields of obscurity, attaining to a higher converse with God and a deeper insight of
his works, and that this breaking forth of light and beauty in them by
degrees and upon search, will both occupy their powers and feed their
joy. Still, that there will be a great and sudden clearing of God's way,
as we enter that world, and a real dispersion of all the clouds that
darken us here, is doubtless to be expected; for when our sin is completely taken away, (as we know it then will be,) all our guilty blindness will go with it, and that of itself will prepare a glorious unveiling
of God and a vision of his beauty as it is.

In what manner we shall become acquainted with God's mind,
or the secrets of his interior life, whether through some manifestation
by the Eternal Word, like the incarnate appearing of Jesus, or partly
in some way more direct, we can not tell. But the divine nature and
plan will be open, doubtless, in some way most appropriate, for our
everlasting study and our everlasting progress in discovery. The
whole system of his moral purposes and providential decrees, his

penal distributions and redeeming works, will be accessible to us, and all the creatures and creations of his power offered to our acquaintance and free inspection. Our present difficulties and hard questions will soon be solved and passed by. Even the world itself, so difficult to penetrate, so clouded with mystery, will become a transparency to us, through which God's light will pour as the sun through the open sky. John knew no better way of describing the perfectly luminous state of the blessed minds than to say,—and there shall be no night there, and they have no candle, neither light of the sun; for the Lord God giveth them light. They dwell thus in the eternal daylight of love and reason; for they are so let into the mind of God, and the glorious mysteries of his nature, that every thing is lighted up as they come to it even as the earth and its objects by the sun—The Lord God giveth them light.

In closing the review of such a subject as this, let us first of all receive a lesson of modesty, and particularly such as are most wont to complain of God, and boldest in their judgments against him. Which way soever we turn, in our search after knowledge, we run against mystery at the second or third step. And a great part of our misery, a still greater of our unbelief, and all the lunatic rage of our skepticism, arises in the fact that we either do not, or will not see it to be so. Ignorance trying to comprehend what is inscrutable, and out of patience, that it can not make the high things of God come down to its own petty measures, is the definition of all atheism. There is no true comfort in life, no dignity in reason, apart from modesty. We wrangle with providence and call it reason, we rush upon God's mysteries, and tear ourselves against the appointments of his throne, and then, because we bleed, complain that he cruelly mocks our understanding. All our disputings and hard speeches are the frothing of our ignorance, maddened by our pride. O, if we could see our own limitations, and how little it is possible for us to know of matters infinite, how much less, clouded by the necessary blindness of a mind disordered by evil, we should then be in a way to learn, and the lessons God will teach would put us in a way to know what now is hidden from us. Knowledge puffeth up, charity buildeth up. One makes a balloon of us, the other a temple. And as one, lighter than the wind, is driven loose in its aerial voyage, to be frozen in the airy heights of speculation, or drifted into the sea to be drowned in the waters of ignorance, which it risked without ability to swim, so the other, grounded on a rock, rises into solid majesty, proportionate, enduring, and strong. After all his labored disputings and lofty reasons with his friends, Job turns himself to God and says—I know that thou canst do every thing, and that nothing can be withholden from thee. Who is he that hideth counsel without knowledge. Therefore have I uttered that I understood not; things too wonderful for me, that I knew not. There is the true point of modesty—he has found it at last! Whoever finds it has made a great attainment.

How clear is it also, in this subject, that there is no place for complaint or repining under the sorrows and trials of life. There is nothing in what has befallen, or befalls you, my friends, which justifies impatience or peevishness. God is inscrutable, but not wrong. Remember, if the cloud is over you, that there is a bright light always on the other side; also, that the time is coming, either in this world or the next, when that cloud will be swept away and the fullness of God's light and wisdom poured around you. Every thing which has befallen you, whatever sorrow your heart bleeds with, whatever pain you suffer, even though it be the pains of a passion like that which Jesus endured at the hands of his enemies—nothing is wanting, but to see the light that actually exists, waiting to be revealed, and you will be satisfied. If your life is dark, then walk by faith, and God is pledged to keep you as safe as if you could understand every thing. He that dwelleth in the secret place of the Most High shall abide under the shadow of the Almighty.

These things, however, I can say, with no propriety, to many. No such comforts, or hopes belong to you that are living without God. You have nothing to expect from the revelations of the future. The cloud that you complain of will indeed be cleared away, and you will see that, in all your afflictions, severities, and losses, God was dealing with you righteously and kindly. You will be satisfied with God and with all that he has done for you, but alas you will not be satisfied with yourself. That is more difficult, forever impossible! And I can conceive no pang more dreadful than to see, as you will, the cloud lifted from every dealing of God that you thought to be harsh, or unrighteous, and to feel that, as he is justified, you yourself are forever condemned. You can no more accuse your birth, your capacity, your education, your health, your friends, your enemies, your temptations. You still had opportunities, convictions, calls of grace, and calls of blessing. You are judged according to that you had, and not according to that you had not. Your mouth is eternally shut, and God is eternally clear.

Finally it accords with our subject to observe that, while the inscrutability of God should keep us in modesty and stay our complaints against him, it should never suppress, but rather sharpen our desire of knowledge. For the more there is that is hidden, the more is to be discovered and known, if not to-day then to-morrow, if not to-morrow, when the time God sets for it is come. To know, is not to surmount God, as some would appear to imagine. Rightly viewed, all real knowledge is but the knowledge of God. Knowledge is the fire of adoration, adoration is the gate of knowledge. And when this gate of the soul is fully opened, as it will be when the adoring grace is complete in our deliverance from all impurity, what a revelation of knowledge must follow. Having now a desire of knowledge perfected in us that is clear of all conceit, ambition, haste, impatience, the clouds under which we lived in our sin are forever rolled away, and our adoring nature, transparent to God as a window to the sun, is filled with his eternal light. No mysteries remain but such as comfort us in the promise of a glorious employment. The light of the moon is as the light of the sun, and the light of the sun sevenfold, and every object of knowledge, irradiated by the brightness of God, shines with a new celestial clearness and an inconceivable beauty. The resurrection morning is a true sun-rising, the inbursting of a cloudless day on all the righteous dead. They wake transfigured, at their Master's call, with the fashion of their countenance altered and shining like his own.

> Creature all grandeur, son of truth and light,
> Up from the dust, the last great day is bright,—
> Bright on the Holy Mountain round the throne,
> Bright where in borrowed light the far stars shone;
> Regions on regions far away they shine,
> 'Tis light ineffable! 'tis light divine!
> Immortal light and life forevermore!

There was a cloud, and there was a time when man saw not the brightness that shined upon it from above. That cloud is lifted, and God is clear in his own essential beauty and glory forever.

THE IMMEDIATE KNOWLEDGE OF GOD.[10]

"For some have not the knowledge of God."—1 Cor. 15: 34.

Who then are these Corinthian disciples, that they have not so much as the knowledge of God? Plainly enough our apostle is not charging them here with ignorance, but with some lack of the divine illumination which ought, if they are true disciples, to be in them. They certainly know God in the traditional and merely cognitive way. Indeed the apostle is discoursing to them here of the resurrection of the dead, which is itself a matter based in Christian ideas. Besides, he adds, "I speak this to your shame;" having it in view that they are not Pagans, but so far informed, as disciples, that they ought to know God in a way more interior.

We shall best understand the point assumed in this impeachment, I think, if we raise the distinction between knowing God, and knowing about God. Doubtless, it is much to know about God, about his operations, his works, his plans, his laws, his truth, his perfect attributes, his saving mercies. This kind of knowledge is presupposed in all faith, and constitutes the rational ground of faith, and so far is necessary even to salvation. But true faith itself discovers another and more absolute kind of knowledge, a knowledge of God himself; immediate, personal knowledge, coming out of no report, or statement, or any thing called truth, as being taught in language. It is knowing God within, even as we know ourselves. The other is only a knowing about God, as from a distance. To put this matter of the immediate knowledge of God in its true doctrinal position, it may be well to say, that we have two denials set against it, both as nearly fatal as need be to any such possibility. One is the denial of the philosophers outside of Christianity, speculating there about the cognitive functions, and making what they conceive to be their specially profound discovery, that knowledges are possible only of things relative. Therefore, God being infinite, can not be known—God is unknowable. They say nothing of faith, they have no conception of any such super-

10. From *Sermons on Living Subjects* (New York: Scribner, Armstrong & Co., 1872), 114–28. Preached at Yale, date of delivery unknown; first published in 1872.

eminent, almost divine talent in our humanity, shut up or drawn away from God by our sin—an immediate sensing power, to which God may be as truly known, as we know the distinct existence of objects perceived by the eyes. Could they simply trust themselves over to God, to live by his tender guidance and true inward revelation, they would never again call him the unknowable. Meantime, there will be many children of sorrow, unlearned and simple, who will easily know the God they have it as their point of philosophy to show can not any way be known! This most false and feeble doctrine of negation, I do not feel called upon to discuss—it will die of inanity sooner than it can by argument.

The other and second form of denial as regards the immediate knowledge of God, sets up its flag inside of the Christian church and among the muniments of doctrine. Here the possibility of faith is admitted, and the necessity of it abundantly magnified. But the faith power is used up, it is conceived, on propositions; that is propositions which affirm something about God. It does not go through, and over, and beyond, such propositions, to meet the inward revelation or discovery of God himself. The accepted doctrine is that we know, or can know God, only so far as we know something about Him, no immediate knowledge of Him being at all possible, or even conceivable. The continually reiterated assumption is that never, in our most sacred, dearest, deepest moments of holy experience, do we get beyond being simply acted on by certain truths we know about God. And when men are called to God, saying, "Come unto me," they understand the meaning to be, that they are called only to believe something about him put in words, and work their feeling or their faith by what the words supply. They do not even conceive it as a possibility, that we should know God himself as a presence operative in us; even as we know the summer heat by its pervasive action in our bodies. We do not know the heat by report, or debate, or inference, or scientific truth interpreting medially between us and it; we do not see it, or hear it, or handle it, and yet we have it and know that we have, by the inward sense it creates. So in what is called the Christian regeneration, our being born of God implies the immediate revelation of God within—all which these teachers can not so understand, but imagine that we are born of something about God rather; that is of truths, affirmations, notions, working medially or instrumentally between us and God.

What then is the truth in this matter? Why it is that human souls, or minds are just as truly made to be filled with God's internal actuating presence, as human bodies are to be tempered internally by heat, or as matter is made to be swayed by gravity, or the sky-space to be irradiated by the day. God is to them heat, gravity, day, immediately felt as such, and known by the self-revelation of his person. So at least it was originally to be, and so it would be now, had not this presence of God internally and personally to souls, this quickening, life-giving God-sense, been shut off by sin. For by this they tear themselves away from God, and become self-centered, separated creatures, even as growths in a cavern, or as fishes on the land, having no longer that immediate knowledge of God which is their normal state of subsistence. Henceforth they know or may know, much about God, but they do not know God. They are shut up as to God, dark to God, except, as by the head, they may think, discover, learn, or reason something about him. Never do they know him till he becomes centered in their soul again as its life, and the crowning good and blessing of its eternity. And this is fitly called being born of God, because it is the entering of God again into his place—to be the beginning there of a new movement and life derivative from him, and fed by the springs of his fullness in the heart. Which entering in of God supposes, in fact, a new discovery of God. Not that the subject is put back now into a new cognitive relation; his cognitive function is nowise altered, and if there were no other, would still be as blind to God as before. The new discovery made is made by faith, opening the heart to receive, and in receiving feel or inwardly sense, what should have been the original and always normal revelation.

Is it then to be said or imagined that, in this new-birth, or new-begun life of faith, the subject really knows God by an immediate knowledge? He may not so conceive it, I answer, but it is none the less true. He will speak, it may be, only of his peace, but it will seem to him to be a kind of divine peace. He will testify that God is wondrously near to him, and he will put into that word *near* something like a sense of Him. He will be conscious and will say that he is, of a strangely luminous condition, as if his whole body, in the words of Christ, were full of light; and all the scripture terms that set forth God as a light, and a sun, and a power opposite to darkness, will come in, as it were, to answer, and to interpret the force of his experience. Still he will not conceive, it may be, of any such thing as that the peace, the nearness, the luminousness of his soul, supposes an immediate knowledge of God now discovered to Him. He may even disown such a conception, as implying a kind of irreverence. Nevertheless that is the exact verdict of his experience, and nothing else can at all give the meaning of it. Indeed, if we can believe it, he was made originally to be even conscious of God and live eternally in that kind of immediate knowledge; which design is now beginning, for the first time, to be fulfilled.

Thus you have every one two kinds of knowledge relating to yourself. One is what you know mediately about yourself, through language, and one that which you have immediately as being conscious of yourself. Under the first you learn who your parents were, what others think of you, what effects the world has on you, what power you have over it, and what is thought to be the science it may be of your nature, as an intelligent being. Under the second you have a knowledge of yourself so immediate, that there is no language in it, no thought, no act of judgment or opinion, you simply have a *self-feeling* that is intuitive and direct. Now you were made to have just such an immediate knowledge of God as of yourself; to be conscious of God; only this consciousness of God has been closed up by your sin and is now set open by your faith; and this exactly is what distinguishes every soul enlightened by the Spirit, and born of God. Whether he says it or not, this is the real account of his experience, that God is now revealed in him, and that he begins to be conscious of God; for it is a fact, as every soul thus enlightened will testify, that he is now conscious, not of himself only, but of a certain *otherness* moving in him; some mysterious power of good that is to him what he is not to himself, a spring of new-born impulse, a living of new life. It is not that he sees God without by the eye, any more than that he sees himself without by the eye, when he is conscious of himself; it is not that he has any mind-view of God awakened in him any more than that he has in consciousness a mind-view of himself. It is only that he has the sense of a sublime *other* not himself; a power, a life, a transcendently great felt Other—who is really and truly God. Hence the rest, and strength, and peace, and luminous glory into which he is born—it is nothing but the revelation of God and the immediate knowledge of God. Probably enough he will not say this, not having been trained or accustomed to this mode of conceiving the change, but he will say that God is *near,* wonderfully, gloriously near, and will press into the word all nearness possible, even such as to include in fact the felt consciousness of God, and the immediate knowledge of his presence.

Observe now in what manner the Scriptures speak on this subject. And the time would fail me to merely recount the ways in which it is given as the distinction of faith or holy experience, that it carries, in some way, the knowledge of God, and differs the subject in that manner from all that are under the blindness of mere nature.

Discoursing thus, for example, of the state of love, it distinguishes that state as being one, in which God and God's love are actually revealed in the soul—"For love is of God, and every one that loveth is born of God, and knoweth God. He that loveth not knoweth not God, for God is love." And accordingly there was never a soul on earth that being born into the great principle and impulse of self-sacrificing love, did not have the sense of God in it, and consciously live, in some mysterious participation of him.

The Holy Spirit, in like manner, is spoken of in a great many ways, as the intercoursing life and immediate inward manifestation of God. Thus he is said to "witness with our spirit," which means that there is to be a consciousness raised of his presence in the soul, and a sense of reciprocity established by what is called his witnessing with us; as if he carried himself into our feeling in a way of internal dialogue. So there is a discerning of the Spirit spoken of, which does not mean a reasoning out, but an immediate knowing of the mind of the Spirit. Christ also declares when promising the Spirit, that "the world seeth him not, neither knoweth him, but ye *know* him, for he dwelleth with you and shall be in you." And in immediate connection—"the world seeth me no more, but ye see me—[know me, that is, in him.] At that day ye shall know that I am in the Father, and ye in me and I in you." And then again—"He that loveth me shall be loved of my father, and I will love him, and will manifest myself unto him." And what is manifestation but immediate knowledge?

This new consciousness of God is plainly declared by the apostle when he says—"That Christ may dwell in your hearts by faith, that ye, being rooted and grounded in love, may be able to comprehend with all saints what is the breadth, and length, and depth, and height, and to know the love of Christ which passeth knowledge; that ye might be filled with all the fullness of God." What language but this, "to know the love that passeth knowledge," to have revealed in conscious participation what can not be known or measured by the notions of the cognitive understanding—what but this can fitly express the sacred visitation of a Christian soul, when through Christ and the Spirit it is wakened again to the eternal consciousness of God.

O this wonder of discovery, the knowledge of God—who can find words for it, or the change it must needs make! It even makes the soul another creature to itself. Now it is no more blank to God, tortures itself no more in guesses dim, sighs no more—"O that I knew where I might find him." It has recovered, as it were, the major part of existence that before was lost; it knows not only itself, but it has the knowledge of God; and in that fact it is raised out of its mere finite speck of magnitude, into the conscious participation of being infinite. Every thing is now become luminous. Old things are passed away, behold all things are become new—great as new, and holy as great, and blessed as holy.

But there is an objection to this mode of conceiving holy experience, as implying an immediate discovery of God, which I am properly required to notice. What is the use, in this view, some will ask, of a Bible, or external revelation? what use of the incarnation itself? Are not these advances on our outward knowledge superseded and made useless, when we conceive that God is offered to immediate knowledge or experience? In one view they are, and in another they are not. Does it follow that because we have an immediate knowledge of heat, we have therefore no use at all for the scientific doctrine of heat, or the laws by which it is expounded? Suppose it is a part of our interest in this article of heat, that we be able to generate more of it, or use it differently and with better economy. So far we have a use in knowing about heat, as well as knowing heat. In the same way it is of immense consequence to know every thing possible about God, that we may find how the more perfectly to know God. We want, in this manner, the whole Scripture, and not least the incarnation and the cross, and the story of the pentecost. These things are matters given to us about God, for the very purpose of showing us how to find God. The inherent use of all medial knowledges, all truths, cognitions, books, appearings, and teachings, is that they bring us in, to know God by an immediate knowledge. So far I would give most ready assent to the Quaker doctrine. We are never to put the book between us and God, to give us second-hand knowledges of him, and there accept our limit. The book is given us to carry us beyond the book, and put us in the way of finding God as others have found him; then and there to be in the Spirit as they were, and know Him by such private interpretation as he will give us. The mine is given, not that we may have the gold already dug, but that we may go a mining for ourselves. And as these great saints of holy scripture were men of like passions with us, it is to be our glorious privilege that they pilot us on, by telling us how to know and grow as they did.

There is also another objection to be noticed here, which moves in the exactly opposite direction, where those who know not God complain that revelation, as they look upon it, does not reveal him, and that God is dark to them still, as they could not expect him to be. If there be a God, they ask, why does he not stand forth and be known as a Father to his children? Why allow us to grope, and stumble after him, or finally miss him altogether? They are not satisfied with the Bible, and if we call it a revelation of God, they do not see it. Why should he be so difficult of discovery, hid in recesses so deep, and only doubtfully and dimly known? If there be a God, is he not of such consequence, that being hid is even a wrong? Is it not also the right most plainly of every human creature, to have an easy and free knowledge of him? I certainly think it is; only we must not make him responsible for the blear and self-blinding of our sin. And if it were not for this, I think we should all see him plainly enough, and always, and every where. For it is the whole endeavor of his management to be known. He not only meets our understanding processes in the facts of his Bible, but he offers himself to be known without any process at all, just as the light is; nay, if we will have it so, to be a kind of second consciousness in us, and be known to us even as we know ourselves. He is even pressing himself into knowledge when our eyes are shut—in our self-will, our hate, our denial, our desolation. O that for one hour you could have the ingenuous mind that is needed to really give him welcome! No more, after that, would you complain of him that he withdraws from your knowledge.

Now this exposition of God's truth, here brought to a close, converges practically, as I conceive, on a single point of broadest consequence; correcting a mistake almost universally prevalent in some greater or less degree; the mistake I mean of being over much occupied in religion with matters of the head. The true evidence of discipleship is knowing God. Other men know something about him.

The Christian knows him, has him as a friend. And there is no substitute for this. Observances, beliefs, opinions, self-testing severities—all these are idle and prove nothing. If a man knows God, it is a fact so grand, so full of meaning, that he wants no evidence beside. All curious explorations and deep searches in this matter are very much as if a man were trying himself carefully, to find whether he sees the day. If a man knows God in the revelation of his Son, he is *ipso facto* full, and wants no more. Therefore he should not even begin to be elaborate in his self-testings, or his questions about himself; the sign is a bad one. When the true day hath dawned, and the daystar hath risen in the heart, the man himself ought to know it without much trouble. Let thine eye be single, serve God, seek God, know God only, and thy whole body shall be full of light.

Now as these keep off the light of their day, by the ever-busy meddling of their understanding, there is another class who have never found the day by reason of their over-busy, over-curious endeavors to make ready for it. They are waiting, and reading, and reasoning, as they think, to get light *for* conversion. They are going to be converted rationally, nursing all the while a subtle pride of this, which only makes them darker, and puts them farther off. They quite misconceive the relation of our previous opinions, knowledges, and wisdoms, to the state of faith or conversion; and putting themselves down upon these, they are all the while at work, as they think, grading a road into the kingdom of God, so that when the road is done, they expect to be steered straight in, guided by, and rested on, the rails they have now finally laid down. But there is, alas! a great gulf of transition here to be passed, that forbids eternally any such conceit as that. There is no such relation between the knowing about God and knowing God, as they think there is. All the speculative preparations made, and roads of knowledge graded, stop inevitably short of the kingdom, and whoever imagines that he is going to be trundled logically along the plane of his notional wisdoms and arguments, into God's bosom, will assuredly find that he is not there, but has fallen infinitely short of it. What then, must you drop out your very intelligence in order to become a Christian? Far from that as possible; you are only required to use your intelligence intelligently. That is, perceiving that all you know, debate and think *about* God is, at best, only introductory to the knowledge of God himself, and some way off, take care rather to let go your speculations and open your heart in faith to the true manifestation of God. After all you have reasoned, faith is still to come. The roads of the natural understanding are in a lower plane, you must rise, you must go up into trust and *know God—God himself*—by the inward discovery of his infinite spirit and person.

What is wanted, therefore, for us all, is summed up in this Christian word faith—faith in Christ, or faith in God; for it makes no difference. Thinking and questioning stir the mind about God, faith discerns him, and by it, as the soul's open window, he enters to be discerned. Would that all of you could know how much this means. Cease then from your questions, all ye that are afar off, not knowing God, and asking sometimes, with a sigh, where shall we find him? Know that he is here in thy mouth and in thy heart; only believe in him, and you shall know the greatest bliss a soul can know, the Father of all glory, manifest within.

SELECTED BIBLIOGRAPHY

The following books are recommended for those who wish to pursue further Bushnell's ideas on the spiritual life. For a well-nigh exhaustive bibliography of writings by and about Bushnell, the reader is well advised to consult James O. Duke, *Horace Bushnell: On the Vitality of Biblical Language* (Chico, CA: Scholars Press, 1984), pp. 95–126.

WORKS BY BUSHNELL

Building Eras in Religion. New York: Charles Scribner's Sons, 1881.

Christ and His Salvation, In Sermons Variously Related Thereto. New York: Charles Scribner, 1864.

Christ in Theology. Hartford: Brown & Parsons, 1849.

Christian Nurture. New York: Charles Scribner's Sons, 1912.

God in Christ. Hartford: Brown & Parsons, 1849.

Moral Uses of Dark Things. New York: Charles Scribner & Co., 1868.

Nature and the Supernatural. New York: Charles Scribner's Sons, 1877.

Sermons for the New Life. New York: Scribner, Armstrong & Co., 1873.

Sermons on Living Subjects. New York: Scribner, Armstrong & Co., 1872.

The Spirit in Man. Sermons and Selections. New York: Charles Scribner's Sons, 1903.

The Vicarious Sacrifice. New York: Charles Scribner & Co., 1866.
Work and Play. New York: Charles Scribner, 1864.

WORKS ON BUSHNELL

Cheney, Mary Bushnell. *Life and Letters of Horace Bushnell*. New York: Harper & Brothers, 1880.

Cherry, Conrad. *Nature and Religious Imagination: From Edwards to Bushnell*. Philadelphia: Fortress Press, 1980.

Crosby, Donald A. *Horace Bushnell's Theory of Language: In the Context of Other Nineteenth Century Philosophies of Language*. The Hague: Mouton, 1975.

Cross, Barbara. *Horace Bushnell: Minister to a Changing America*. Chicago: University of Chicago Press, 1958.

Duke, James O. *Horace Bushnell: On the Vitality of Biblical Language*. Chico, CA: Scholars Press, 1984.

Munger, Theodore. *Horace Bushnell: Preacher and Theologian*. Boston: Houghton, Mifflin & Co., 1899.

Smith, David L. *Symbolism and Growth: The Religious Thought of Horace Bushnell*. Chico, CA: Scholars Press, 1981.

INDEX TO INTRODUCTION

INDEX TO TEXTS

DATE DUE
